Banksy: Completed

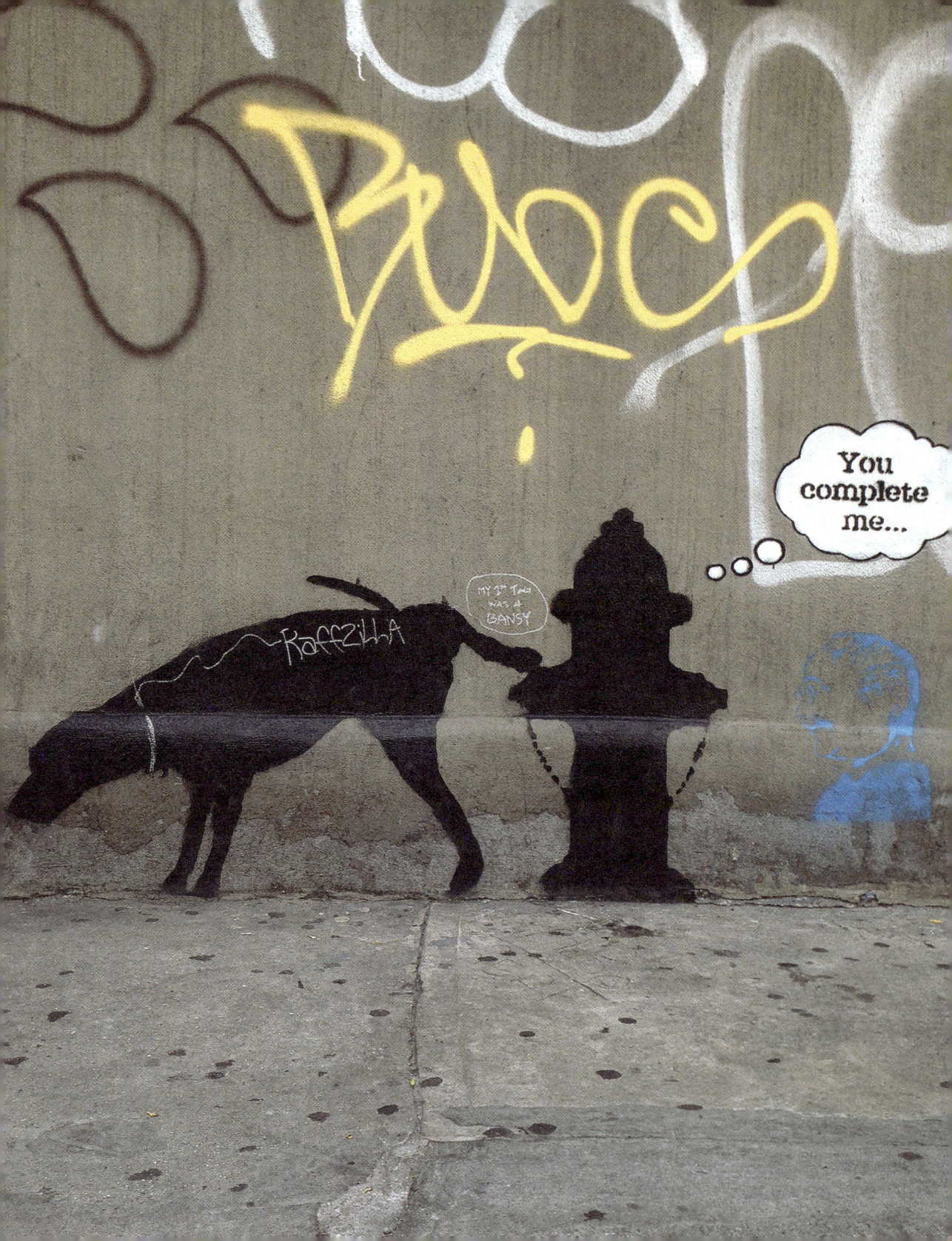

Banksy: Completed

Carol Diehl

The MIT Press
Cambridge, Massachusetts
London, England

Library of Congress Cataloging-in-Publication Data
Names: Diehl, Carol, author.
Title: Banksy : completed / Carol Diehl.
Description: Cambridge, Massachusetts : The MIT Press, [2021] | Includes bibliographical references and index.
Identifiers: LCCN 2020047105 | ISBN 9780262046244 (hardcover)
Subjects: LCSH: Banksy--Criticism and interpretation. | Banksy--Influence. | Art and society.
Classification: LCC ND497.B254 D54 2021 | DDC 759.2--dc23
LC record available at https://lccn.loc.gov/2020047105
10   9   8   7   6   5   4   3   2   1

To Robert Irwin, who showed me what art is

Table of Contents

Introduction

The poet produces poems
The painter produces paintings
The criminal produces crimes
If you can do all three at once
You'll really confuse the shit out of them

Banksy

Banksy is the last person I ever thought I'd be writing a book about. A regular visitor to England since 1999, I'd been aware of the British graffiti artist, but because the astronomical prices his work commanded at auction conflicted with my idea of street art credibility, I dismissed him as simply an attention-seeker. It was my son Matt who encouraged me—or rather insisted, as is his nature—that I take Banksy seriously as an artist. Matt had just been to see *Barely Legal*, the free, one-weekend-only event in a lofty but decrepit Los Angeles industrial building that Banksy had filled with paintings and installations—and where the elephant in the room was an actual thirty-seven-year-old pachyderm painted red with gold fleur-de-lis to match the brocade wallpaper. Billing it as a "vandalized warehouse extravaganza" in one of LA's most derelict areas, Banksy focused his first large-scale exhibition in the United States on themes of global poverty, injustice, and the Iraq War, then at its height in 2006. In one wall-size painting, a motley group of street kids hoisted an American flag atop the shell of a burnt-out car, a twist on the famous World War II photo of soldiers raising the Stars and Stripes at Iwo Jima. The side of a graffiti-covered truck included a stenciled painting of Dorothy from *The Wonderful Wizard of Oz* holding a noose, while on the back, a shiny black and yellow sticker inquired, "How's my bombing?" with a phone number later revealed to be that of an army recruitment center.

Grit met glamour as crowds were drawn by an underground word-of-mouth buzz such as might have announced a rave, as well as a savvy publicity effort to attract Hollywood's famous to view, ironically, the work of an artist who refuses to reveal not only his face, but his identity. Standing behind Sasha Baron Cohen in the queue to get in, Matt was given a handout that read, "1.7 billion people have no access to clean drinking water. 20 billion people live below the poverty line. Every day hundreds of people are made to feel physically sick by morons at art shows telling them how bad the world is but never actually doing something about it. Anybody want a free glass of wine?"

When I asked what impressed him most, Matt, a rock music journalist with a background in art, was unequivocal. It was a two-minute video showing Banksy, face electronically obscured, entering Disneyland with a backpack and jumping the fence of the Big Thunder Mountain ride. There he quickly inflated a life-size doll dressed like a Guantánamo detainee and placed it in full view of the riders. In orange prison garb, manacled hand and foot, with a face-and-vision-obscuring black hood, the figure highlighted the grim situation at the US military prison in Cuba where only months before three inmates, tortured and detained indefinitely without trial, had committed suicide. The blow-up sculpture remained undiscovered for approximately ninety minutes, after which park authorities, fearing for public safety, had it removed and the ride shut down.

Disneyland, of course, is commercialized myth and fantasy taken to an extreme, and one aspect of fantasy is hope. Guantánamo is a place of no hope. Both are highly controlled manmade environments with specific rituals and costumes: one designed to elicit pleasure, the other, pain. Matt pointed out that Disneyland at Anaheim, only thirty miles away, is part of the fabric of the Los Angeles experience. "Everyone seeing the video had been there as kids, or with their kids. Banksy was injecting this political tragedy directly into our world."

A few years later, I saw Banksy's film *Exit Through the Gift Shop* and found it brilliant, as my Brit friends would say. Billed as "the world's first street art disaster movie," it was nominated in 2011 for an Academy Award in the documentary feature category. For those who haven't seen *Exit*, I won't spoil it with description, except to say that it qualifies as yet another Banksy prank, and after several viewings, I remain more confused than ever. A Hollywood film editor told me that it's regarded as a groundbreaker in her field, and film critics wrote almost uniformly positive reviews—with the *Guardian*'s Peter Bradshaw going so far as to call Banksy "Britain's newest national treasure."

• • •

So who is Banksy? Possibly the world's most famous living artist (sorry, David Hockney!), and definitely the most notorious. Since surfacing in Bristol's underground art and music scene in the 1990s, Banksy has left his distinctive stencil-based spray-painted images and caustic anti-establishment slogans on streets, walls, and bridges in public urban spaces worldwide, stirring things up as he goes. His images include rats, birds, chimpanzees, children, the police, and workers such as maids and housepainters, often surprised in the middle of a mundane act; if there is a single expression that appears throughout his work, it's perplexed. Symbols of war abound—tanks, gas masks, bombs, soldiers, planes—often in innocent and therefore ironic juxtaposition, such as in *The Mild Mild West*, an early and still-existing Bristol piece, in which a teddy bear is aiming a Molotov cocktail at a team of riot police. Particularly poignant is the painting, one of nine that appeared in 2007 on the West Bank barrier wall between Israel and Palestine, of a little girl frisking a soldier. And in 2007, when Banksy organized Santa's Ghetto in Bethlehem with twenty other artists to raise awareness and contributions for Palestine, his welcoming painting was of a peace dove wearing a bulletproof vest.

Having branched out into sculpture and installation, Banksy took over the entire Bristol Art Museum in 2009 with 100 works in a surprise exhibition, *Banksy Versus Bristol Museum*. Then, in October 2013, Banksy generated daily headlines as one work per day appeared somewhere on the streets of New York City during the month-long self-described "residency" he entitled *Better Out Than In*. More recently, incorporating the work of fifty-eight other artists and running for five weeks in 2015, Banksy produced his magnum opus, *Dismaland*, in Weston-super-Mare, a small resort town on England's west coast, where he fashioned a derelict water park into an anti-Disneyland—a 2.5 acre dystopian "family theme park unsuitable for children." Dedicated to the failure of capitalism, *Dismaland* featured concerts, film, miniature golf (or rather miniature "Gulf" with an appropriate oil spill), a whacked-out Cinderella's castle, games that were impossible to win, a terrifying carousel, disgruntled park guides, vegetarian food stands, and an art gallery.

0.1 *following pages*
Banksy, *The Mild Mild West*, spray painting, 1999,
Bristol, England. Photo: author.

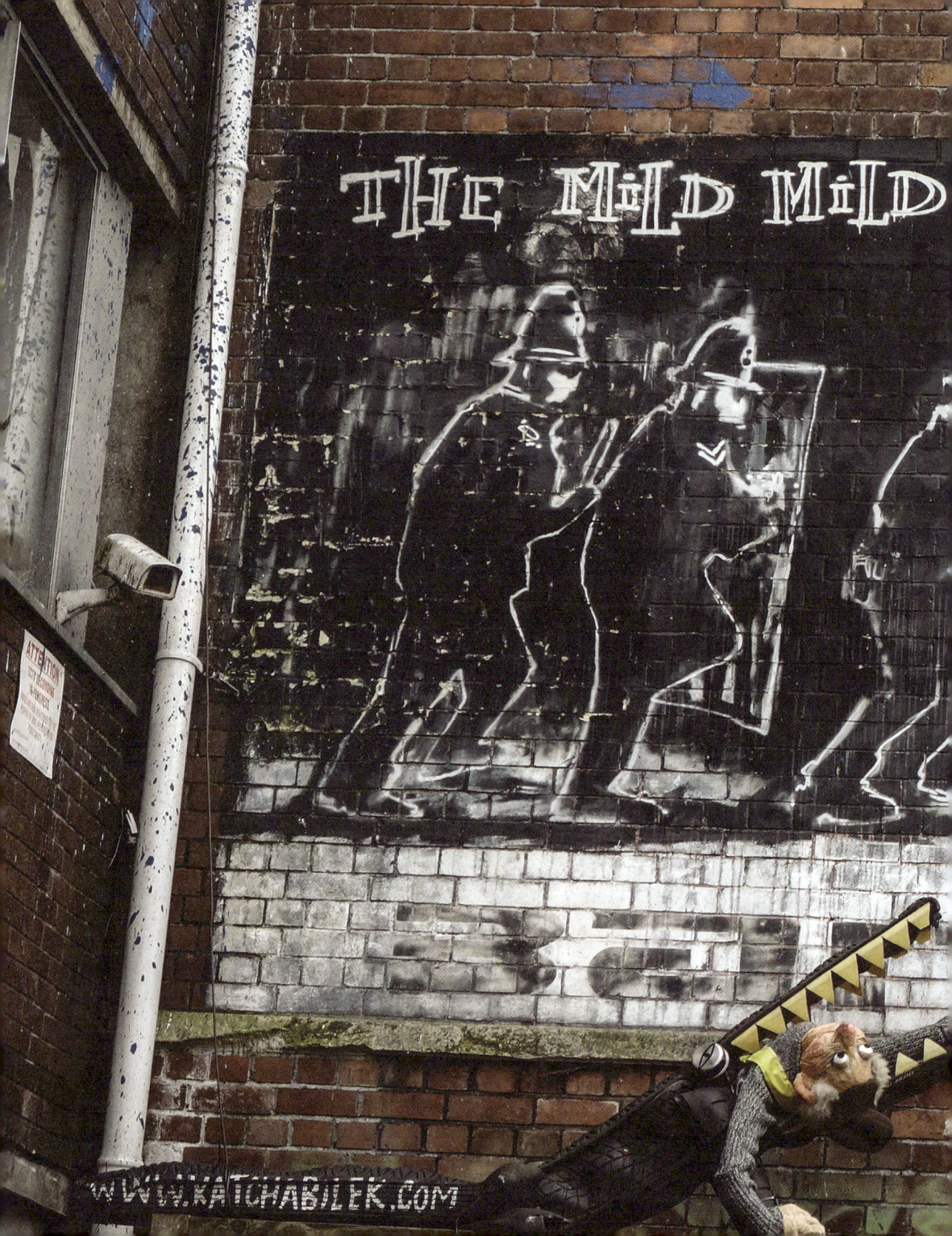

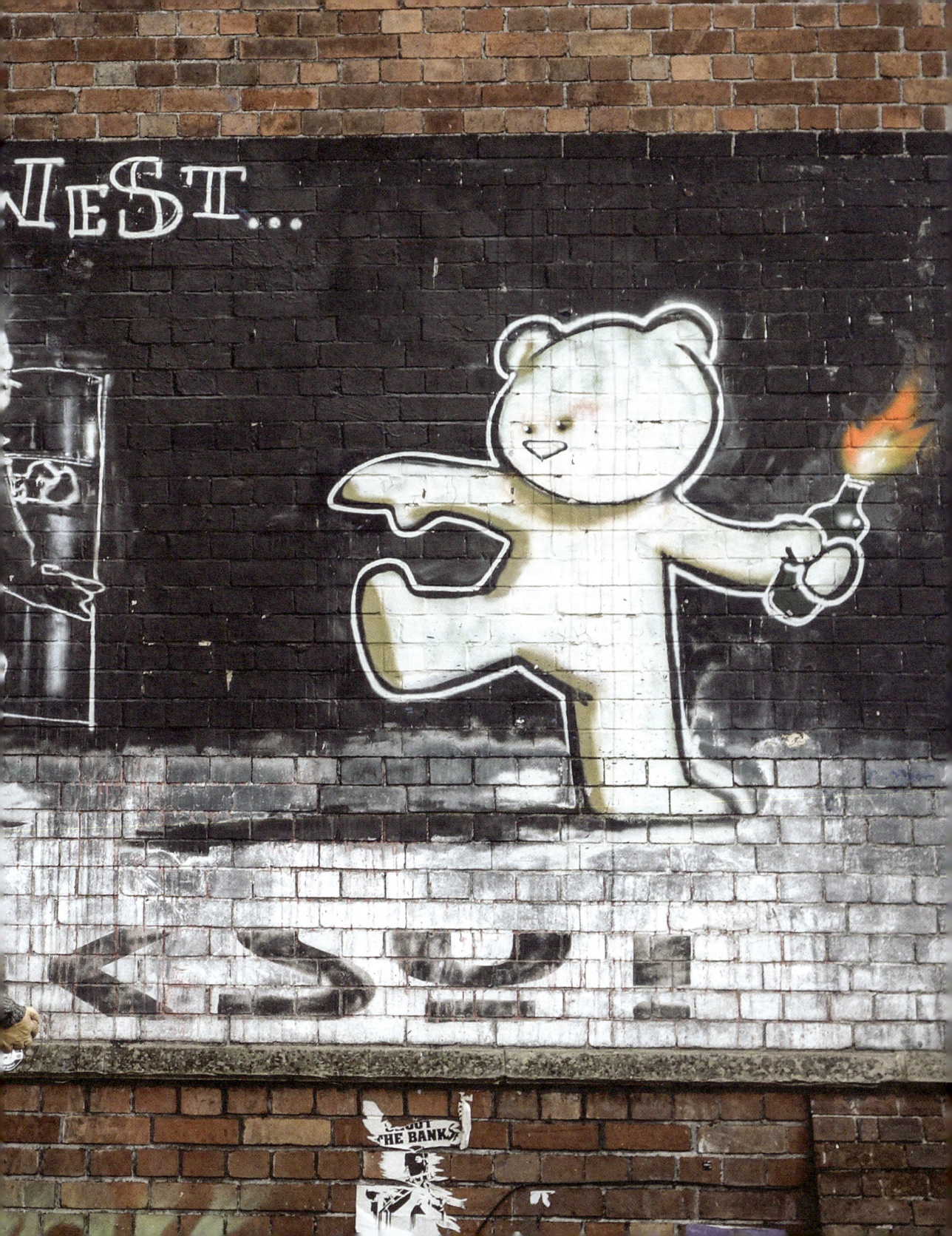

Dismaland was followed by a venture even more ambitious: *The Walled Off Hotel*, a fully functioning guesthouse with a museum and gallery that opened in March 2017. Located in the West Bank town of Bethlehem, it features "the worst view in the world," as it overlooks the massive security barrier built by Israel to enclose the Palestinian territory. Filled with his artwork and that of others, *The Walled Off Hotel* is a floor-to-ceiling work of art intended to spark dialogue and attract visitors from Tel Aviv and beyond, as well as create jobs in the area.

Banksy's carefully guarded anonymity provokes much conjecture. Is Banksy a woman? A collective? The alter ego of English superstar artist Damien Hirst? The speculation is no doubt more interesting than the reality—which is why, in 2016, when scientists at the Queen Mary University of London claimed to have identified him using an advanced system of geographic profiling usually employed to track serial criminals, the public and press seemed more taken with the detective methods than with the conclusion that Banksy is a middle-aged bloke who grew up near Bristol and went to a Catholic prep school. Superman, after all, is infinitely more compelling than Clark Kent.

And the name Banksy? It could have been derived from a number of sources. Appropriate to his somewhat Robin Hood persona, the guerrilla artist started out signing his work with the name Robin Banx as in "robbin' banks" (get it?). Also, after moving to London around 1999 and shifting toward anonymity, he favored painting on walls in places with the word "bank" embedded in the name, such as Embankment, Bankside, and South Bank. Additionally, it has been reported that he got the moniker, same as the nickname of legendary English goalkeeper Gordon Banks, while playing football for a local Bristol team. If so, he must have been very good.

That Banksy has managed to keep his identity secret all these years is something of a miracle, no doubt wrought by a combination of extreme loyalty and lawyers with piles of nondisclosure agreements. A management company, Pest Control Office (aptly named given that so much of Banksy's work has featured rats), authenticates his work and protects him from the inquisitive public. Banksy hid under a black hoodie and had his voice electronically altered when he appeared in *Exit Through the Gift Shop*, and that same year, when *Time* magazine named him one of the world's 100 most influential people, had himself photographed with his head under a brown paper bag on which he'd drawn a smiley face.

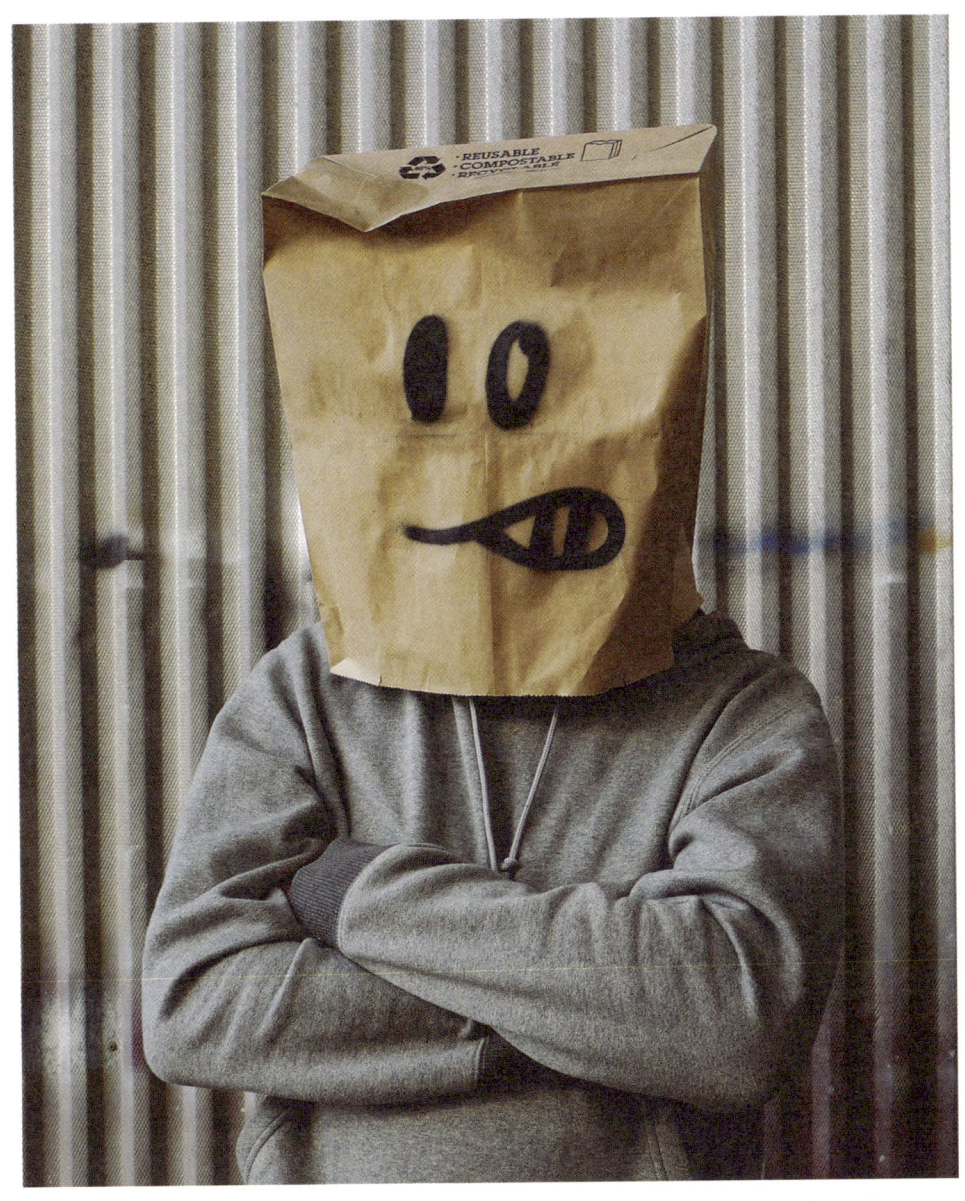

0.2
Banksy, *The TIME 100*, photograph, 2010, courtesy of
Pest Control Office.

As his following grew, so did the value of Banksy's paintings and prints. In 2007 his mind-blowing prices at auction made tabloid news when Brad Pitt and Angelina Jolie, known to their fans as "Brangelina," bought a painting for £1 million. The Banksy record-breaker, however, was *Keep It Spotless*, an original Damien Hirst painting of colored dots to which Banksy added the image of a uniformed hotel maid attempting to sweep under it, as if it were a curtain or the proverbial rug. Estimated at $350,000, *Keep It Spotless* ultimately sold at Sotheby's in 2008 for $1,700,000.

Banksy's rise coincided with a boom in the art market for certain contemporary artists, predominantly young and male, whose mushrooming prices often seemed to have more to do with hype than talent. "There are people out there pushing these artists like IPOs [initial public offerings]," said adviser Mia Romanik in a *Bloomberg* article on "flipping," a relatively recent phenomenon where a work might change hands five or six times in a single year, increasing in value each time while pumping up the prices in the artist's current catalog. It's a bubble that, as of this writing, has not yet burst. Those who make up what might be called the "critical" art world to which I belong—the artists and writers who don't directly profit, if they profit at all—tend to look askance at these fiscal shenanigans. We want artists to be successful, but only up to a point. Those whose interest in making art appears to be mostly pecuniary, such as the aforementioned Damien Hirst, are barely taken seriously.

Other than British writer Mark Hudson, who has also called Banksy a "national treasure," and the London *Times*' Rachel Campbell Johnston, who said, "He uses art as a weapon . . . sharp as a political cartoonist's joke," art critics have been scathing—the late Brian Sewell going so far as to say "Banksy should have been put down at birth." Matthew Collings has called the respect given to street art "puerile and idiotic," and regarding Banksy asks, "Do you like adolescent entertainment? Do you have the mentality of a teenager? Do you find Cezanne a bit overrated? If the answer is yes, yes and yes, then I don't know what to do with you. You are a childish philistine literalist." And finally, in complete agreement is Jonathan Jones in the *Guardian*: "[Banksy] appeals to people who hate the Turner prize. It's art for people who think that artists are charlatans."

Obviously, art critics just can't cope when an artist becomes too popular with the public. Aside from simple snobbery, which cannot altogether be denied, this attitude may have its roots in the work of political theorists of the 1960s who deplored "spectacle" and theatricality in art, which, they said, by not leaving room for active contemplation, reduced the viewer's role to that of a passive consumer of entertainment. In this was couched the fear that people would again be seduced by the pomp and circumstance of fascism, which in the '60s was not so long ago, as well as caution in the face of the growing consumerist culture and a world that was quickly becoming inundated with advertising.

As recently as 2008 these considerations were evident in a review by Roberta Smith, senior critic for the *New York Times*, where she mentioned fascism and spectacle when discussing public art, lauding the subtlety of Olafur Eliasson's only moderately popular waterfalls in New York's East River, while denouncing as "ostentatious" *The Gates*, Christo and Jean-Claude's 2005 installation of 7,503 saffron-colored banners in Central Park, which generated unmitigated public enthusiasm.

Ironically, capitalism and consumerism—as well as encroaching fascism in the form of the surveillance state—are some of Banksy's primary targets. In his book *Wall and Piece*, he writes: "We can't do anything to change the world until capitalism crumbles. In the meantime we should all go shopping to console ourselves."

• • •

Along with my son Matt's vigorous endorsement, operating in Banksy's favor was my captivation with street art, which began in the 1980s when graffiti culture was thriving in New York. At that time, the outsides of the subway cars were so ablaze with color that tourists came from Europe just to view them, and I looked forward to seeing what would roll into my local station each morning. As the art world was becoming more commercialized, I couldn't help but admire artists who were willing, quite literally, to risk their lives for their art. Being a subway passenger in those days was exciting in many ways, most of them undesirable, as it meant dealing with extreme temperatures, gross odors, rampant crime, rodents, panhandlers, and mechanical malfunctions; having to leave cars filled with smoke was an almost weekly event for those of us who rode the subway regularly. Graffiti made the interiors of the cars claustrophobic, with black felt-tip marker tags scribbled across every surface, even the windows. The exteriors, however, were glorious.

I became friends with several of the train writers when I was exhibiting my paintings with the Sidney Janis Gallery, which happened to be the first blue-chip gallery to feature graffiti-inspired art. Sidney, then an octogenarian, was one of the most influential art dealers in the world. A fearless early adopter, he was willing to take on artists he believed in, regardless of how the work might be received or even whether it would sell—starting with, among others, Picasso, Brancusi, Mondrian (whom Sidney supported with weekly checks even though there were no sales), and Marcel Duchamp, whose works, Sidney and his wife Harriet wrote in 1945, "are scarcely recognizable as the products of creative activity: they are so unorthodox, and so far removed from patterns, centuries-old, of the material and conceptual substance of painting and sculpture." Sidney's son, Carroll, told me about how, when he was eleven, Duchamp asked him and his brother to bounce a ball back and forth in the middle of a Duchamp exhibition and, if anyone questioned them, to say, "Mr. Duchamp said it was okay."

Sidney showed Jackson Pollock early on, as well as other major abstract expressionists whom he represented for ten years until, in 1962, he included Warhol and Lichtenstein in the first exhibition of what would come to be known as pop art, and his horrified AbExers, with the exception of de Kooning, quit the gallery in protest.

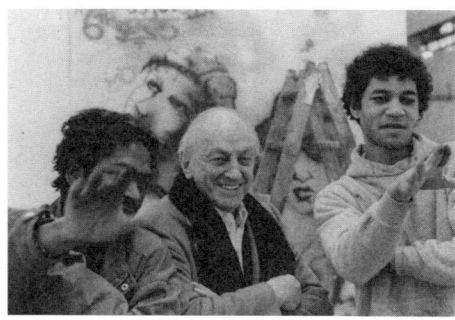

0.3
A-One, Sidney Janis, and Daze, Basel, Switzerland, 1984, courtesy of Chris Ellis. Photographer unknown.

I shudder to think what the disgruntled AbExers would have thought of Sidney's next passion, graffiti, which he came to through his interest in self-taught art (including Rousseau and Grandma Moses)—an enthusiasm that was not shared by the rest of the art world during most of his lifetime. When I interviewed him for *Art & Antiques* in 1984, he said that although he was initially annoyed by graffiti, the creative lettering on the trains won him over. Graffiti artists, Sidney said, "create their own expression, which comes from the inside, not the outside. They're not subject to what André Breton called, 'the stain of art education.'"

Only a few years short of ninety, wearing dapper suits and his trademark bow tie, Sidney hit the streets of the Bronx to seek out talent, and brought spray-painters Crash, Daze, Toxic, A-One, Lady Pink, and Rammellzee, who was also a musician, to perform and make impromptu paintings at the usually uptight Basel Art Fair in Switzerland. This is where I got to see graffiti artists at work up close, and to marvel at the technical sophistication—"can control"—that it takes to wield aerosol paint with finesse, the intricate maneuvering of fingers and wrists that makes for clean lines, variations of width and shade, and a wide array of effects.

While commercial and critical interest in graffiti fizzled in the 1990s, with few other than superstars Keith Haring and Jean-Michel Basquiat successfully crossing the boundary between high art and popular culture, it stayed with me on a personal level. Being exposed to Sidney's ability to recognize art wherever it existed, not just within the confines of the art world, enabled me to see graffiti through a broader lens than most of my contemporaries, and it ended up being an unintentional but significant influence on my own work. In my paintings, I'm always striving for graffiti's sense of immediacy coupled with palimpsest, the random layering that occurs when street artists write over each other's tags on a wall, and in the last few years have made wide use of stencils and spray ink. No one else has picked up on it, but when Charlie Ahearn, who made *Wild Style*, the classic early-1980s film about graffiti and hip-hop, visited my studio recently, he saw it right away.

Also I, too, am something of a self-taught artist, having avoided "the stain of art education" by not being admitted to the School of the Art Institute of Chicago. Instead I discovered contemporary art in an evening painting class at a suburban art center and became immersed in the short-lived but influential art scene that flourished in Chicago in the 1970s. I started writing then as

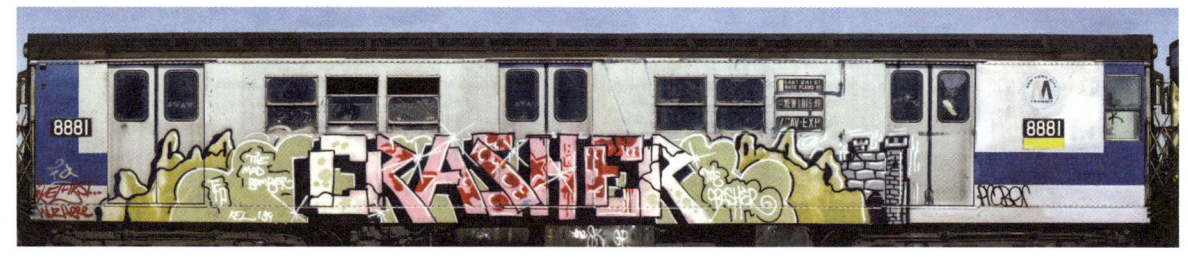

0.4
Crash, spray painting, 1979. Photo: Henry Chalfant.

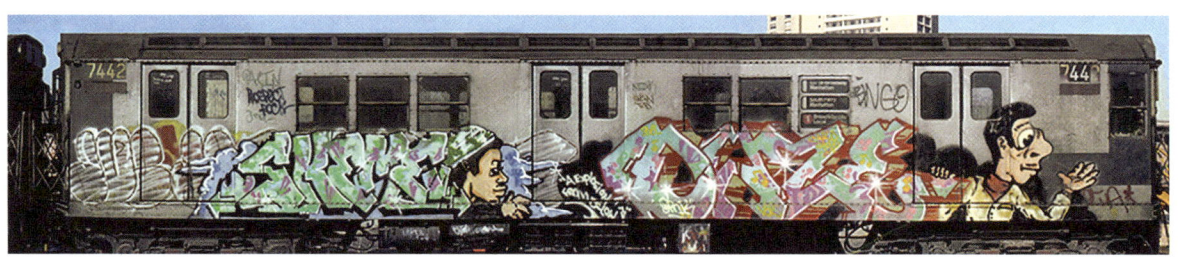

0.5
Daze, spray painting, ca. 1979, courtesy of Chris Ellis.

well, schooled by Jane Allen, editor of the fledgling local art journal the *New Art Examiner*. Jane was another outlier—an academic who was also a lone crusader against "artspeak," who insisted, shockingly at the time, that writing about art could be both intellectually rigorous and enjoyable to read. With my move to New York in 1976 to work for editor John Coplans at *Artforum* magazine and the association with the Janis Gallery, my involvement in the art world was complete. While there have been moments when I've regretted my lack of university degrees (when applying for a tenured teaching job, for instance), I think that although I'm now an insider, my biggest asset may be the sense I still have of being an outsider who doesn't take anything for granted.

Therefore, in 2013, when Banksy came to New York for his month-long residency, I was excited to see what he would do. But along with Mayor Bloomberg and the *New York Post*, whose tabloid front page howled for the police to "GET BANKSY!," my art world colleagues reacted with annoyance bordering on indignation. With the exception of *New York Times* writer Deborah Solomon who, in a radio interview, compared Banksy to eighteenth-century political satirist William Hogarth, their reviews were singularly negative. It also became evident that these otherwise scrupulous critics felt research was unnecessary when reviewing an artist they'd decided in advance was unimportant. These are the same writers who can be found railing against art school dogma and the hegemony of mega-galleries such as Gagosian, which represents Damien Hirst (it's said that almost one-third of solo shows in US museums go to artists represented by only five galleries, and the same is no doubt true worldwide), yet when an artist appears who's not part of the system, they see no need to do their homework.

This irritated me so much that I resolved to do their job for them. Convinced that there was more depth to the elusive artist's work than anyone had previously realized, I decided to devote my attention to all things Banksy—his images, books about him, books by him, his film, and news stories. What I found was enough to convince me that Banksy is one of the geniuses of our time, a worthy bearer of the torch passed by Marcel Duchamp. Along with exposing society's many hypocrisies, Banksy challenges the culture to reconsider what art is, as well as its value and purpose. If that weren't the case, there wouldn't be so many people so upset about a guy visiting New York for a month and painting on the sides of buildings. The handwriting, quite literally, was on the wall, and the status quo was digging in its heels.

B anksy: Completed

"Better out than in" is a colloquial British way of acknowledging a burp or fart, but for Banksy it has a double meaning, referring also to impressionist painter Cézanne whom he quoted on his website: "All pictures painted inside, in the studio, will never be as good as those done outside." Befitting an artist who seems unable to be entirely serious (or, for that matter, entirely frivolous), Banksy chose *Better Out Than In* as the title for his self-described 2013 New York "residency," for which he generated at least one work per day during the month of October—as well as a storm of controversy.

Not since Christo and Jeanne-Claude's *The Gates* in 2005 had the New York public been so engaged with art—and when the public likes something too much, art critics get nervous. This dim view of popular intelligence was expressed by *New York* magazine's art critic Jerry Saltz, who wrote, "People like Banksy because other people have liked Banksy and liking Banksy becomes a way of feeling like you're part of something, participating in the group mind." As Banksy devoted October to producing artwork on the streets of New York and on his website, Saltz, in an unprecedented number of articles as well as television and radio appearances on a single subject, devoted the month to dissing the "bad artist" he dubbed "Mr. Meh." If the more than five hundred responses to each of Saltz's Facebook posts about Banksy could be seen as indicators, the rest of the New York art world was in fervent agreement, closing rank against the upstart outsider with whom most, surprisingly, seemed to be unfamiliar. Also weighing in on Banksy's lack of artistic prowess was Roberta Smith, *New York Times* critic and married to Saltz, who described his output as "distracting" and

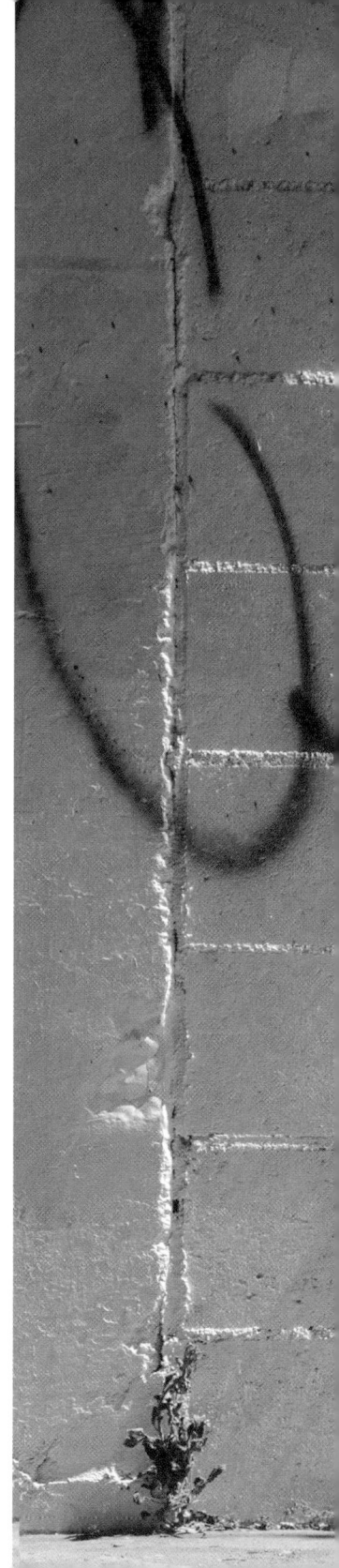

1.1
Banksy, *Better Out Than In*, 2013, spray painting,
New York, courtesy of Pest Control Office.

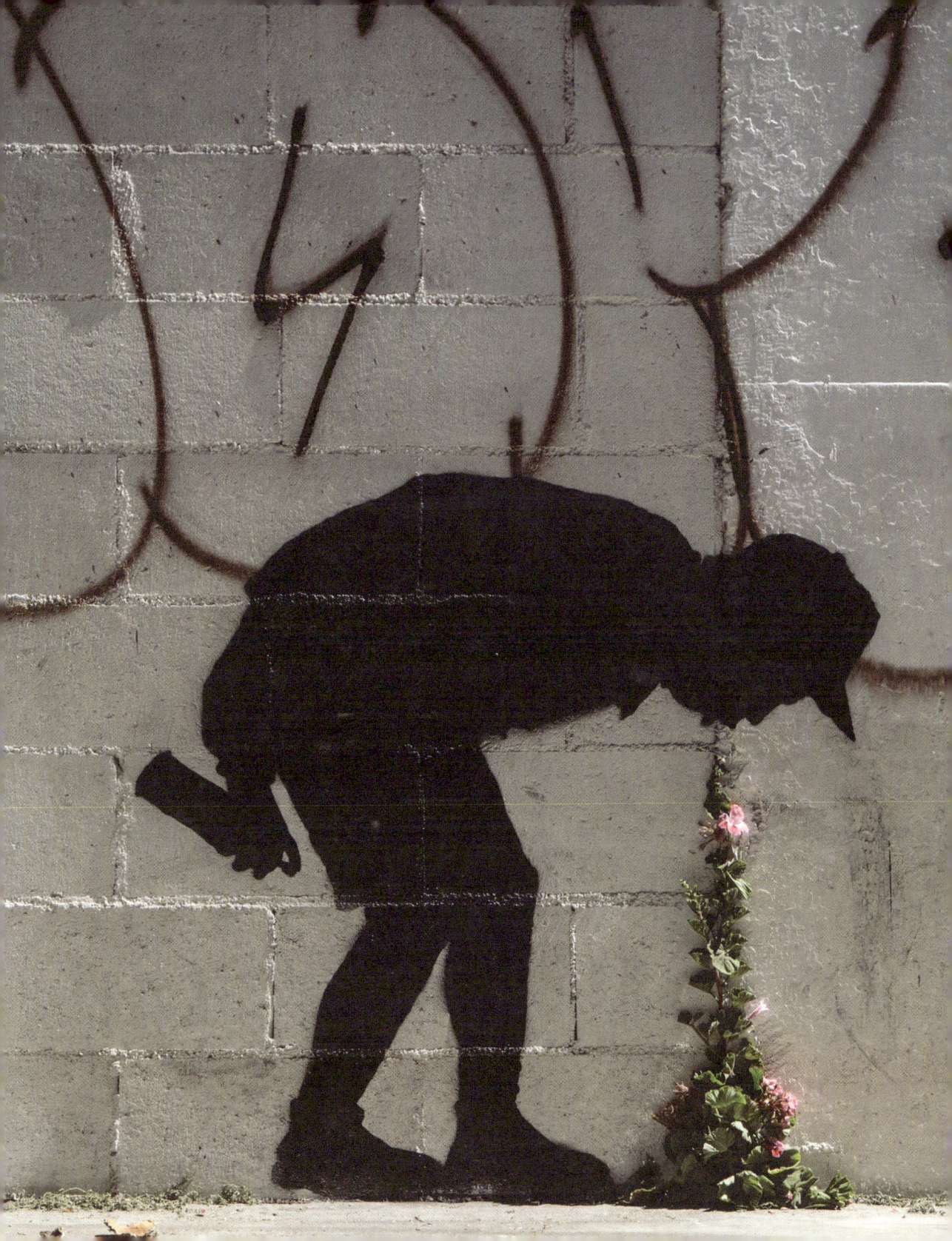

1.2

Banksy, *You Complete Me*, 2013, spray painting, New York.
Photo: Joshua Tjaden.

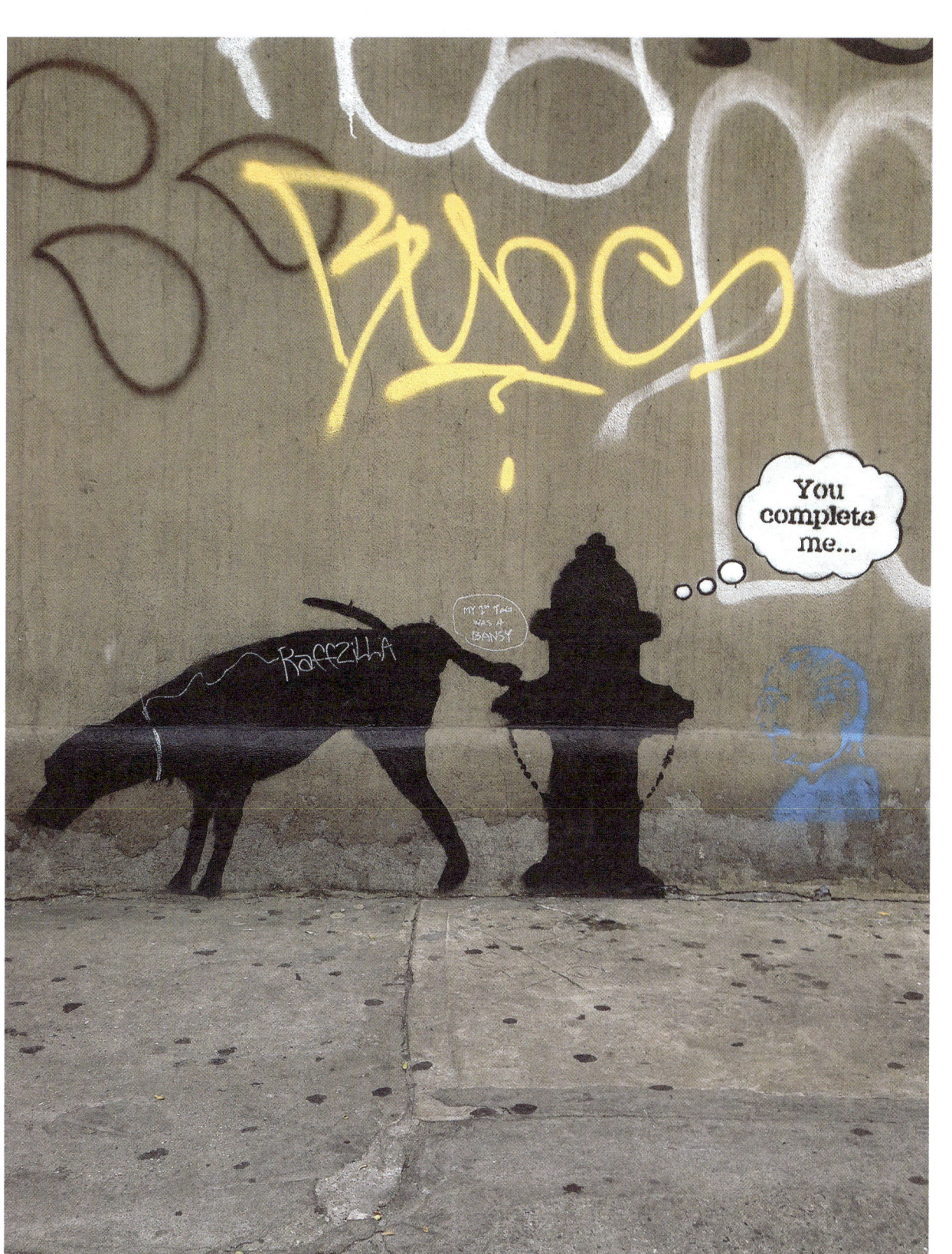

"frothy," while asking, "But what of these works as art? . . . His October offerings have had a made-by-committee variety, full of adman jokes and sight gags that emphasize a clear punch line over visual style."

Our opposing views of Banksy caused Saltz and me, old friends that we are, to go head to head on Facebook, each insisting that the other had lost their critical marbles. He faulted me, in a message, for having "a weak eye," while I held out the hope that if Saltz were to assess the breadth of Banksy's output, look at the video and "audio guides" posted daily during the month on Banksy's website, peruse his books and watch *Exit Through the Gift Shop*, he might have a greater understanding if not appreciation of his work. At least he wouldn't have described Banksy in *New York* magazine as "the subject of a big-time documentary film," when those who have seen *Exit* know that Banksy's role in the mindbender he produced is supporting at most, and the question of whether it's a documentary or a "mockumentary" remains frustratingly unanswered. (On Facebook, in the beginning of November, Saltz allowed he still hadn't seen the film but that "Everyone says it's great!")

Meanwhile Banksy's opinion of art critics matches their opinions of him. When veteran critic Brian Sewell said he was "a complete clown," the artist responded, "When criticising art in return for money, please try to remember who the parasite is in this relationship."

By focusing on the images alone and comparing hasty spray paintings on exterior walls to showpieces in galleries and museums, Saltz and Smith overlook not only the history and intention of street art, but the essence of Banksy, each of whose endeavors is more like an intervention, action, or Happening—which, John Cage said, "should be like a net to catch a fish the nature of which one does not know." The videos and "audio guides," the context, the reaction, what happens to it later (painted over? not painted over? removed and sold by others for profit? stolen? destroyed?) comprise a synthesis of contextual and conceptual art, social commentary, political protest, and relational aesthetics played out, not in museums at twenty to twenty-five dollars a head, but where it can have the most effect: on the street, in the real world.

Saltz: Another day, another Banksy . . . an idiotic dog-shadow peeing on a firehydrant thing. There's a thought balloon drifting from the hydrant that says, "You complete me." Really? That's what people think is "so great" and "important" and so politically pointed? Really?

Key here is the cryptic phrase "You complete me," from the 1996 film *Jerry Maguire*, which became a meme before there were memes. And by acting the art critic and figuratively "pissing" on the piece, Saltz unwittingly "completes" it—as Banksy clearly anticipated in his "audio guide" for that day, where a casual American male voice says:

> You are in Midtown Manhattan. Are you looking at one of the great artworks of the twenty-first century? If so, you're in the wrong place! You should be looking at a stencil of a dog peeing on a hydrant. (I call it "spay" art . . . heh heh). It's a well-known truism that the mark of a great artist is their ability to capture light. So you will note that this piece is rendered entirely in silhouette. At first glance, this may seem a thin faux comical cartoon aimed at providing a small glimmer of light relief to local commuters. But look again and what do you see? That's right! A structural re-contextualizing of the juxtaposition between form and surface . . . welcome to the art world! Perhaps Bansky *[sic]* is playing with the notion that graffiti is the territorial spraying of feral youth. After all, wouldn't the architecture foisted on our cities be incomplete without the maverick stains of those answering back? Or perhaps, as some would argue, this is a broader comment on the nature of abusive relationships . . . *(voice fades into Muzak-like accompaniment).*

Soon Banksy had provoked a number of others into appearing stuffy and silly, while simultaneously operating as his unpaid publicity agents—like Mayor Bloomberg, who presents himself as a supporter of the arts, whose statement in a press conference that "Graffiti is a sign of decay and loss of control" caused the *New York Post* to fill its tabloid front page with just two words: "GET BANKSY!" Then the editors of the *New York Times*, whose rejection of Banksy's op-ed piece criticizing the bland architecture of the new One World Trade Center (now stuck with his term "shyscraper") became a story in itself, possibly getting him more international coverage than if they'd published the original.

In his book *Wall and Piece*, Banksy recounts a fable where a king's court painter was pitted in competition with a "dirty and disheveled stranger" who claimed "*he* was the greatest painter in the land." After "thirty days of working feverishly, day and night," the artists presented their paintings, both hidden by a cloth, to the king. The court painter's, presented first, was so realistic a bird flew down and tried to snatch a painted grape. When the vagabond refused to pull the covering from his painting, the king tried in vain to pull it away himself: "You see, said the tramp quietly, there is no blanket covering the painting.

This is actually just a painting of a cloth covering a painting. And whereas your famous artist is content to fool Nature, I've made the king of the country look like a clueless little twat."

Banksy attributes the story to "a man in a pub," when actually it's his adaptation of a Greek legend about two fifth-century BCE painters, Zeuxis and Parrhasios, who stage a contest to prove who is the better artist. The French psychoanalyst Jacques Lacan, whose writing greatly influenced critical theory, uses the legend as an example when discussing *trompe-l'oeil*, saying that "if one wishes to deceive the man, what one presents to him is the painting of the veil, that is to say, something that incites him to ask what is behind it."

Trompe-l'oeil, of course, is one of Banksy's primary tools. Often it's literal, in the form of signs or markings that mimic official ones, such as the stenciled sign for a "designated graffiti area" that carries an authentic-looking crest (lifted from a cigarette package). But it's also active in the way he incorporates existing elements and blends his images so thoroughly into their surroundings that they look as if they'd always been there. Banksy's images don't shout for attention, but sidle obliquely into your consciousness so you have to pull yourself back and question them, while questioning yourself: "Did I really see that? Does that wall under that surveillance camera really say 'One nation under CCTV'? And if they're watching, how did it get there?"

"Adept at creating and unmasking deceit, proficient at hiding his tracks and at seeing through the devices used by others to hide theirs" is how scholar and cultural critic Lewis Hyde, in his book *Trickster Makes This World*, describes the archetype that appears throughout world mythology. The trickster is a boundary-crosser, a traveler and thief who, Hyde writes, "is amoral not *immoral*. He embodies and enacts that large portion of our experience where good and evil are hopelessly intertwined. . . . When he lies and steals, it isn't so much to get away with something or get rich as to disturb the established categories of truth and property and, by so doing, open the road to possible new worlds." Tricksters are necessary, Hyde argues, for the reason that "no self-contained world can induce its own fundamental change, because self-containment means it knows nothing beyond its own givens."

In Greek mythology the trickster is Hermes, whom Banksy evoked when configuring the fiberglass replica of Ronald McDonald that appeared on the sidewalk outside a different McDonald's every lunchtime for a week in mid-October, accompanied by a real live boy who sat shining his shoes.

From the "audio guide" of Day 16, spoken by the same wry, soft-spoken man with the American accent:

> What you see before you is a sculpture entitled *Shoe Shine* dating from the summer of 2013 depicting the powerful figure of Ronald McDonald waiting impassively while his ridiculously oversized clown shoes are buffed to a fine shine. Ronald was adopted as the official mascot of the McDonald's fast food corporation chain in 1966. Fiberglass versions of his likeness have been installed outside restaurants ever since, thus making Ronald arguably the most sculpted figure in history after Christ. For this piece the artist has reproduced Ronald McDonald in perfect detail single-handedly—if by perfect detail you mean roughly, and by single-handedly you mean with two people helping. The result is a critique of the heavy labor required to sustain the polished image of a mega-corporation. Is Ronald's statuesque pose indicative of how corporations have become the historical figures of our era? Does this hero have feet of clay? And a massively large footprint to boot? But take a closer look, and you may notice something familiar about this clown. His face is that of the Greek god Hermes, carved by Praxiteles in 340 BC. Is this a wry, oblique reference to Greek mythology? Or, did the artist have such difficulty trying to sculpt the face that he simply plonked on the nearest replica bust he could find? We will never know. *[Whisper]* It's the second one.

Even if one doesn't recognize that Banksy's Ronald McDonald is modeled after Greek sculpture, his face and bearing read subliminally as representative of the patriarchy. His attitude is disdainful and, given his stance, Ronald's foot might as well be on the back of the boy. Of course as Banksy no doubt expected, the piece was regularly ticketed for obstructing pedestrian traffic, thereby forcing the police inadvertently into the position of being protectors of the McDonald's brand. One weird aftereffect of Banksy's version of Ronald McDonald is that once you've seen it, the original statue appears downright pervy.

It's also amusing to consider, in the context of McDonald's, that Hermes is a god associated with cattle. He is also the god of overland travel, represented by the mounds of rough stones called "cairns," used from prehistory to the present to mark trails and landmarks—remarkably like Banksy's one-thirty-sixth replica of the Great Sphinx of Giza made from smashed cinderblocks that appeared on October 22 in an abandoned lot in Queens. Leaving "no turn unstoned," he titled it *Everything but the Kitchen Sphinx* and advised visitors "not to drink the replica Arab Spring water."

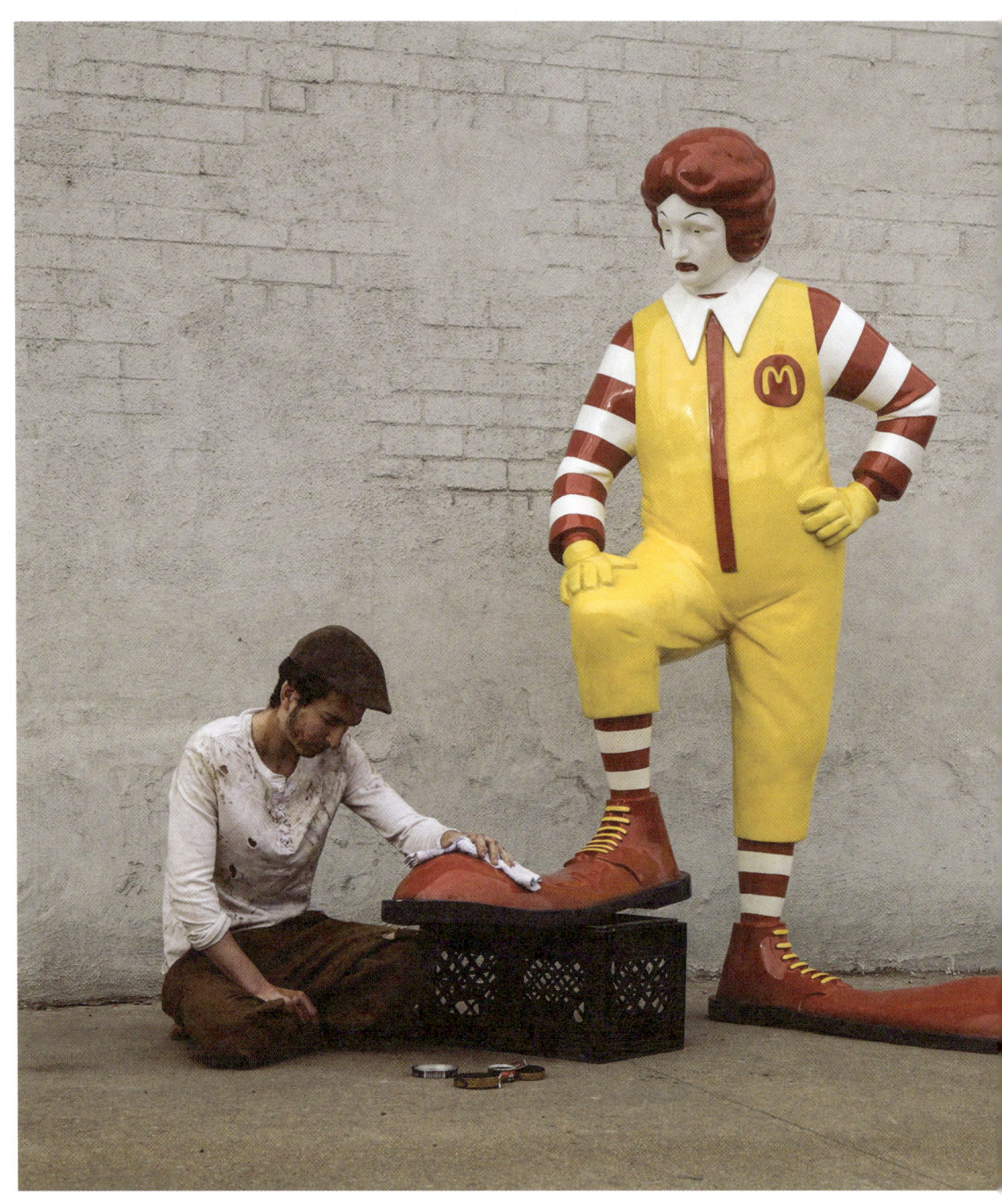

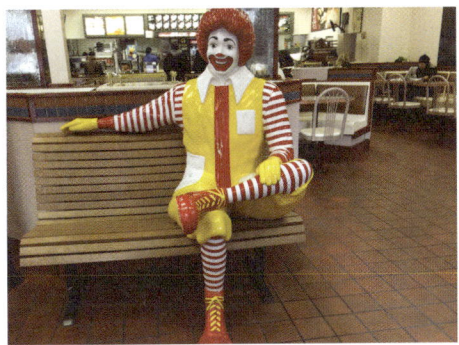

1.3 *left*

Banksy, *Shoe Shine*, 2013, fiberglass, paint, New York, courtesy of Pest Control Office.

1.4

Ronald McDonald, New York.
Photo: author.

1.5 *following pages*

Banksy, *Everything but the Kitchen Sphinx*, 2013, concrete, brick foam, New York, courtesy of Pest Control Office.

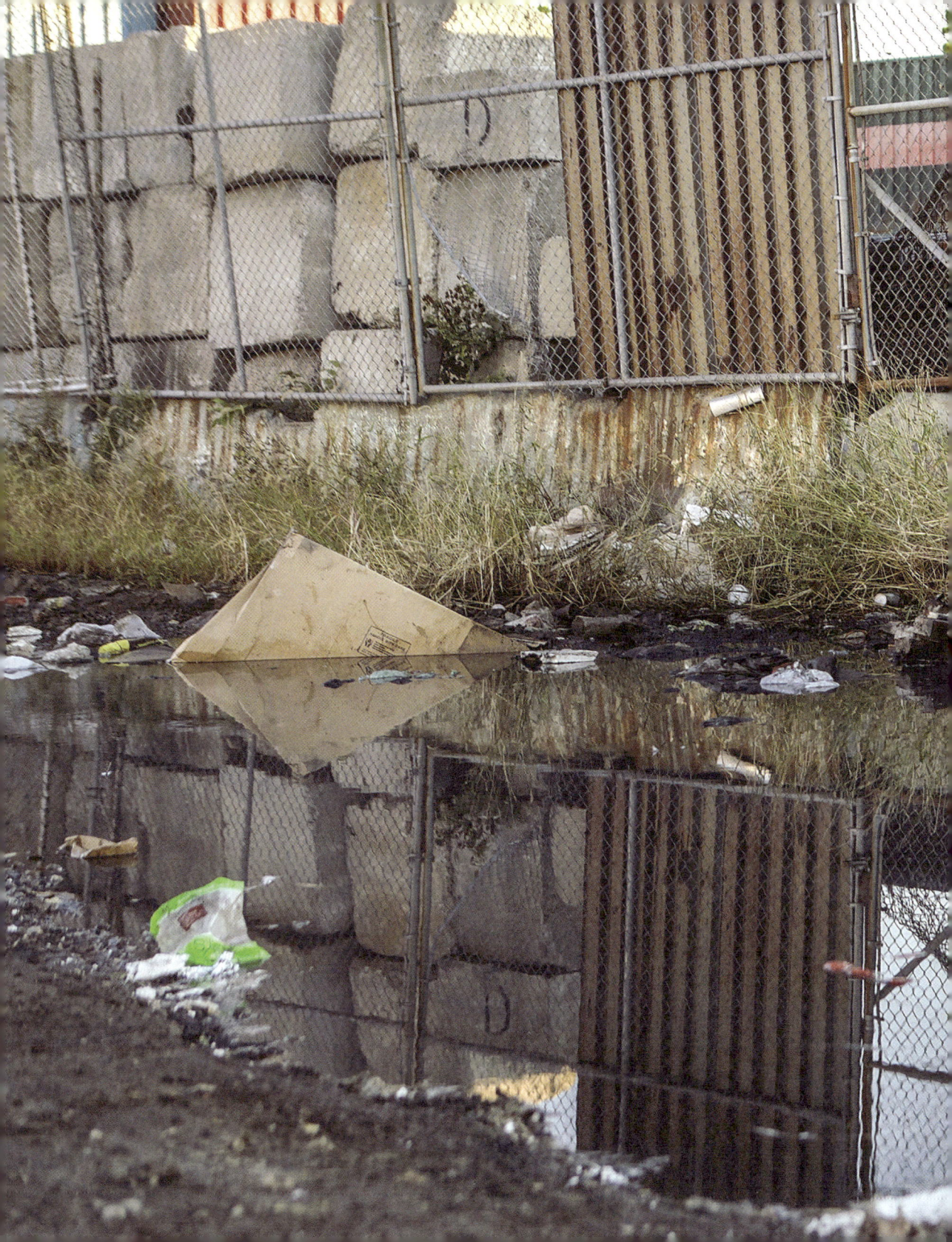

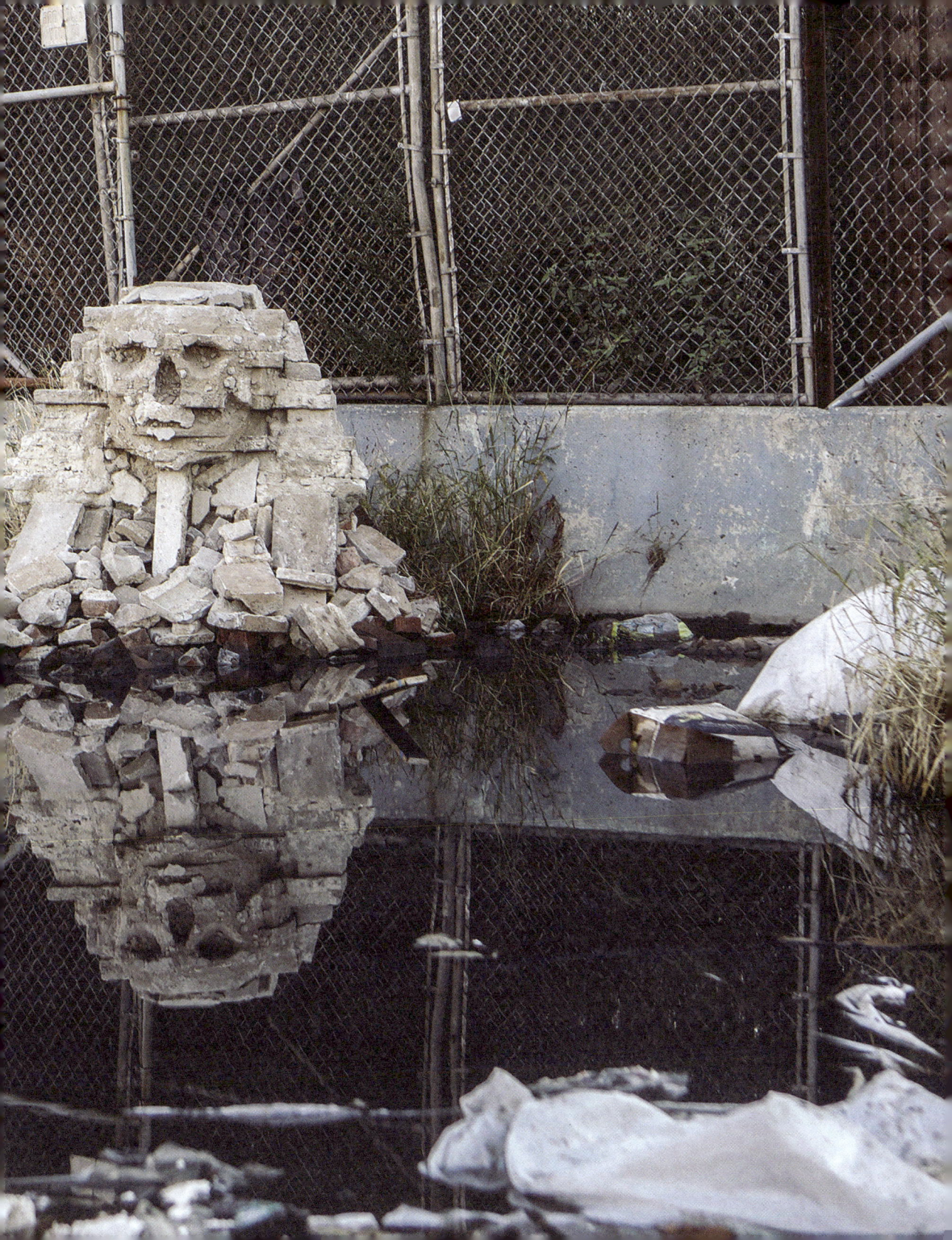

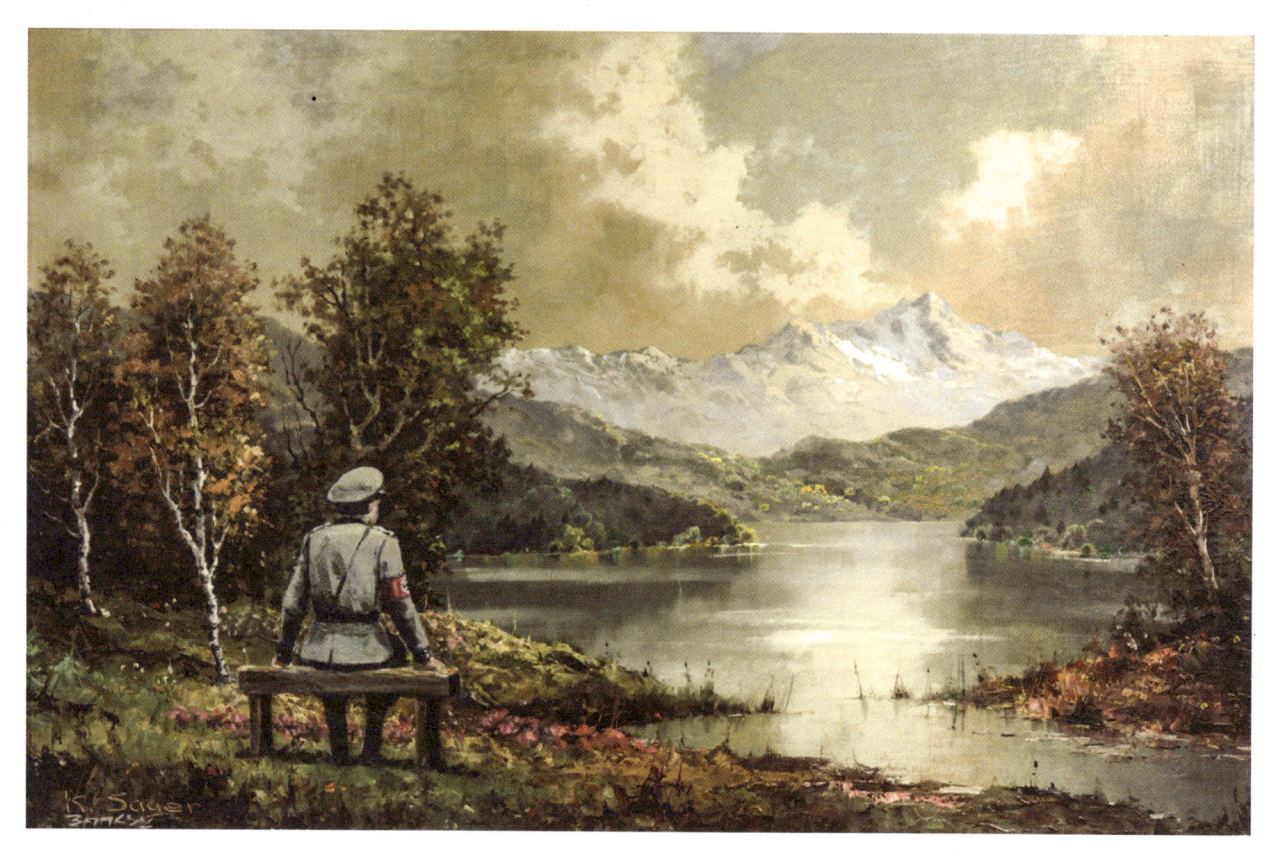

1.6

Banksy, *The Banality of the Banality of Evil*, 2013, oil on oil on canvas, courtesy of Pest Control Office.

Capitalism, imperialism, greed, and war are Banksy's primary targets, which segue into issues of morality, accountability, culpability, legitimacy, value and values, law and regulation, all of which he tackles with dark humor. These themes converged when Banksy repurposed an original artwork, an over-wrought pastoral oil painting purchased for fifty dollars from the Housing Works thrift store. With his painted addition of a solitary Nazi officer seated in contemplation on a bench, the painting of an autumn forest by a river with snowy mountains in the distance is transformed from kitsch Americana to Caspar David Friedrich-esque German romanticism, the falling yellow leaves now signifying the decline of the Nazi regime as well as a warning, perhaps, of our own social and political decline. Scrawling his signature under that of the original artist, Banksy, on his website, titled the work "*The banality of the banality of evil*, oil on oil on canvas, 2013," and described it as "a thrift store painting vandalized then re-donated to the thrift store," with the intention that the proceeds go to the Brooklyn-based nonprofit that benefits homeless people living with HIV/AIDS. Housing Works auctioned it off and ultimately, after much bidding drama, netted at least $450,000.

On the *Village Voice* blog, writer Raillan Brooks no doubt Googled "the banality of evil" to discover that it was associated with Holocaust escapee and philosopher Hannah Arendt's "theoretical reckoning of the Nazis' rise to power." Brooks concluded, however, that the phrase more likely had "something to do with Banksy not really caring much about what he's actually saying"—when it's clearly the key to Banksy's philosophy, and the theme that underlies his subversive enterprises.

A Report on the Banality of Evil is the subtitle of Arendt's 1963 book *Eichmann in Jerusalem*, an eyewitness account of the Nazi criminal trial of Adolf Eichmann, who was accused of engineering the extermination of European Jews. Writing originally in the *New Yorker*, Arendt expressed shock that Eichmann did not come across as a monster, but "terribly and terrifyingly normal," a man whose thinking was so conventional that he spoke only in clichés. This insight led Arendt to develop her thesis that beyond Hitler's vile nature, it was the mediocrity of his functionaries, their unwillingness to think for themselves while attempting to fulfill their mundane needs and individual ambitions—hence their banality—that enabled the Nazi atrocities. Therefore, Banksy's title has to do with the original painting being itself a cliché, the work of a painter who is trying to please others rather than thinking for himself, and by inserting the Nazi officer, Banksy is adding a symbol of banality to banality, with "oil on oil."

While being tried as a war criminal, Adolf Eichmann insisted on his innocence, saying he never killed anyone or ordered that anyone be killed, nor did he have a grudge against Jews. He was a man eager to get ahead, and his job, which he fulfilled efficiently, was to arrange for the transportation of Jewish prisoners to the death camps. To do otherwise, he explained on the stand, would be to break the law at the time, and he was not a law-breaker. Their destination was not his responsibility.

This concept is at the heart of Bernhard Schlink's 1995 novel *The Reader*, later made into a film. One of two main characters, Hanna, is being tried for a war crime, but she's not an officer—nothing like it—simply a guard who never considers the possibility that she could defy orders and unlock the burning church in which most of her prisoners die. Like Eichmann, what's chilling about Hanna is her ordinariness; she's just doing her job. Arendt suggests that evil is more accidental than intentional, less a result of ideology and conviction than a by-product of petty ambition and the drive for personal security.

> *Banksy:* The greatest crimes in the world are not committed by people breaking the rules but by people following the rules. It's people who follow orders that drop bombs and massacre villages. As a precaution to ever committing major acts of evil it is our solemn duty never to do what we're told, this is the only way we can be sure.

It is therefore significant that Banksy's Nazi officer is depicted not as an ogre but as a lover of nature, which makes him all the more normal and therefore frightening. In that context, Banksy's entire crusade can be seen as against what one Arendt scholar famously summed up as a "failure to think"—in other words, mediocrity and banality in all its forms.

Because Banksy's work is also political and often incorporates silhouettes, Jerry Saltz compares him negatively to one of our best-known gallery artists, saying, "Banksy's art is conventional political realism and doesn't pack anywhere near the formal or psychological incendiary wallop of, say, the artist Kara Walker, who's been making cutout paper silhouettes of slave life for almost twenty years." While we can't be reminded too many times of the horrors of American slavery, what about now? While Banksy risks arrest (or bullets, as when he "bombed" the West Bank barrier wall), Walker is not painting her images on barns in KKK land; her audience is those who can afford to see her work in museums and the multimillionaire collectors who buy it—of whom it could be said that they are thereby enabled to make a show of being on the right side without having to otherwise do anything about it. Patrick Potter and Gary Shove, in their book *Banksy: You Are an Acceptable Level of Threat*, would call this "cash for credibility." "It's a bit weird buying agit-prop to decorate your dining room with," they write, noting the inherent contradiction in "taking radical gestures and absorbing them into a narrative that supports capitalism."

The effectiveness of institutionalized protest, or rather the lack of it, was brought home to me in 2011 when I went to the Metropolitan Opera to see Philip Glass's *Satyagraha*, about Gandhi and nonviolent resistance, after which guards were employed to steer the exiting audience clear of the actual Occupy gathering taking place outside.

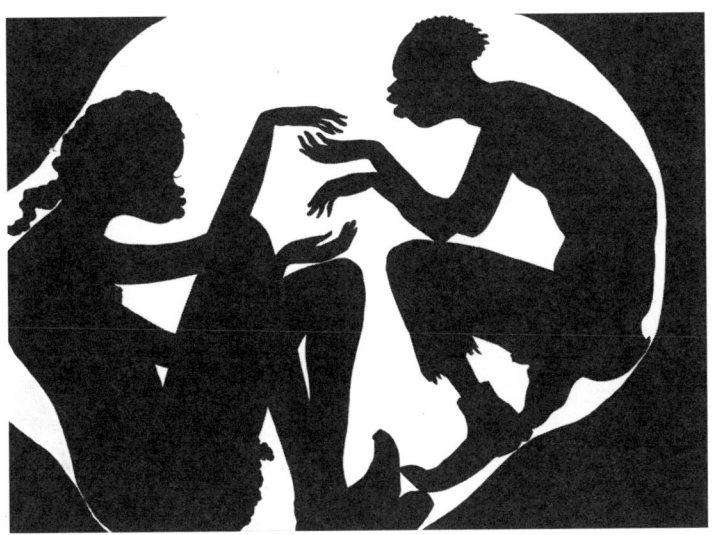

1.7
Kara Walker, *Event Horizon* (detail), 2005, mural/public art installation, Arnhold Hall, The New School, New York. Photo: author. © Kara Walker.

What no doubt leads Saltz to accuse Banksy of being "anarchy-lite" is the very thing that makes his work sophisticated and radical: it vilifies no one. With some exceptions (such as when he placed the blow-up figure dressed and shackled like a Guantanamo prisoner in a Disneyland ride), Banksy doesn't condemn but rather chides as he presents alternatives to the status quo: What if there wasn't "another crap advert" here? What if two male bobbies could kiss freely? What if children could play safely on Palestine's West Bank barrier? Living, as we do, in a culture that's constantly pitting one side against another, such an attitude can be confusing, especially when dealing with matters of life and death.

This gentle humanism is evident in the video Banksy posted on October 6 in which, in just ninety seconds, he makes a convincing case that war is mindless cruelty. The video is a parody of an attack by Syrian rebels that incorporates, among other things, actual footage and audio from a recent military skirmish; however, the menace they shoot from the sky turns out to be . . . Dumbo. While the soldiers jump on his back and jubilantly shout praises to God ("Allahu Akbar! Allahu Akbar!"), a child comes onto the scene and, seeing his beloved cartoon elephant in distress, kicks his gun-toting elder angrily in the shin.

Along with the *Voice*'s still baffled Raillan Brooks, who wrote: "It's unclear what this is supposed to mean," the pundits engaged in conjecture:

The Independent: Commenters believe the clip reflects the way we've been granted an insight into the Syrian conflict through videos uploaded onto the internet."

Business Insider: "There's some speculation that the video is a reference to the DUMBO section of Brooklyn. Perhaps it will be the location of the artist's next piece."

9News.au.com: "The clip has been criticised online with some commentators suggesting Banksy is indifferent to the plight of Syrians and has trivialised their struggle."

The Washington Post: "The video has been received poorly by Syria-watchers, some of whom have described its 'crude politics' as an over-simplification of the conflict."

Robert Mackey on his *New York Times* blog: "Many close observers of the conflict in Syria were either confused or unimpressed by the artist's gnomic commentary."

Meanwhile, it was a comment on Reddit that perfectly summed up the piece: "It's a view of war from the eyes of the child. The adults . . . feel victorious for ideological reasons. . . . The child doesn't have these ideas and only sees that the adults killed something beautiful. So he goes over and kicks the guy as if to say 'great work you fucking doofus.'"

Exactly. Why does the public get Banksy when the critics don't? Most likely because the public knows more about Banksy than the "experts" who, perceiving a sudden opportunity for publicity, appear to be rushing to judgment without doing their homework. Further, the public has no vested interests to defend. Banksy's critics, however, unconsciously "complete" the work (or expose themselves as "twats") by revealing how the lens of self-interest limits observation. Imbedded in their own narrative and hampered by their preconceptions, they seem to fear they will lose their authority if they succumb to the antics of the trickster.

Another example is Karl Sharro, a Lebanese architect and online satirist based in London, who tweeted about the video: "None of that is related to art, he's a crude propagandist and that's if you want to flatter him. . . . 'Banksy's art makes you think.' How dumb do you have to be to need something to remind you to think?"

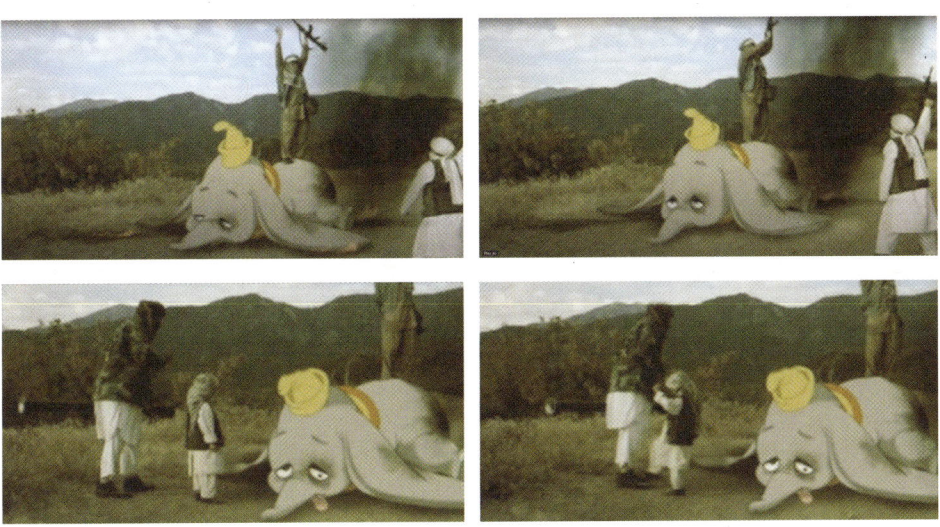

1.8

Banksy, *Rebel Rocket Attack*, 2013, video, courtesy of Pest Control Office. Screenshots: author.

Sharro doesn't need to be reminded to think, perhaps, but to notice that an essential component of propaganda—ideology—is lacking here. If Banksy's work does invite us to "think," it is by asking us to imagine a world without these cultural givens, to observe it with the innocence of the children who appear so frequently in his work and who, as in the Dumbo video, just might have a clearer understanding of what's important than the adults whose decisions form their world.

And finally, as a reminder that nothing is random or accidental in Banksyland, Wikipedia tells us that Dumbo was the code name used by the US Navy during the 1940s and 1950s to signify search and rescue missions by long-range aircraft flying over the ocean.

> *Banksy:* When the time comes to leave, just walk away quietly and don't make any fuss.

Some followers expected that Banksy would mark his tenure in New York by going out with a bang on the last day. Instead, in the wee hours, on the side of an abandoned building on the Long Island Expressway in Queens, Banksy installed an inflated blow-up spelling out his name in the bubble letters we've come to associate with graffiti. Those who called in heard the accompanying "audio guide," where, over the background of Frank Sinatra's "New York, New York," the now-familiar narrator intoned:

> Well, this is the last day of the show, and I'd like to say we're going out on a high note. And, I guess in a way, we are. [Cue "New York, New York"] This is a sideways take on the ubiquitous spray-painted bubble lettering that actually floats. It's an homage of sorts to the most prevalent form of graffiti in the city that invented it for the modern era. Or, it's another Banksy piece that's full of hot air.
>
> So, what does the artist hope to have achieved with this so-called residency? Shame it didn't get any press. He told me, "If just one child has been inspired to pick up a can of paint and make some art—well that would be statistically disappointing considering how much work I put in."
>
> It's been an interesting experiment, but is there a cohesive message behind it? I gave the artist two minutes to think of one.
>
> Banksy asserts that outside is where art should live, amongst us. And rather than street art being a "fad," maybe it's the last thousand years of art history that are the blip. When art came inside in service of the church and institutions. But art's rightful place is on the cave walls of our communities, where it can act as a public service, provoke debate, voice concerns, forge identities.

The world we live in today is run, visually at least, by traffic signs, billboards, and planning committees. Is that it? Don't we want to live in a world made of art, not just decorated by it?

Thanks for coming.

[Fireworks]

On his website Banksy wrote "An inflatable throw-up on the Long Island Expressway. And that's it. Thanks for your patience. It's been fun. Save 5pointz. Bye." The 5Pointz Banksy wanted to save was a former water meter factory turned artist studios, whose entire exterior was covered with street art to the point that it attracted international visitors. The landlord's decision to demolish the building and build a luxury residential complex ignited protests that were covered in newspapers all over the world. Ultimately the building was demolished, but the semi-good news is that the celebrated court case resulted in the owner being ordered to pay twenty-one artists $6.7 million in damages.

Banksy's piece stayed up until midday when three men scaled ladders to take the letters down. They were arrested for "criminal mischief"—as we don't yet have official terminology to apply to those caught vandalizing vandalism—and the police confiscated the work. In such cases, unclaimed property is held for up to eighteen months, after which it's considered abandoned and then either destroyed or auctioned off to benefit the city's general fund. So, yes, the police *could* have auctioned the piece off and gained $200,000 or $300,000—but only if they designated it as art, which would have put them in the untenable position of condoning Banksy's illegal efforts. It was a quiet move on Banksy's part, but one that left the police with the job of defining what is and isn't art.

Trickster to the end, when he left town, Banksy also removed his website, so that the only record of his activities is in reflections of the others who "complete" the experience—as I am doing now by writing this and you by reading it.

1.9 *following pages*
Banksy, *Balloon Banksy*, 2013, inflatables, New York, courtesy of Pest Control Office.

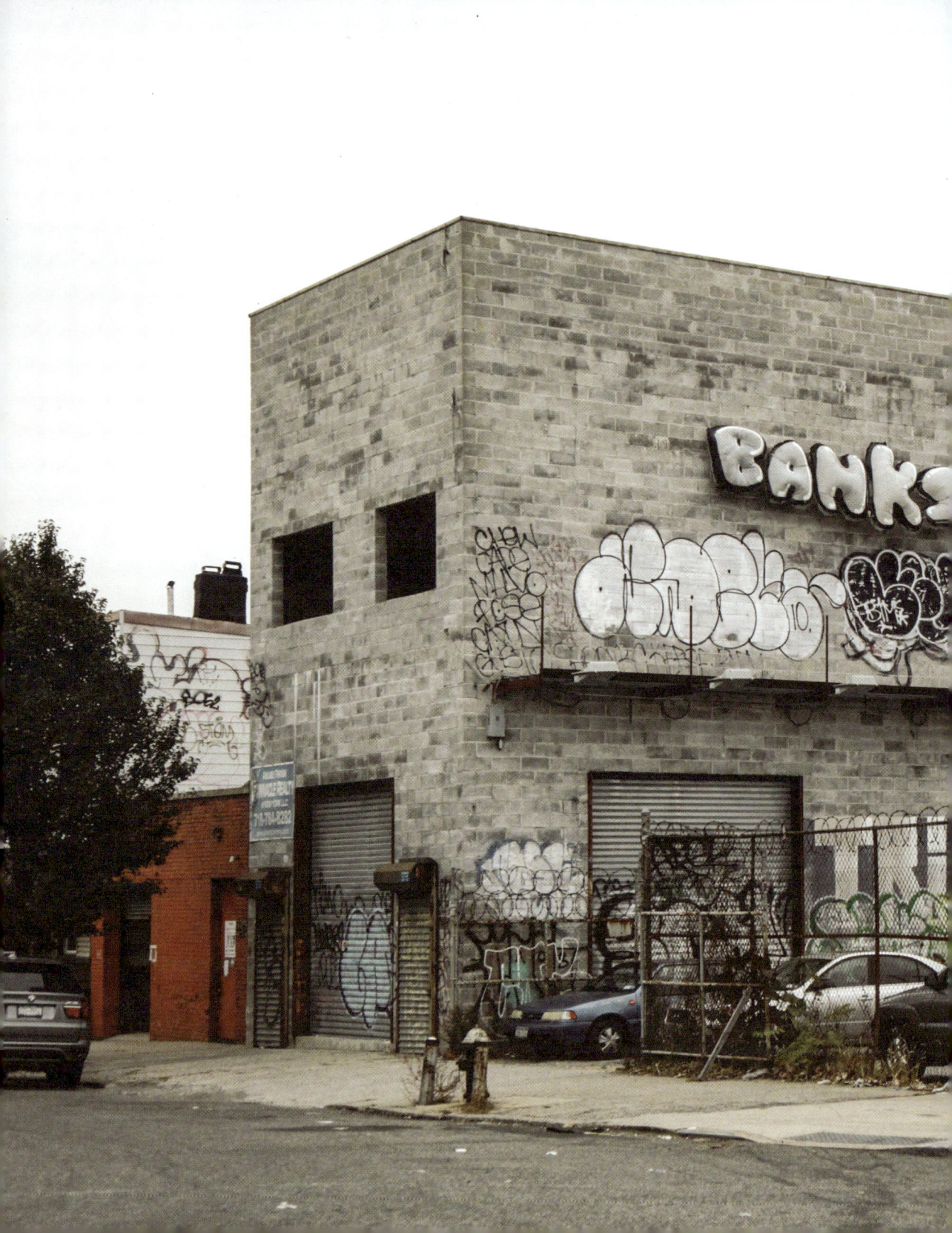

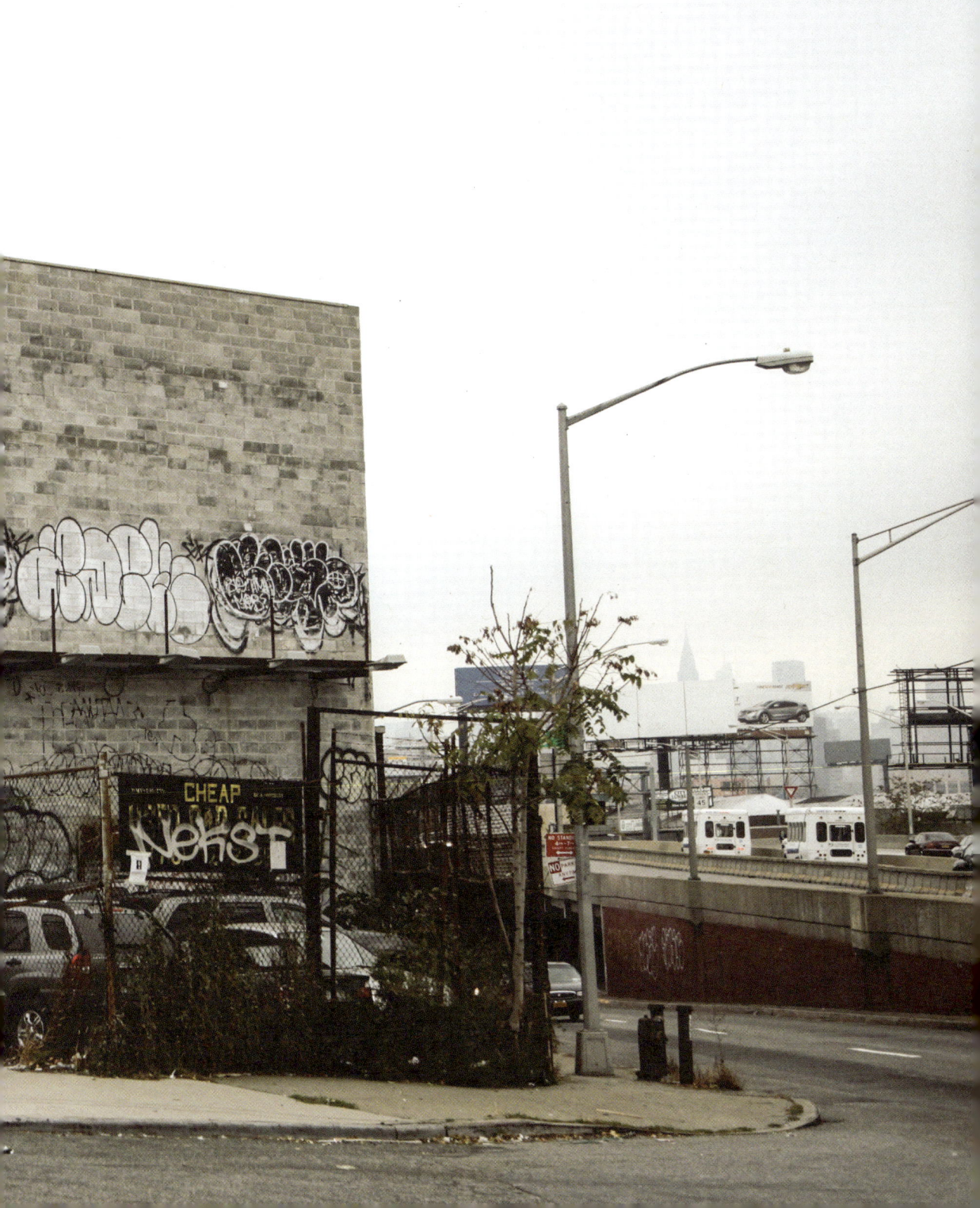

B anksy in Folkestone

In the fall of 2014, I attended a weekend art symposium in the southern coastal town of Folkestone, England, where some two hundred artists, writers, curators, and academics pondered "The Sculpture Question," as in "How might sculpture, as a discipline of fine art, continue to be taught and defined today?" The event marked the finale of the third Folkestone Triennial where, for two months, more than twenty-four international artists, including Andy Goldsworthy and Yoko Ono, took over public spaces to exhibit newly commissioned artwork that was intended to be specific to Folkestone, engaging with, as the press release explained, the town's "rich cultural history and built environment." At the conference, which was kicked off with a keynote address by the director of the Tate Britain, art world luminaries, having recognized that "sculpture" was no longer confined to the pedestal but had come to embrace installation, architecture, and performance, seemed to conclude that it could be understood as "anything that isn't painting." Presenters and panelists discussed ways in which art could encourage community involvement, social engagement, political activism, and other aspects of "relational aesthetics," the now universal term coined by curator and critic Nicolas Bourriaud who, looking the part of the French intellectual with rumpled hair and black turtleneck, was present to extrapolate it.

2.1 *following pages*
Banksy, *Art Buff*, 2014, spray painting, Folkestone, England, courtesy of Pest Control Office.

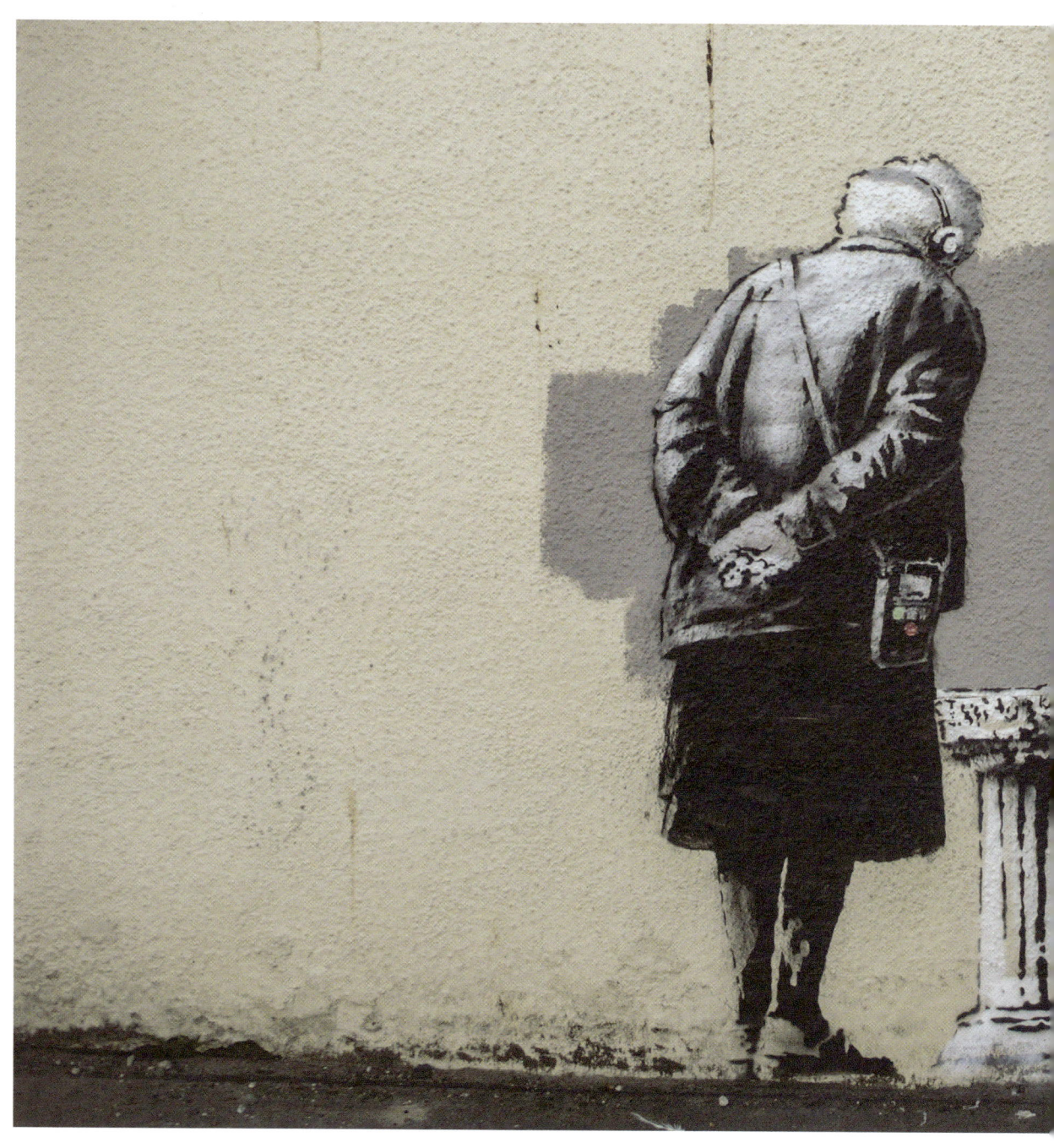

Chapter 2

Meanwhile, on a building atop a hill overlooking the conference hall, Banksy, the previous month, had bestowed on Folkestone his own unauthorized Triennial contribution, which he titled *Art Buff*. On a beige concrete wall where earlier graffiti had been covered over or, as they say on the street, "buffed" with a hastily brushed cloud of gray paint, Banksy applied, in his inimitable stencil and spray manner, a columned Greek sculpture pedestal, as if to display one of the buffs. Depicted peering at it is an older woman who some thought could be the queen, although she'd hardly show up in a padded jacket and sensible shoes. With hands clasped behind her back and wearing headphones like those from a museum audio tour, she looks as if she's trying to figure the whole thing out. She's an "art buff" grappling with "the sculpture question." To confirm that this was his work, Banksy, as is his custom, placed a slideshow of the painting on his website, banksy.co.uk, with the words: "Part of the Folkestone Triennial. Kind of."

Now, as we listened to the presenters in the conference hall, workmen were at the site erecting scaffolding over the painting. When drilling was heard coming from the interior of the building, some bystanders concluded that the piece was to be cut out and turned around so it could be safely viewed from the inside. Holes were drilled into the clear acrylic panel that had been put in place by the District Council after the Banksy had twice been "vandalized" by graffiti writers—one who spray-painted atop the pedestal a large erect penis that was later removed (police called it "criminal damage"). A crowd swarmed to the scene, and by late afternoon five police cars had arrived in response to reports that town artists were trying to tear down the scaffolding. No arrests were made, the excavation continued, and by 8:00 p.m. *Art Buff* was gone. Word had it that the artwork was to be sold.

Artist and arts organizer Diane Dever, who was seen angrily opposing a policeman in a photo that later appeared in the press, told me she went into the bar where her friends were gathered and demanded, "What are you all doing drinking in here? They're taking the Banksy out!" She was, she remembered, quite emotional. "It was not right," she said. "I felt it belonged to the town, and was not theirs to sell. The opportunism! And then the void in the wall that was created when it was torn out. It really cranked me up!"

Rumors flew—that Banksy himself was one of the workers and had colluded with the owners of the building to remove and sell the piece at auction so they could all cash in, or that it was Banksy who ran into the fish and chips shop opposite shouting, "They're taking it out! They're taking it out!" Finally it was revealed that the Godden family, whose amusement arcade occupied the building, had made an arrangement with one Robin Barton, the owner of a gallery in London, artfully named Bankrobber, which specializes in the sale of Banksy's retrieved work. Interviewed on the radio, Barton said, "It's being sold because the Goddens are heartily fed up with keeping it safe and they've decided they want rid of it. . . . Being magnanimous, they don't really care [what anyone thinks]. Rochelle Godden's husband, Jimmy Godden, died of cancer a few years ago, and she's going to put any funds from it to her cancer trust."

Some days later, new graffiti appeared on the rebuilt portion of the wall *Art Buff* had once occupied: "Fuck Jim Godden. Charity my arse. Art is for the artists."

When *Art Buff* first appeared unannounced in Folkestone in September, it generated national and international headlines. "People flocked to it," Diane Dever recalled. "I've never seen so many people from all different walks of life approaching an artwork continuously over days. Kids were getting on buses to come to Folkestone to look at the Banksy, when they'd never come for the Mark Wallinger, or whatever else was in the Triennial. Older people, mums, dads . . . flashy cars pulling up. . . . Also the place it held at the top of the compound, looking down over the Creative Quarter, made it almost processional. It was a real moment, a sign that Folkestone was happening, that it had arrived."

And Folkestone desperately needed to arrive. A thriving Kent shipping port since the thirteenth century with sweeping views of the Channel and adjacent white Dover cliffs, Folkestone was once known as the "gem of the south coast." Only seventy miles from London, with grand hotels lining its waterfront promenade, the town had once been one of Britain's most fashionable destinations. There, King Edward VII could be spotted through the arched windows of the Grand Hotel having tea with his mistress, Alice Keppel, great-grandmother of Camilla, Duchess of Cornwall (it's said that the expression "monkey business" came from the king and his friends being viewed by passersby like "monkeys in a cage"). That majestic brick mountain of a hotel, with its seaside view, potted palms, and black and white marble tile floors, was also the temporary home of Agatha Christie while writing her 1934 thriller, *Murder on the Orient Express.* Other authors, such as H. G. Wells, George Bernard Shaw, Joseph Conrad, Ford Maddox Ford, and Henry James, stayed in the town or nearby. After it was no longer a draw for high society, Folkestone continued to attract tourists into the 1950s.

But cheap airfare to warmer European vacation spots brought a downturn in tourism, the fishing industry slumped, and the coal mines closed. When the opening of the Channel tunnel caused the end of local ferry service, Folkestone's fifty-year decline hit rock bottom. The population was ageing, the schools were failing, and unemployment, teen pregnancy, drug use, and crime were on the rise. The historic town center, where fishermen's houses clung to the steep streets above the harbor, seemed on the verge of collapse. While the beachfront around the Grand Hotel had retained some of its Edwardian charm when I first visited Folkestone over fifteen years ago—friends there being the only draw—the rest of the town felt like a halfway house.

Then, against all likelihood, a savior emerged: Sir Roger De Haan, a multimillionaire who is exceptional among philanthropists in that the bulk of his largesse is devoted to a single town, one he has not left since his parents brought him to Folkestone as an infant. Young Roger's first job was carrying bags for guests at his father's hotel, and later he joined the family business as it morphed into a group of companies with over two thousand employees called Saga, best known for selling holidays to the over-fifty market. When his father retired, De Haan became chairman, launching Saga-branded radio stations to accompany the group's holiday, insurance, and financial services, and in 2004 sold the entire Saga Group for £1.35 billion.

Noted for his extraordinary drive as well as unassuming manner, De Haan, at fifty-six, was not in the mood for retirement, but instead devised a massive campaign to make the town economically viable by reinventing Folkestone as a major art center. Since 2002 the Creative Foundation, which De Haan founded and funded, has bought and restored over ninety buildings in the once derelict old town area, transforming it into what's now known as the Creative Quarter, giving affordable, 125-year leases to artists and creative industries, as well as establishing a university extension, an adult education center, and art programs with local schools, overall creating more than five hundred jobs. The enterprise includes the Quarterhouse, the £4 million architect-designed performance and conference center where the symposium I attended took place, but by no means stops there.

In 2008, the Triennial was inaugurated, with big-name curators inviting internationally recognized contemporary artists to make public work that would, as De Haan put it, "be connected to Folkestone and reflect something of the place, its culture and its people." Six works out of each Triennial are purchased for permanent display toward the goal that the entire town will ultimately become a gigantic urban sculpture park.

While at first there was resentment that blockbuster artists were being favored, the event has brought wider audiences to local artist initiatives such as Strange Cargo, which produces public art projects involving participation by the towns-people, and the Folkestone Fringe, run by Diane Dever and her sister, Denise, which curates art, architecture, sound, and performance to coincide with the Triennial, and organizes arts activities in the intervening years.

The confluence of cheap rents, nearby universities, and access to the wider art world makes for a thriving creative scene where as much happens in the cafés as in the studios. "I've lived all over the world," artist and musician Andi Elliot told me, "and Folkestone is the most buoyant place I've been, bordering on Berlin, and I love Berlin." Andi and Cathy Burton, his wife of some thirty years, ran the tiny Lime Bar Café (since closed), a music venue and bar in the Creative Quarter. "There's a crackling cross-fertilization of disciplines," he says, "anything is possible, every day there's something new, and it's garrulous—everyone's got an opinion and will voice it."

The Creative Quarter, however, was just the beginning of De Haan's vision for Folkestone. In 2006, after having bought Folkestone Harbour from ferry operators for £11 million, he unveiled a master plan designed by the firm of "starchitect" Norman Foster, calling for an £800 million overhaul of the whole of Folkestone's eighty-nine-acre waterfront, including a revamped marina, a thousand low-rise homes, leisure and commercial space, an ice rink, a performing arts wing of Canterbury Christ Church University, and possible resumption of fast-ferry service to France.

There was, however, a complication, in that the District Council already had a master plan and another contender for the harbor development who, like De Haan, owned a substantial portion of the essential property—Jimmy Godden.

Outside of their comparable age and attachment to the area, the two tycoons couldn't have been more different, and their wrangling over the coastal real estate, which entertained newspaper readers for eighteen months (a "living soap opera," one account called it), represented a clash of class, aspiration, and values.

Jimmy, as he was known (apparently only his intimates called him "Jim"), operated amusement ventures and as such was a major South Kent property owner and employer whom, it seems, Folkestonians either loved or hated. His £100 million proposal, which the District Council was inclined to approve, included a mega-casino, a bowling alley, a cinema, retail outlets, and a contended fourteen-story apartment block on what had long been a desolate concrete strip.

Born in Folkestone, Godden had an entrepreneurial spirit that kicked in early when he carved out a nocturnal niche as a twenty-four-hour emergency glazier, chasing police cars to pub brawls on the chance a window might need replacing—an endeavor that enabled him, at nineteen, to buy his first flat. Later he went to work for his first wife's father at the Rotunda Fun Park on the Folkestone beach that later became his, the beginning of an empire that for decades provided Kent's seaside towns with its classic arcades, cafes, ice cream parlors, and pleasure parks, ultimately including Dreamland in Margate and Pleasurama in Ramsgate. The twenty-acre Folkestone park was special, however, because it boasted the largest concrete dome in the world. Built in the 1930s and donated to the town by an earl, the Rotunda was an attraction in itself, and when Godden had it demolished in 2002, townspeople said it was "the end of an era." At the time his intention was to redevelop the spot as a supermarket—but that was before he got bigger ideas.

After his death from cancer in 2012, Godden was described in the press as a "straight forward [sic], shrewd broker who had an old-fashioned way of closing business deals, often on a handshake or a word," someone who could "cut to the heart of any issue with a simple one-liner," and that "once a person had earned his respect, it would be reciprocated. A promise made was a promise kept." However, a short online search will also reveal that Jimmy Godden was not above taking shortcuts that skirted the law, and was known for a string of fires that just happened to erupt on his properties after they'd served their purposes. One was the massive 1998 blaze that destroyed Pleasurama, after which its acres lay derelict while the developer further enraged residents with empty promises. Godden ceded the property in 2001, after a controversial offer allowed him to keep the insurance money in exchange for not contesting the purchase. As one blogger wrote, "I do feel sorry for Jimmy Godden as it appears that anything he owns seems to catch fire."

Godden also once narrowly escaped prison after being convicted of an attempted £12,000 bribe to a councilor to get permission for a major development. Another time he made the news for being a victim of a crime when armed robbers broke into the family home and demanded that his partner, Rochelle, get cash from one of their businesses, while Jimmy and his eighteen-month-old son were held hostage. The family was released, but the culprits were never caught.

Then in 1999, an eight-year-old girl died when she fell out of a rollercoaster at the Rotunda Fun Park. During a five-and-a-half-week trial, Dreamland Leisure Limited denied failure to ensure the safety of passengers; it took a jury of twelve less than four hours to find the company guilty. The girl's parents' marriage broke down and her father later committed suicide. While his publicist said of Godden that the incident "hurt him more than anyone will ever know," if measured in pounds, his sincerity was not all that deep, given that the multimillionaire's compensation to the family didn't amount to more than £15,000.

When, in 2000, Godden was arrested (but not ultimately charged) on a tax matter, it was reported that the appetite for bad Godden news was so avid that one Folkestone newspaper sold every copy of the edition that carried the story.

The painfully drawn-out negotiations between De Haan and Godden were finally concluded in 2007 with Godden agreeing to sell his property for an undisclosed but no doubt hefty sum. After Jimmy's death, the District Council approved De Haan's plan which, because of the recession, was somewhat downsized and no longer included Sir Norman Foster. As work on the harbor project was beginning, De Haan no doubt figured his Godden entanglements were over.

He hadn't counted on Banksy.

• • •

The Folkestone townspeople clearly felt Banksy's *Art Buff* was a gift, that it was theirs, and now it had been stolen. Some even marched in protest. "It was the opportunism that really got us," Diane Dever told me. "The Goddens said they'd give the money to charity and we were like . . . yeah, right. There was no trust there." And now it was on its way to New York to be restored and then to Miami to be sold for big bucks, courtesy of Robin Barton of Bankrobber Gallery.

It seems that if you're clever enough to find a niche, you can make a business out of almost anything. So just as Jimmy Godden had scored with his late-night glazing scheme, Barton in London and Stephan Keszler of Keszler Gallery in

New York have formed a cottage industry in the sale of recovered Banksy street works, which are often worth considerably more than the buildings on which they're found. In 2011, they teamed up to restore and sell two famous Banksys that had been pried out of their original locations in Bethlehem—*Wet Dog* from a highway bus stop and, from a butcher shop, *Stop & Search*, an image of a little girl frisking a soldier. The locals, who had removed them from their original sites, intended to sell the pieces on eBay but after storing them for three years, realized it just might be too difficult to move nearly six tons of work across tightly monitored border controls. Believing he had enough evidence to support the provenance of both pieces, Barton stepped in, and after the artworks had been shipped, restored, and marketed, each ultimately sold, Keszler assured me in an email, "in the high six figures."

Does Banksy profit from any of this? Not beyond Barton's grandiose assertion that he's doing Banksy a favor by "keeping his name in the public eye" and that he and Keszler are preserving art that might otherwise be destroyed. As far as Banksy is concerned, he has made it clear that street art in general, and his work in particular, is only meaningful in its original context, and is therefore valueless, indeed no longer a Banksy, once it is removed. Not only that, his firm refusal to acknowledge such work makes it harder to sell (museums, for instance, are restricted from accepting art, even as a gift, which is not properly authenticated).

When another group organized a 2014 auction of his purloined work in London and charged visitors an entrance fee to the exhibition, Banksy put out a statement: "This show has got nothing to do with me and I think it's disgusting people are allowed to go around displaying art on walls without getting permission." Of course, Banksy also doesn't ask permission, so his policy of not certifying works is additionally designed to protect him from implication in criminal activity. Authenticating his street art, Banksy has said, would be like "a signed confession on letterhead."

Pest Control, the organization Banksy set up to monitor the authenticity of his output, had similarly slammed Barton and Keszler in 2011, when they exhibited the artist's Bethlehem work along with a number of his other excavated street pieces in Southampton, New York. In a statement to the online magazine *Artnet*, Pest Control said, "We have warned Mr. Keszler of the serious implications of selling unauthenticated works, but he seems to not care." Keszler, who knew the policy before acquiring the pieces, appeared to take this personally, as if he were the victim and the artist was unreasonably interfering with his business. "We do not know," he said, "why Pest Control is releasing self-penned 'admonishments' about our exhibition and the artwork, [unless they are trying] to manipulate the marketing of the street works or as an attempt to damage the gallery's reputation."

Before *Art Buff*, both Keszler and Barton justified their dealings with Banksy's work by emphasizing that they were never involved in physically removing works from their original walls. "I would view that as grave-robbing," Barton was once quoted as saying—a high-minded stance he seems to have jettisoned once the opportunity in Folkestone arose, where he was seen supervising the excavation.

Although expected to fetch nearly $600,000 at auction in Miami, *Art Buff* didn't sell. Barton, however, was undaunted, saying that to make such a deal could take up to three years, no doubt because of the authentication issues. So the intent was that he and Keszler would hold on to it and keep trying to sell it— which didn't happen because of a rather significant error: Barton failed to ascertain that the Goddens actually owned the building their business, Palace Amusements, was occupying, and that they had the right to the artwork or even to alter the wall. "I work on handshakes only, so it was a mistake on my part," Barton told the BBC. Given the amount of real estate the Goddens hold, it was a surprise to learn that they didn't own that particular property, but were actually leasing it from . . . De Haan's Creative Foundation. As they say, you can't make this stuff up.

Did Banksy know all this? Did he do the research that Barton, in his eagerness to make a bundle, did not? Some think it's sheer coincidence (Folkestone artist Leigh Mulley, for one, who told me, "Street artists don't research the buildings they paint on") while others, knowing that Banksy has been associated with other graffiti writers in the area, find it hard to believe it wasn't thought out. Regardless, the townspeople wanted the artwork back and De Haan, the determined champion, was again embroiled in a protracted dispute involving the Goddens.

• • •

Admittedly, the Goddens were in a bit of a bind. The District Council had charged Palace Amusements with keeping *Art Buff* safe, without any indication of how that might be achieved for the long term, and their fear that it could become a shrine for Banksy followers and attract even more graffiti was not unreasonable. In a perfect world, however, the Goddens might have consulted with the Creative Foundation regarding *Art Buff*'s future and come up with a plan. Instead, their decision to remove the artwork and send it to auction met with an outcry that went all the way up to a Conservative MP, who raised the issue in the House of Commons.

Banksy reminds me of an old-time American comic strip personality, *Li'l Abner*'s Bald Iggle, whose gaze compelled anyone he looked at to tell the truth—to the point that Iggle was declared a menace by the FBI ("The life it ruins may be your own"). Likewise, Banksy is a somewhat invented character who operates outside the law, whose actions goad people into revealing their basic natures. Certainly, in this instance, the central players acted true to expected form, with De Haan and the Creative Foundation coming to the rescue. Early in 2015, their lawyers obtained an injunction in the High Court against Dreamland Leisure Limited and Jimmy's sons, Jeremy and Jordan Godden, preventing them from selling or otherwise dealing with *Art Buff*, thereby kicking off a lengthy legal battle.

Almost nine months later, Judge Richard Arnold ruled that the tenant had "no reasonable prospect of establishing that it was entitled, let alone obliged, to remove the mural" and ordered that *Art Buff* be brought back to Folkestone to be delivered up to the Creative Foundation—the first example of a Banksy, or perhaps any street art, being returned to public ownership. The *Law Society Gazette* cited it as one of the first cases ever to consider the ownership of street art. In a public statement, Alastair Upton, chief executive of the Creative Foundation, said he hoped the case would inspire others in the future. "People should fight to keep these works in the public realm," he said. "That's how they came about and where they were intended to stay." He admitted, however, that he had no idea of Banksy's intentions, whether the artist would approve or not—or, one might ask, if he cares at all.

· · ·

Just as we can't surmise Banksy's intentions for the piece after he left it on the wall, we also don't know what he was thinking when he made it. Certainly, the image of the woman peering over the pedestal (who appears quizzical, even from behind), is the perfect response to "The Sculpture Question," as it was posed in the Triennial symposium. But was it, as the *Folkestone Herald* and most other local news sources saw it, "a massive high five" for the regeneration of the town?

Talking with another local artist and organizer, Matt Rowe, a different interpretation emerges. He suggests that *Art Buff* could be marking the moment when "regeneration tiptoes into gentrification," the woman in the painting in this case representing "the ordinary Folkestone person, retired, or here on a Saga holiday, looking at what's going on and trying to figure out what it has to do with her."

And indeed, despite the improvements to the area, poverty and unemployment are still widespread and drug use is a major concern—the same high-speed train that has brought visitors and investors to Folkestone has also made it more accessible to city drug lords. While there are trendy shops and bars on Tontine Street in the Creative Quarter, the High Street still feels a bit dreary, with stores that look as if they've passed their expiration date, frequented by pensioners in mobility scooters, young moms with toddlers, and teenagers for whom the town appears to offer little stimulation. This is the population that was well served by Jimmy Godden's amusement parks, and it's unlikely that an encounter with an artwork by superstar Tracey Emin could begin to fill the gap—Emin's effort for the first Triennial, bronze simulacra of baby clothes left outside in random places, was an attempt to highlight the pressing issue of teen pregnancy, but it would be farfetched to think it could have had an effect. When the young clerk in Boots' chemist, inquiring about my accent, heard I was from New York, her eyes widened in disbelief. "You're from New York and you're visiting *Folkestone*?"

This societal disparity was sadly played out in 2014 when German artist Michael Sailstorfer's participatory work for the Triennial, *Folkestone Digs*, turned into, as the *Guardian* put it, "a documentary of despair." Sailstorfer, no doubt intending it as a lark, had buried thirty bars of bullion worth a total of £10,000 in a strip of sand beach just inside the harbor, but along with middle-class families and art fans came those who were unemployed or low-waged and digging out of desperation. The priest of a nearby parish, where a third of the children and 20 percent of the adults were living in poverty, told the *Guardian* it was "in questionable taste at the very least to bury gold under the noses of the poor as an art stunt."

Matt Rowe, however, is positive about the changes in Folkestone, and emphasizes that without the Creative Foundation, the town would be nothing. "But at the same time," he says, "I struggle with the possible loss of my cultural identity. While Roger [De Haan] is providing the aspiration, there's the London market coming in, developers desperate to build, estate agents writing blogs about how Folkestone is the cool place to be, everyone trying to get rich—yet the populace still gets screwed. Banksy knows a whole subculture of people who grew up in Folkestone when it was a shithole but are not really getting perks from the new initiatives. It's possible that he's reacting to the gentrification and the inclusion of the international art scene which, in the end, is all about money, and choosing to paint his piece on the Goddens' wall is his way of giving the finger to the whole endeavor."

Folkestone's particular issues aside, *Art Buff*, which shows buffed-out graffiti being elevated by a classical pedestal (an aspect missed by the news accounts, all of which reported that the woman was viewing an "empty plinth") could be seen as looking forward to a time when street art is taken as seriously as other forms of art and be considered deserving of the cultural weight that such a pedestal or a museum audio tour conveys. Perhaps "sculpture" might be broad enough to include not only installation, performance, and architecture, but street art as well.

• • •

So *Art Buff* came back to Folkestone. In October 2015, Terry Perk, an artist and professor who helped organize the sculpture conference, happened to see a van quietly pull up to the back of the Quarterhouse and a crate being taken inside, so by chance was among a small group, including Creative Foundation chief Alasdair Upton, a university chancellor, and some students, who were gathered informally in the back of the Quarterhouse theater when it was unpacked. "It was dark," Terry told me, "and they turned the lights on in just that section, which made everything overly dramatic. When they took the top off the crate, you could see how fragile and crumbly the piece was. It felt like some kind of religious relic, like that moment in the first Indiana Jones movie where the Nazis are pulling away the casing to look at the Ark of the Covenant, which turns out to be their demise, of course, and I commented to someone, 'We'd better close our eyes.'"

Since then, *Art Buff* has been in secret storage and as of this writing a decision has not been made about where it should ultimately be placed. Inside? Outside? Down by the harbor? So far no one has found a match for its original Acropolis-like spot at the top of the hill, with the steps going up to it through the park and the view of the Creative Quarter.

Meanwhile, Terry, letting his imagination run, is thinking of how, after the Russian Revolution, every May 1 those celebrating International Workers Day would carry various structures, such as the model for Vladimir Tatlin's famous ziggurat-like tower, throughout the city. "We shouldn't install it," he says, "but just parade it around once a year, like the secular icon it is."

• • •

I'd end the story there, except Banksy provided an addendum. On the eve of the May 2017 French presidential election, which was seen as an unofficial referendum on membership in the European Union, a new Banksy work mysteriously appeared (and was verified on his official Instagram account), this time located just north of Folkestone in Dover, which faces France at the Channel's narrowest point. Large enough that its square azure field could be seen from afar, the three-story-high "Brexit Banksy," as it was dubbed, showed a workman on a tall ladder chipping away at one of the twelve yellow-gold stars that represent the unity of EU member states.

The French election, definitively won by the pro-EU candidate Emmanuel Macron, "solidified France's place at the center of the European Union," as the *New York Times* put it, "and highlighted Britain's position on the outside looking in." Coming up was the general election called by Prime Minister Theresa May, who was hoping the outcome would reinforce her anti-EU position.

Kent News reported that the new Banksy piece, which could be seen from the busy A20 coming into the port town, was largely welcomed by locals, almost two-thirds of whom had voted to leave the EU in the previous year's referendum. It quoted one resident who described Dover (which is even more economically depressed than Folkestone) as "a little bit on the grotty side," and added about the Banksy, "It's a marvelous thing, because nothing much happens here." Residents were amazed at the suddenness of its appearance, one neighbor remarking, "We only live up the road and didn't notice anything. . . . If I want to put a ladder up outside my house I have to get planning permission . . . so I don't know how he's done it so quickly."

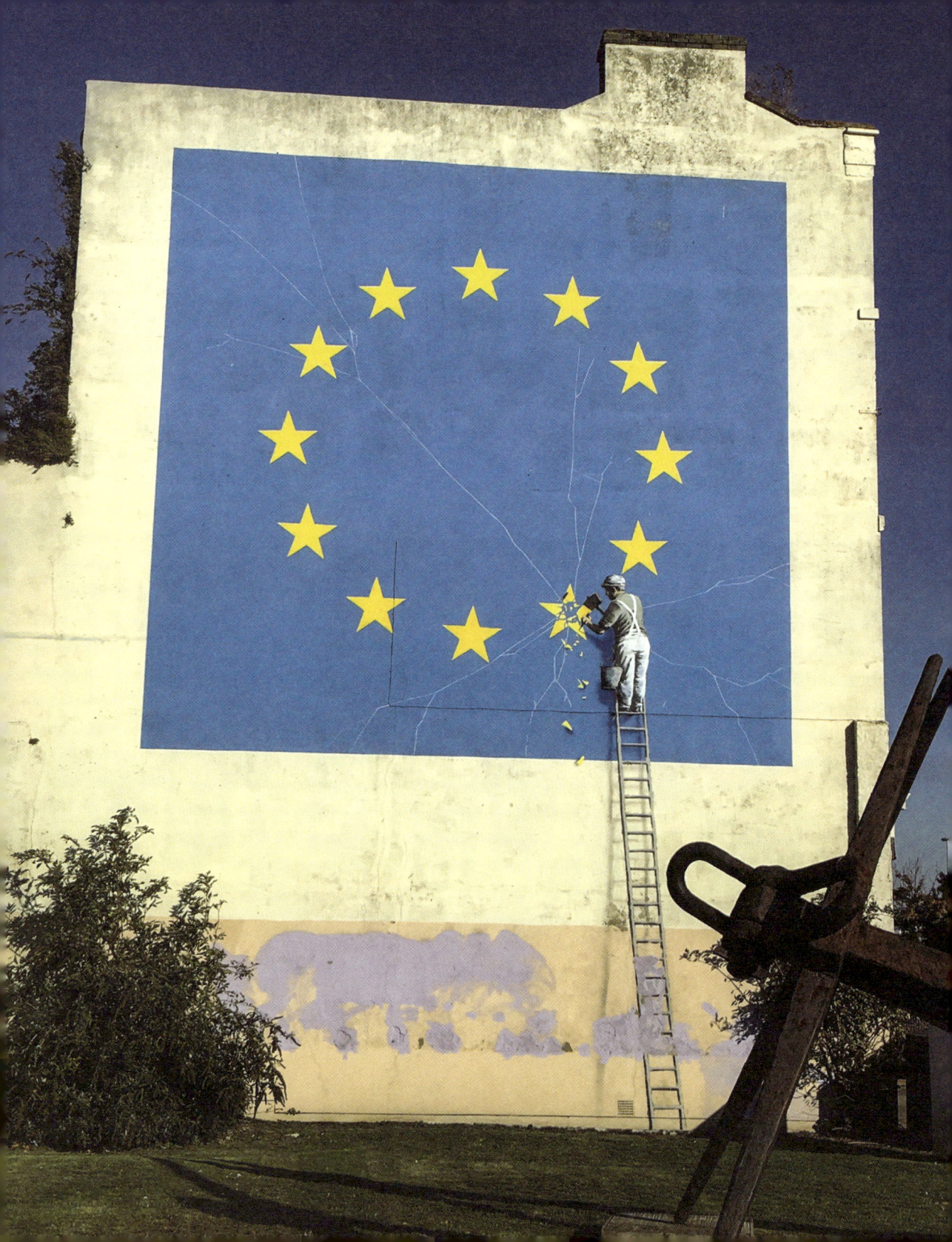

And its fate? A local MP immediately launched a "Save Our Banksy" campaign to keep the artwork in Dover, writing to Historic England requesting that the piece be listed, and asking the arts minister, at a meeting in the House of Commons, to help maintain the artwork. "I told the minister how much it is loved in the town and why we must protect it," the MP was reported in *KentOnline* as saying. "The Banksy may be worth millions—but to the people of Dover it is priceless. The new waterfront development should have this Banksy at its heart—as a central attraction. Renewal is about more than just new buildings," he added. "This is about protecting a piece of our culture and history."

Meanwhile, the Dover District Council chiefs met to discuss the Banksy's future, saying that although it was a matter for the landowner, they would explore available options "as a matter of urgency," while local residents gathered to protest the possibility of its demolition and sale. That prospect was denied by restoration experts, who were quoted as saying that not only was the artwork too big and the wall too unstable for it to be retrieved and preserved, it would be difficult to find a buyer for a work of that size. The owners seemed determined to sell, but after considering their options with a London art gallery, in September 2019 they had the wall scaffolded and mysteriously whitewashed over—although no one knows whether the intention was to destroy the artwork or protect it.

This time, however, there is no question: the building is owned by the Goddens.

2.2
Banksy, 2017, spray painting, Dover, England.
Photo: author.

3

The Case for Graffiti

What is art? Who gets to say it's art? And where does it belong? Clearly, as the debate at the Folkestone conference indicated, our culture is moving away from identifying art solely with objects, such as painting and sculpture, toward an understanding that art can be any experience that generates elevated ways of seeing, thinking, or feeling.

Musician and artist Brian Eno writes, "Stop thinking about art works as objects and start thinking of them as triggers for experience. . . . We don't have to argue about whether photographs are art, or whether performances are art, or whether Carl Andre's bricks or Andres Serrano's piss or Little Richard's 'Long Tall Sally' are art, because we say, 'Art is something that happens, a process, not a quality, and all sorts of things can make it happen.' . . . What makes a work of art 'good' for you is not something that is already 'inside' it, but something that happens inside you—so the value of the work lies in the degree to which it can help you have the kind of experience that you call art."

Fortunately, our access to music, film, and literature has never been greater, and there the public has an influence—we get to vote with our purchases of tickets, books, and MP3s. Books are at the top of the best-seller lists for the simple reason that we've bought them. Popularity at the box office has an influence on a film's distribution. However, given how photographic representations of artworks can vary from the originals in size, color, and quality, most visual art cannot be as effectively reproduced and shared. There's no way a Monet on your phone, or even on a large flat screen, can replicate the experience of actually standing in the Musée d'Orsay and absorbing the vast sweep of the real thing.

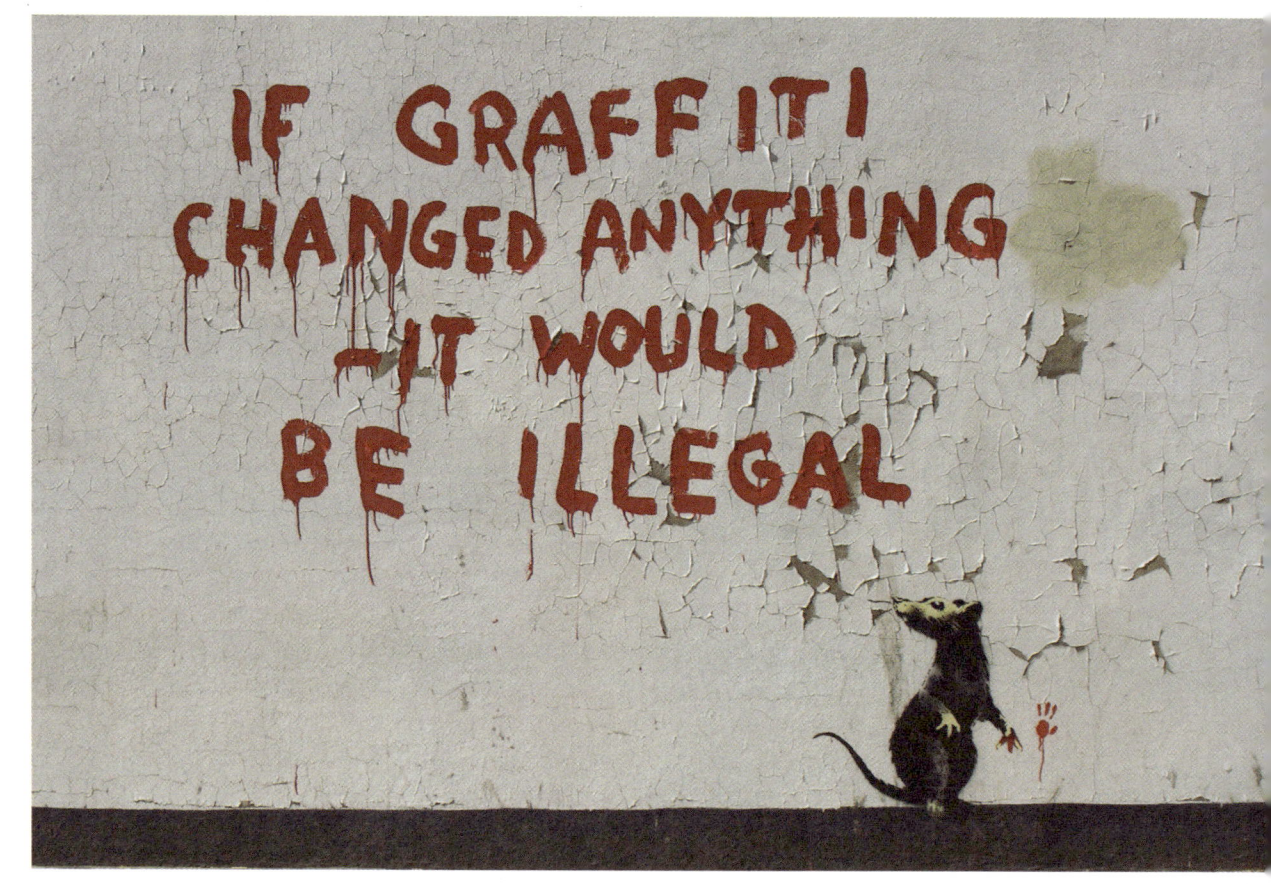

3.1

Banksy, *If Graffiti Changed Anything, It Would Be Illegal*, 2011, spray painting, London, courtesy of Pest Control Office.

To truly take in the texture, scale, color, and dimensionality of an artwork, you must exist with it in the same physical space. So, while it's good that *something* still requires the intimacy of one-on-one, this exclusivity puts innumerable gatekeepers in the way—an administrative layer of curators, collectors, and gallerists who are in the business of deciding what we see. Often, they sift out the rude and raw (as well as the unprofitable) or, as *New York Times* critic Michael Kimmelman once colorfully put it, the "radical qualities art used to have when it could still call itself radical and wasn't like a barnacle clinging to the cruise ship of pop culture."

> *Banksy:* Art is not like other culture because its success is not made by its audience. The public fill concert halls and cinemas every day, we read novels by the millions, and buy records by the billions. "We the people" affect the making and quality of most of our culture, but not our art. . . . The Art we look at is made by only a select few. A small group create, promote, purchase, exhibit and decide the success of Art. Only a few hundred people in the world have any real say. When you go to an Art gallery you are simply a tourist looking at the trophy cabinet of a few millionaires.

These days the arbiters include former New York mayor Michael Bloomberg, who, at the time of Banksy's New York "residency," made a public statement that caused the *New York Post* to fill its tabloid front page with two words: "GET BANKSY!" To Bloomberg, graffiti is "a sign of decay and loss of control." "Art is art, and nobody's a bigger supporter of the arts than I am," said the billionaire, an art collector who has also donated millions to the city's artistic institutions. "You running up to somebody's property, or public property, and defacing it is not my definition of art."

Of course, the irony is that New York hardly presents a harmonious aesthetic that begs not to be disrupted, but is instead a place where one is assaulted on all sides with a cacophony of advertising. I thought for sure all possible display surfaces were usurped until advertisers discovered new real estate on subway turnstiles, the risers on subway steps, and figured out how to shrink-wrap ads on entire subway cars (this, of course, after getting rid of the gloriously tagged trains of the 1980s). Los Angeles is no different—when driving its boulevards, I'm constantly imagining how beautiful the city would be if there were no billboards (where is Lady Bird Johnson's anti-billboard campaign when we need it?). In Paris and Barcelona, where they really do care what the city looks like, the absence of ads is visual fresh air. To me, *advertising* is a "sign of decay and loss of control" to the capitalist powers Bloomberg represents. I would also suggest that graffiti doesn't lead to social and physical decay, but rather such decay is the result of inequality, and graffiti is its protest. As Banksy says, "The people who truly deface our neighborhoods are the companies that scrawl giant slogans across buildings and buses trying to make us feel inadequate unless we buy their stuff."

Brandalism
People abuse you everyday [sic]. They butt into your life, take a cheap shot at you and then disappear. They leer at you from tall buildings and make you feel small. They make flippant comments from buses that imply you're not sexy enough and that all the fun is happening somewhere else. They are on TV making your girlfriend feel inadequate. They have access to the most sophisticated technology the world has ever seen and they bully you with it. They are The Advertisers and they are laughing at you.

However, you are forbidden to touch them. Trademarks, intellectual property rights and copyright law mean advertisers can say what they like wherever they like with total impunity.

Screw that. Any advert in a public space that gives you no choice whether you see it or not is yours. It's yours to take, re-arrange and re-use. You can do whatever you like with it. Asking for permission is like asking to keep a rock someone just threw at your head.

You owe the companies nothing. Less than nothing, you especially don't owe them any courtesy. They owe you. They have re-arranged the world to put themselves in front of you. They never asked for your permission, don't even start asking for theirs.

Banksy, *Wall and Piece*

For me, graffiti is often the only humanizing element in a soulless corporatized environment that's constantly being configured, in one way or another, to get us to spend money. As with all forms of expression, there's good graffiti and bad graffiti, but I'm not sure it's wise to give those who would foist advertising on us the authority to decide which is which, or where it should go. The "war on graffiti" is less about aesthetics than it is about control—after all, when graffiti is painted over, it's usually done badly, and with a color that doesn't even match the wall.

Philosopher, activist, and linguist Noam Chomsky, who has spent a lifetime connecting the dots between language and power, has said, "When people in power believe something firmly, it's worth paying attention to them. And I think they believe firmly that you should not have revolutionary popular art in which people participate. Actually, that's one of the reasons, I think, for destroying the graffiti on the New York subways." To which social critic Adam Mansbach adds, "It is . . . telling that from 1972 to 1989, New York City spent over three hundred million dollars on a 'war on graffiti'. Any movement a city is willing to spend that kind of money to eradicate deserves careful examination."

Banksy: Imagine a city where graffiti wasn't illegal, a city where everybody could draw whatever they liked. Where every street was awash with a million colours and little phrases. Where standing at a bus stop was never boring. A city that felt like a party where everyone was invited, not just the estate agents and barons of big business. Imagine a city like that and stop leaning against the wall—it's wet.

All attempts at graffiti legislation ultimately become a struggle between our concepts of property ownership and freedom of expression. And in reality, there are only three legislative options: bless it wherever it appears, make it entirely illegal, or designate areas where it can be practiced unmediated—solutions that will make no majority happy. Thankfully, just when anyone thinks they have it all figured out, Banksy comes along to muddy the waters.

It's important here to make the distinction between "street art," which is spontaneous, and "murals" which, after going through a vetting process, occupy sites designated by the real estate cartel. Paul Downton, an Australian art activist, has written, "Graffiti that is sanctioned by authority loses its outlaw power to disturb and challenge. When a city provides graffiti walls for its citizens, isn't it simply extending its hegemony?" Brazilian graffiti artist Lu Olivero goes one step further, insisting that graffiti "needs the law so that it can function outside of it. This is where innovation is born," he says, "and this is what pushes the art to evolve."

Banksy would agree, having said in a rare emailed interview with the *Village Voice*: "When graffiti isn't criminal, it loses most of its innocence."

This "innocence" is the basis of my interest in graffiti. I believe that for art to breathe and grow, it is essential that there be places where it can be expressed without review and judgment—and seen for free by all layers of society.

In contrast, the so-called art world, now better described as the "art market," is all about review and judgment—by those who stand to profit from it. Dominated by the auction houses, mega-galleries, billionaire collectors, art fair industry, and art school system, art has become just another part of the corporate economy, and the perfect vehicle for money laundering and insider trading. Art costs money to see, often twenty-five dollars per person for entrance to museums and upward of fifty dollars for art fairs, and requires money to participate in. Most galleries won't even consider an artist who doesn't have a master of fine arts (MFA) degree, which could run $60,000 to $100,000 for a two-year program. Then, of course, to teach in those university programs, one must have an MFA, in addition to a substantial exhibition record. Add to that the newly hot field of "curatorial studies," where a master's comes with the same hefty price tag, and you have a system where teachers, artists, students, and curators, culled from a limited social and economic demographic, are all operating within the same narrow set of values and ideas that have been circulating since the 1980s.

Insular and exclusionary as it is, the art world doesn't have a secret handshake—yet—but it does have its own language, semi-affectionately known as "artspeak." Pretentious, impenetrable, and laden with buzzwords that obscure any possible meaning, it infuses a blight of artists' statements, catalog essays, magazine articles, and museum wall text. Like the weather, everyone complains about artspeak but no one does anything about it—perhaps because it may have a commercial function. Artist David Levine, who has studied the phenomenon, suggests in the *Guardian*: "The more you can muddy the waters around the meaning of a work, the more you can keep the value high." Or possibly, once indoctrinated, you can't get away from artspeak even when grumbling about it, like Levine's colleague, Alix Rule, when she explains, "This language has enforced a hermeticism of contemporary art." Apparently, once you've fallen into a dialectic of unreality informed by a juxtaposition of the mundane and the transcendent, you can't get up.

Meanwhile, art criticism seems to no longer have a place in the field that bears its name, a truth that was abruptly brought home to me when a magazine editor, for whom I'd written for many years, told me that I was "too opinionated." Art historian and critic Sven Lütticken has noted, "In contemporary art magazines, and even more in catalogues and related publications (even if they are termed 'critical readers'), discourse is likely to be positive and celebratory; criticism tends to become highbrow copywriting. When debates do take place, they are often thinly disguised jockeying for positions and symbolic capital." The dialogue around particular artists who might actually be controversial is tightly controlled, as Black feminist writer and cultural critic Michele Wallace discovered after writing a catalog essay, one of several commissioned by different authors, for Kara Walker's 2003 exhibition at Minneapolis's Walker Art Center. Rejecting the essay on the basis of Wallace's negative assessment of Walker's work, the museum agreed to pay her in full if she would delay publication elsewhere for at least a year, which she did. "These days," she posted on Facebook, "I sometimes make more money to write stuff that doesn't get published than I do for the work that does."

Demonstrating just how hegemonic the art world has become, the *Art Newspaper* conducted research which revealed that nearly a third of solo museum exhibitions in the United States between 2007 and 2013 featured artists from just five galleries: Gagosian, Marian Goodman, Pace, Hauser & Wirth, and David Zwirner. Their artists accounted for 90 percent (eleven out of twelve) of the major solo exhibitions at New York's Guggenheim Museum, 45 percent at MoMA, and 40 percent at LA's Museum of Contemporary Art. Even New York's New Museum, which was based on founder Marcia Tucker's commitment to "living artists who did not yet have wide public exposure or critical acceptance," clocked in at 40 percent.

Faced with these odds, artists clearly have to take things into their own hands.

Banksy: Writing graffiti is about the most honest way you can be an artist. It takes no money to do it, you don't need an education to understand it, and there's no admission fee.

Banksy and "Real Art," Part I

If you think my graffiti is overrated, you'd be right. I only hope that one day I get the lack of recognition I deserve.
Banksy

In his determination to prove that Banksy is inconsequential, *Guardian* critic Jonathan Jones joins the swarm of writers eager to dis Banksy while using him as clickbait—and who in doing so are tricked into revealing not Banksy's shortcomings but their own. In 2009, Jones invoked Banksy to promote an article ("Should Banksy Be Nominated for the Turner Prize?") that had nothing to do with the artist, the subject being Jones's excitement at being named a judge for the Tate Britain's prestigious annual art award. That Jones would use Banksy's name to draw readers to an article where he also declared that "Banksy is no longer hot" was a paradox not lost on those who commented. And when, in 2017, Banksy was still "hot" enough that his wall painting of a little girl reaching for a heart-shaped balloon was proclaimed, in a poll, to be Britain's best-loved artwork—ahead of a landscape by early nineteenth-century painter John Constable—Jones went ballistic.

"People are stupid," Jones exclaims in another article ("Britain's Best-Loved Artwork Is a Banksy. That's Proof of Our Stupidity"), pointing out that he was "merely paraphrasing the Victorian art critic John Ruskin, who in his book *Modern Painters* opined that 'the average intellect and feeling of the majority of the public' give them zero competence 'to distinguish what is really excellent.' Only a critic, such as [Ruskin]," Jones says, while no doubt also thinking of himself,

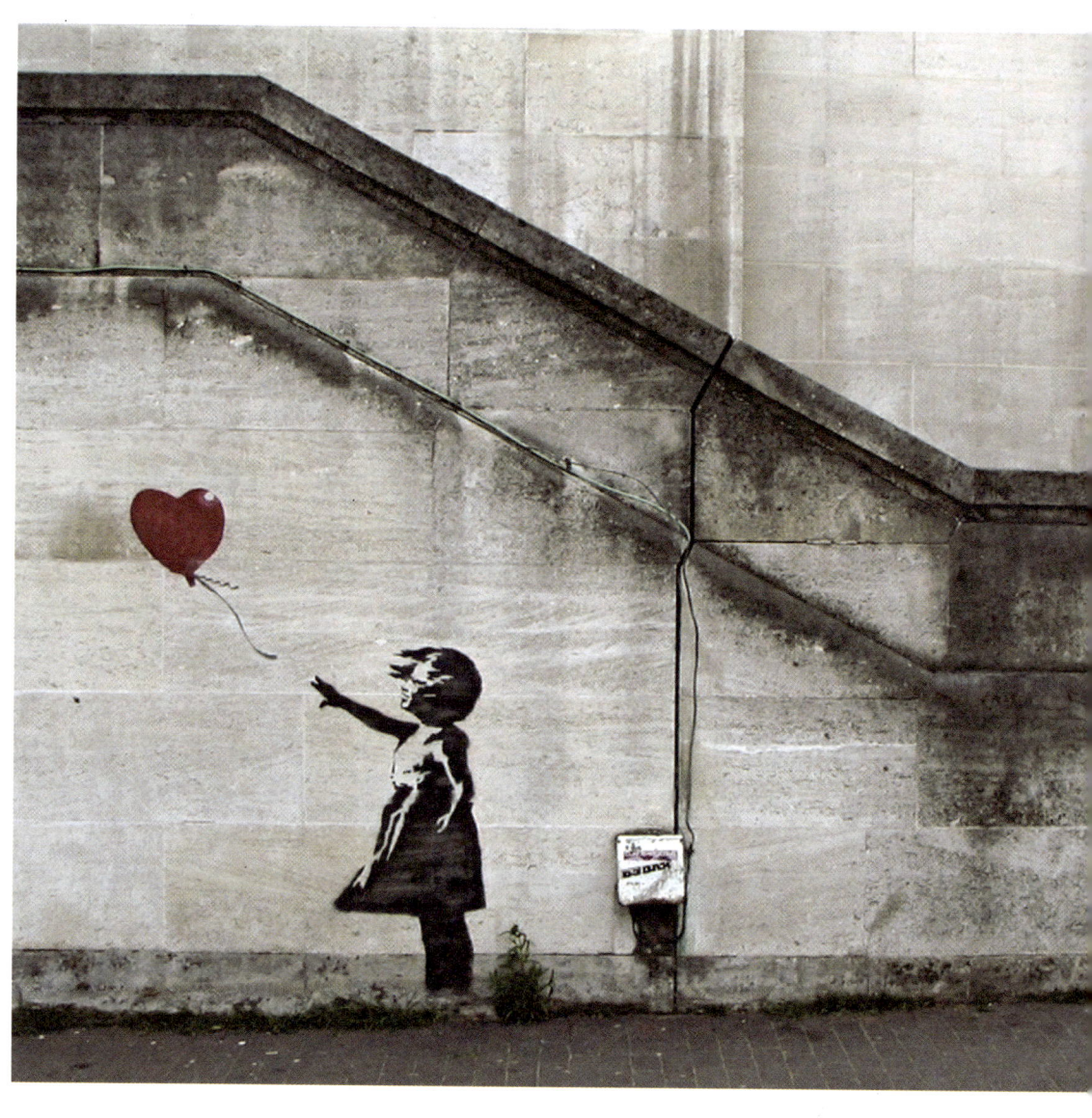

4.1
Banksy, *Girl with Balloon*, 2004, spray painting,
London, courtesy of Pest Control Office.

Chapter 4

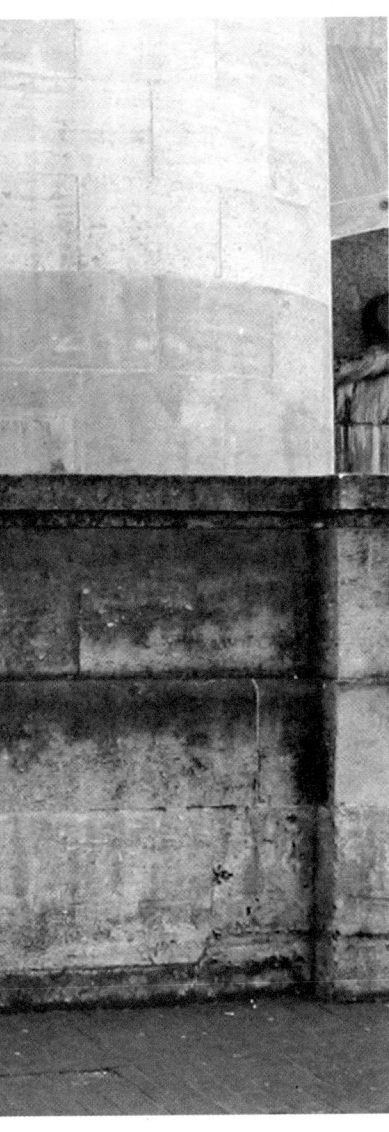

"with superior sensibility and knowledge can judge what is truly great in art." The problem, according to Jones, is that "Banksy's work gives up its entire meaning immediately," where "*real art* [emphasis mine] is elusive, complex, ambiguous and . . . always difficult"—this from the critic who has deemed Tracey Emin's condom-strewn unmade bed "one of the most enduring and poetic works of our time." To Jones, *Girl with Balloon* is "kitsch pathos," "the kind of sentimental tosh our great grandparents too would have voted as Britain's best-loved."

Of course, Ruskin also said, "The world is full of vulgar Purists, who bring discredit on all selection by the silliness of their choice; and this the more, because the very becoming a Purist is commonly indicative of some slight degree of weakness, readiness to be offended, or narrowness of understanding of the ends of things."

Were Ruskin alive today, I like to think he'd be able to discern the difference between artists who indulge in "sentimental tosh" because they lack imagination and Banksy, who uses nostalgia and a certain sentimentality purposefully, almost defiantly, as contrast to the disturbing realities of our lives.

Context is everything. It's one thing to see *Girl with Balloon* (2004) as an isolated image on the internet, another to come across the painting in the location for which it was intended, a wall in London's Southbank, then in the grip of rapid gentrification. High on another wall behind the little girl, the artist scrawled "There is always hope." The girl's innocence not only is incongruent with the background of urban decay, but clashes with the tenor of the times. Consider that when the image first appeared around 2002, the world was still reeling from the shock of 9/11, the Middle East was in chaos, fundamentalist attacks were erupting, systemic child sex abuse in the Catholic Church was being revealed, millions were diagnosed with AIDS in Africa and Asia . . . and on and on. Because we're so used to confronting violence with violence, anger with anger, Banksy's images of children are almost shocking in their gentleness, reminders that our adult conflicts are a choice, our choice. The fragile balloons Banksy uses signify the children's yearning for a way out, as in the image he painted in 2005 on the Palestinian side of the West Bank barrier—a silhouette of a young girl being lifted over the wall by a cluster of balloons.

Another complaint in Jones's diatribe is that the girl in *Girl with Balloon* "is depicted as a simplified black shadow on the wall." "Instead of portraying a rich human being with mysterious emotions," he says, "Banksy gives us a one-dimensional icon whose pathos is instantly readable."

Hmmm . . . I think that's called *symbolism*. A single image of a girl who is Every Girl—or Every Child—the kind of visual shorthand that has been used throughout art history. And what gives it emotional impact is that very lack of specificity Jones deplores. It's *supposed* to be "instantly readable" as you walk or drive by. I'm not convinced that the wall of an urban building is an appropriate site for a work of great complexity and contemplation.

Jones again: "One anecdote [Banksy] does tell about his origins is how, when he was painting graffiti as a teenager, he was chased by the police: hiding under a van, he saw a stencil-like plate on its chassis and decided there and then to use stencils to design his street art. That way he could paint faster and elude the law; but this also meant he could paint better, becoming something far more like a proper artist. Banksy's stencil technique is now what makes his style so recognisable, like Andy Warhol's silkscreens."

I'm not one who measures the quality of an artwork by the amount of time spent on it, but rather judge its quality by how the execution contributes to its overall impact. The spraying or rolling of paint onto a surface through a pattern cut into paper, cardboard, or other media is a method long used in graffiti to create images that are easily reproducible. This doesn't mean there's no craft involved, of course, just that most of the effort takes place in advance. In Banksy's case, the complexity of his stencils indicates a certain amount of premeditation for a result that appears utterly spontaneous. "The holy grail," according to Banksy, "is to spend less time making the picture than it takes people to look at it."

"Better the rudest work that tells a story or records a fact, than the richest without meaning," says Ruskin.

Banksy's staple characters, most often working people and children, appear in attire and accoutrements as if they've emerged from the earlier part of the twentieth century—and it's this approach that's made his style so consistent over more than twenty years, as any allegiance to contemporary fashion would look dated not long after the work appeared. Therefore, his famous maid is wearing a frilly white apron over a black dress and a little white headpiece in her hair, as in a movie in the 1930s, and the men he depicts hail from a time when you could identify their occupations by their garb—the painter in white overalls, and detectives in ill-fitting trench coats. Banksy's children are similarly attired; instead of tees and capris, the little girls play in dresses, and his mischievous boys are rendered in longish shorts, sometimes the old-fashioned knee pants Americans call "knickers," and wearing baseball or even newsboy caps—to make for images that remind us not so much of our own childhoods as the idealized innocence portrayed in children's book illustrations of the early twentieth century.

While Western culture today sees childhood as a protected period of education and enjoyment, this concept is relatively modern, and as it developed in Victorian England, led to labor reform that moved children from the workplace to compulsory state schooling. It also resulted in the emergence of child-specific activities and products: recreational games, organized sports, factory-made toys such as the Teddy bears and dolls Banksy's children sometimes clutch, and a genre of children's books more humorous and fanciful than Grimm, with marbled endpapers, gilt-embossed bindings, and mounted full-color plates with elaborate illustrations. Most prominent among the illustrators was Arthur Rackham (1867–1939), whose books are still in print and much-beloved today, with the originals in museum collections.

One of Rackham's illustrative innovations was his development of the silhouette, with its clever use of negative space, and the similarity to Banksy's silhouettes is immediately clear (as it is to those of Banksy's contemporary, African American artist Kara Walker). More economical to produce than full-color prints, Rackham's silhouettes allowed for wider distribution of the books that featured them. In Banksy's case, the silhouette is uniquely suited to stencil reproduction.

What Banksy shares with Rackham, who illustrated the *Peter Pan* books, is this notion of the sanctity of childhood, the period of life that deserves to be care-free, protected from grownup preoccupations and dangers. While the threats children face in Rackham's illustrations are products of the imagination— goblins, monsters, and looming anthropomorphic trees—Banksy's message is aimed at adults; the children he depicts are endeavoring to play, but confronted with restrictions (such as the West Bank barrier wall, signs prohibiting graffiti and ball games, poor children made to work, blackboard resolutions starting with "I will not . . .") as well as the ultimate constraint: war.

In image after image, Banksy juxtaposes symbols of childhood innocence with those of combat. One of his earliest wall paintings in Bristol, *The Mild Mild West* (1999), shows riot police advancing on a Teddy bear armed with a Molotov cocktail. *Kids on Gun Hill* (2003), a silhouette most evocative of Rackham, presents the viewer with the image of a boy and girl with a Teddy bear and a heart balloon, standing atop a mound of lethal weapons. In other instances, Banksy uses flowers to represent love and purity of intent, as in his well-known *Flower Thrower* (2002), where a rioter or protester is gearing up to hurl a bouquet, or the open-winged peace dove (*Armored Dove*, Palestine, 2007) bearing an olive branch in its beak while wearing a flak jacket with a heart-shaped target on its breast—the heart being another frequent symbol. And the pair of male bobbies (*Kissing Coppers*, 2004), of course, are kissing.

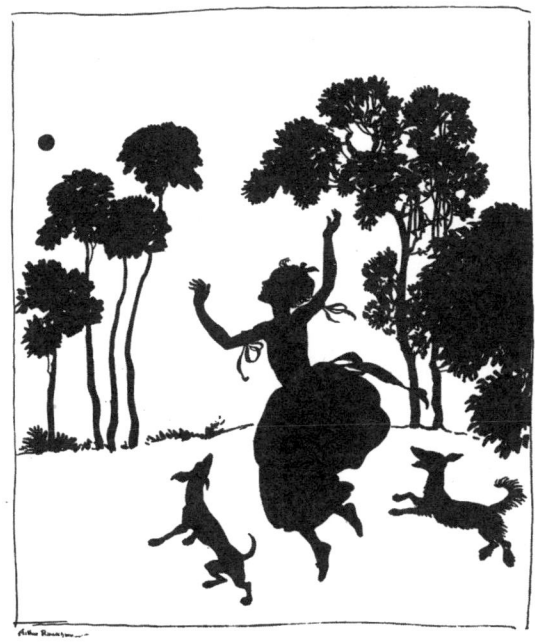

4.2
Arthur Rackham, "Cinderella," book
illustration, 1919.

Meanwhile, the stencil technique frequently employed in graffiti, which Banksy has adopted, is a by-product of war, used by the US Army in World War II to mark equipment as well as inscribe information and directions on the walls and streets of devastated towns (as Banksy did in 2015, when he sprayed his name and arrows on the sidewalks of Weston-super-Mare to guide visitors from the train to his temporary art project, *Dismaland*). American soldiers tagged tanks, artillery, and helmets with motifs of skulls or angels (and sometimes amalgamations of both), either to scare the enemy or raise morale, while the Nazis did the same with the swastika and fire bolts. After the war, dovetailing with the invention of canned aerosol spray paint, stencils became a popular tool of civilian resistance, covering European cities with rebellious antigovernment slogans, and in the Americas supporting the rise of Fidel Castro and Che Guevara.

Thus the simple, powerful graphic style that once represented oppression and fascism came to represent its opposition: protest, solidarity, and revolution—and, since morphing into this leftist, populist permutation, persists in forceful, nuance-free visual messages that present themselves as demands.

So yes, what we find in Banksy's work are "instantly readable" emotions. However, unlike Hallmark cards, they don't exist on their own, but are part of a blending of opposites that requires us to simultaneously negotiate contradictory feelings, such as sympathy and outrage. Banksy marries motifs of peace, innocence, and love with those of warfare, authoritarianism, and runaway capitalism in a stencil style that reads as a call to revolution. Often the combinations are so absurd (a rioter throwing flowers, cops kissing) and at the same time so instinctively reasonable (of course we should be throwing flowers instead of bombs and kissing instead of arresting people) that the irony—and the truth—make us laugh.

"Truth," of course, is relative, but there are certain values we almost all agree on—that life should be enjoyed, war is abominable, childhood should be protected, and we should not be constantly spied upon. By staying with higher ideals and not being politically specific—no grotesque images of Trump here—Banksy's work can speak to and challenge those on both sides of the ideological fence, rather like John Lennon ("Imagine all the people, living life in peace . . ."). Not being so specifically topical has another advantage in that an image may apply to many situations at once and remain relevant for a much longer period of time.

The deftness with which Banksy combines opposing concepts is his strong point, which becomes especially clear when we analyze the few instances where his amalgamations fall flat. One such is *Napalm (Can't beat the Feeling)* (ca. 2004), where he isolates the image of a fleeing nine-year-old girl on fire from napalm (from the 1972 photo by Nick Ut, one of the horrific photos that many credit with finally stopping the Vietnam War) and places her holding hands and skipping between the two major childhood icons of American consumerism, Mickey Mouse and Ronald McDonald. Perhaps I'm just too sensitive, but I find using the figure of the burning girl to make a point trivializes her agony, which is too much to bear looking at. Combined with the grinning cartoon characters, the ability to empathize becomes overloaded; the result is paralyzing.

This is similar to the claustrophobic violence of his elaborate Cinderella installation inside the crumbling castle at *Dismaland* (2015), where mannequins reenacted the death of Princess Diana in the Disney vernacular, Cinderella's lifeless body spilling out of the upended pumpkin carriage, surrounded by paparazzi whose cameras flashed like strobe lights. Indeed, we are shocked, but the situations depicted are so far out of our grasp, we end up feeling helpless. Author and teacher Joseph Campbell held that "Art that repels is didactic," in that by offering some kind of moral lesson, one is distracted from the art itself—a frequent failing of what the art world calls "social practice," and one that Banksy largely manages to avoid.

My guess is that Banksy's exceptional popularity with the public has to do with his ability to approach divisive subjects in a way that, while unsparing, is also delicate and humorous—thereby engaging people of different backgrounds and persuasions to consider topics with which they might not otherwise be concerned. Further, he does this in a manner that doesn't preclude a result, but allows for agency. In Banksy's world, even if the vehicle is as fantastical as a balloon, there is a way out. "There is always hope."

In 2014, our friend Jones wrote, "The political content of Banksy's art is generally so accepted and enjoyed that it has become tame." However, that statement was part of an article where, in a head-spinning if temporary reversal, Jones waxed lyrical about a Banksy on the wall of a boathouse in the town of Clacton-on-Sea. The painting appeared only days before a closely fought special election where the local Conservative Party lawmaker, Douglas Carswell, was attempting to retain his Parliament seat after switching his allegiance to UKIP, a right-wing populist party that promotes British nationalism and independence, reduced immigration, and the deportation of illegal immigrants. The painting depicted a mob of fat gray pigeons toting signs saying, "Migrants not welcome," "Go back to Africa," and "Keep off our worms," while advancing on a single, colorful, exotic bird. Jones wrote:

> This satire is in the tradition of Aesop's fables or St. Francis of Assisi when he preached to the birds—it's a lovely little vignette. For birds do not, of course, wave racist placards. Only humans do.
>
> The contrast between the ugly pigeons and the pretty swallow could hardly be starker or more telling. Plainly, we're meant to be on the side of the swallow. Banksy has cleverly exploited two contrasting wall textures to put the pigeons and the swallow in contrasting worlds: the place where the pigeons are is not very attractive and yet they defend it brutally, to the last worm.
>
> Clearly the African swallow is not a threat but an enriching presence. It's the "locals" who are grim. And the joke goes deeper. Banksy is pointing out that migration is not just a good thing—it is a natural fact. Migratory birds have been part of our landscape for a very long time. The little Britain defended by those who fear outsiders is an illusion—even the birds in our trees are citizens of the world.

Even before Banksy could claim the image on his website, it was gone. A local resident had complained to the town council who, unaware of its provenance, deemed it "offensive" and "racist" and immediately had the piece painted over. Despite the outcry that ensued, with locals lamenting potential losses in tourism and revenue, the authorities defended their position and in their clumsy struggle to save face—such as their invitation to Banksy to come back and do something "appropriate" on any of their seafronts—only amplified what might have remained a regional event into a story that went around the world.

While Banksy was unable to keep Carswell from winning, he provoked discussions in publications as far-flung as Baltimore, Milan, Mexico, and Turkey about racism, immigration, national identity, political correctness, and the identification and effectiveness of satire, as well as the conditions under which, if ever, graffiti should be saved and whether its eradication can be considered censorship. As a result of Banksy's challenge to authority, which caused its removal, the art acquired more significance in its absence than it would have if it had continued to exist. Is this or is this not "real art"? And do we care?

Banksy: It's not art unless it has the potential to be a disaster.

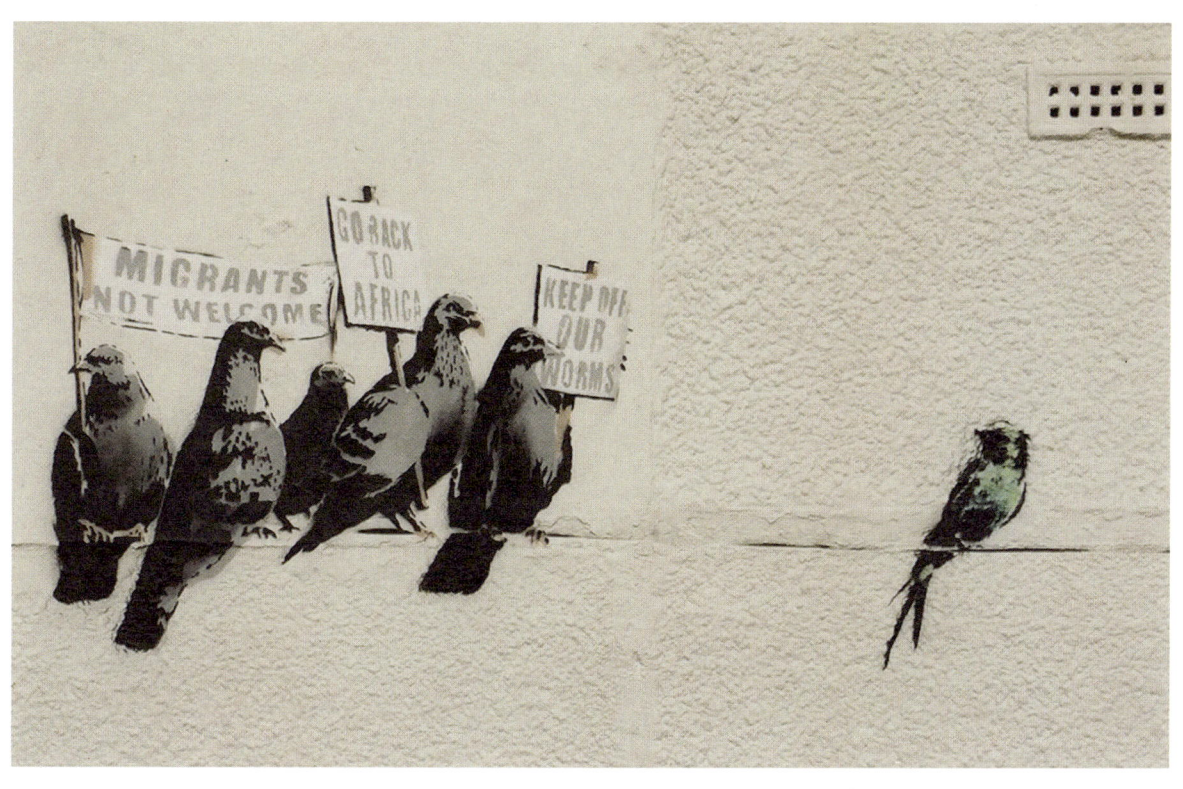

4.3

Banksy, 2014, spray painting, Clacton-on-Sea,
England, courtesy of Pest Control Office.

B anksy and "Real Art," Part II

5

To be an artist is not a matter of making paintings or objects at all.
What we are really dealing with is our state of consciousness
and the shape of our perception. But any tool you'd use is legitimate.
The key to the tool is whether it has the dimensions to deal with
what have become your questions.

Robert Irwin

It might come as a surprise to learn that my understanding of Banksy developed from years of looking at art through the lens of an artist who, on the surface, couldn't be more different—Californian Robert Irwin, whom I've gotten to know while writing in depth about his work, whose art engages neither images nor objects, but space and light.

Irwin's main premise has to do with what he calls "conditional art," where every aspect of the work is wholly determined by the facts and conditions of the site—"the object existing not in a vacuum of its own meaning, but in the real world, affected by the real world." This approach is very different from that of much public art, where a work is conceived without a certain location in mind and plopped in front of an office building ("the turd in the plaza," Irwin has called it)—as, for example, Henry Moore's bronze sculptures, made in editions, have proliferated throughout the world. Beyond that is the work we consider "site-specific," where artists configure their trademark materials and styles to suit particular locations, as Alexander Calder did when he designed his bright red fifty-three-foot-high stabile for Chicago's Federal Plaza. Some of these solutions, like Calder's, are successful. Irwin, however, wants his art to draw *all* of its cues from its surroundings, so that the response may be "monumental or ephemeral, aggressive or gentle, useful or useless, sculptural, architectural or simply the planting of a tree or maybe doing nothing at all." Regardless of approach, Irwin says, "if you do it right, it makes perfect sense and looks as if it's been there forever."

Irwin sees everything that affects the visual, emotional, and intellectual experience as part of the art, such as light, temperature, sounds, smells, comfort and discomfort, and so on. These effects can include even the expectations kindled by photographs and publicity describing the work before it's encountered, or the interpretation presented by wall text in a museum—anything that has the possibility of becoming the frame through which the art is seen before viewers have a chance to assess their own reactions.

Starting as a painter, Irwin was gradually moving toward installation when, in 1970, he staged a guerrilla intervention in an unused gallery at New York's Museum of Modern Art (MoMA) with the support of curator Jennifer Licht after the museum turned down her request to show his work. By changing the fluorescent tubes in the ceiling lights to alternating cool and warm, Irwin achieved a slight rainbow phenomenon, and by adding a stretched veil of translucent scrim fabric and a wire painted white, he created an evanescent "it's there/ it's not there" effect, variations on which he has explored in many ways since. MoMA, when finally aware of Irwin's intervention, refused to legitimize or promote it but let it stay, as long as there was an identifying label. Determined to avoid diluting the experience, Irwin hired someone to take the label down each day. "So when you walked into this thing," he said later, "you had to go through the process of asking yourself 'Is this an empty room? Is this intended?'"

Irwin, now in his early nineties, had never heard of Banksy when I told him a few years ago about how my understanding of "conditional art" had led to my interest in Banksy's work. To illustrate the connection, I described the Banksy in Folkestone, how it was not just a case of putting any old Banksy any old place, but how *Art Buff* was clearly exploring the "Sculpture Question" posed by the Triennial, the role of street art, and the gray area between public and private ownership—and how the location itself, occupied by a private business in a nonprofit building overlooking the conference hall and philanthropic Creative Quarter, put a spotlight on these issues. Hearing it described in this way, Irwin totally got it, and was tickled at the idea of his concepts being extended to street art.

Thinking along these lines led me to also consider how preparation, timing, promotion, and duration affect the art experience and, even more, can be regarded as *part* of the art experience. For example, in 2003, Icelandic-Danish artist Olafur Eliasson took the notion of "conditional art" to another level with the planning of his installation, entitled *The weather project*, at London's Tate Modern. Combining three sensorial elements—light, vapor, and reflection—the artist mirrored the massive Turbine Hall's already high seventy-five-foot ceiling, doubling its perceived height, and softened the atmosphere with fog, transforming the vast cold expanse into a misty cathedral-like infinity into which visitors were drawn by a large yellow aureole of light, like a dim winter sun, at the far end.

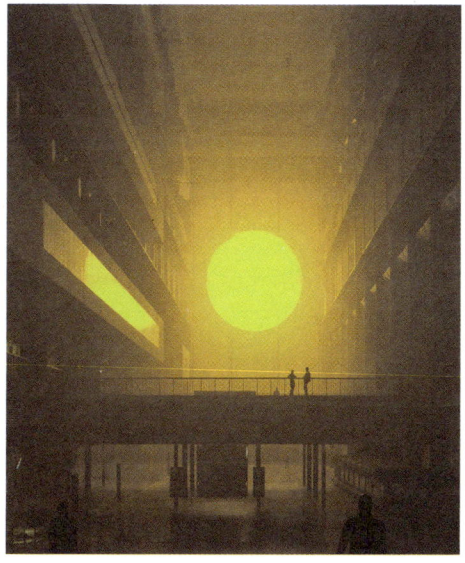

5.1
Olafur Eliasson, *The weather project*, 2003, installation view, Tate Modern, London, courtesy of Studio Olafur Eliasson.
Photo: Jens Ziehe © 2003.

As an art student in Denmark in the 1990s, Olafur (Icelanders are formally referred to by their first names) was greatly influenced by Lawrence Weschler's book about Irwin, *Seeing Is Forgetting the Name of the Thing One Sees*. Before beginning his project, as part of his study of the site, Olafur visited each of the Tate's departments, from curatorial to maintenance, in an effort to understand how their work might impact his and vice versa. And in another Irwin-like gesture, which resonated with me later when I began to think of Banksy's use of surprise as an artistic element, Olafur didn't allow photos or descriptions of the piece in the catalog or prepublicity because he wanted visitors to arrive without any preconception of what they would see.

No one was prepared for the installation's success, however. In planning, the museum predicted *The weather project* could expect about 100,000 visitors. By the end, what BBC critic Will Gompertz recently described as "the most famous piece of immersive art in the world . . . an instant masterpiece that was the making of Tate Modern and Olafur Eliasson" had drawn a million—some say two million—visitors. But when the Tate wanted to extend *The weather project*'s run, as the terms of the contract would have allowed, the artist objected, and the museum deferred to his wishes, removing it on schedule. In talking with Michael Kimmelman of the *New York Times*, Olafur explained his decision by saying, "The time after a show is just as interesting to me, because then it becomes an object of memory and its meanings change." He may also have seen the possibility that the excitement around *The weather project* was overshadowing the work itself, as later he told me that visiting it had become "almost a ritual," and its removal "preserved its integrity as an artistic project."

Writing this about Olafur, I thought of how much more emotional resonance architect Louis Sullivan's Stock Exchange, demolished in 1972, has for Chicagoans than does his Auditorium, which is still standing. And then, relating this idea of impermanence to street art, I remembered descending into New York's Spring Street subway station in the early 1980s, and discovering new, mysterious, and then unattributed Keith Haring chalk drawings of spaceships, angels, or babies. These cartoonlike white-on-black manifestations seemed otherworldly, as if they had dropped down from some ethereal, supernatural place. Never existing long enough to become background noise, their poignancy was heightened by their transitory nature. Later I found out that Haring (to whom Banksy has paid tribute, painting a hooded figure walking a Haring barking dog on a

London wall) was highly influenced by a lecture he heard by the sculptor Christo, which introduced him to ways of involving the public with his art.

Learning about this connection was exciting because Christo has also been part of my history, and yet another path to my understanding of Banksy, especially when considering ways artists can work without sponsors and outside the system. Christo's financial independence was particularly impressive given that his environmental interventions of landscape and fabric (undertaken in partnership with his wife, Jeanne-Claude) were massive and took years of planning, to exist only a short time. Christo's final project, the wrapping of the Arc de Triomphe in Paris, delayed until 2021, is a work he first conceived sixty years before, but will exist for only two weeks. New Yorkers will remember *The Gates* where, for sixteen days in 2005, orange banners hung from 7,503 vinyl gates along 23 miles of pathways, enlivening a wintery Central Park. The fabric Christo and Jeanne-Claude used gave all their work a "fragile, sensual, and temporary character," as their website characterizes it. The history of each piece from conception to actualization, their engineering and logistical challenges, their complex dealings with local authorities, and the chance element introduced by the unpredictability of weather are aspects Christo and Jeanne-Claude always considered facets of their art—as I consider these part of Banksy's.

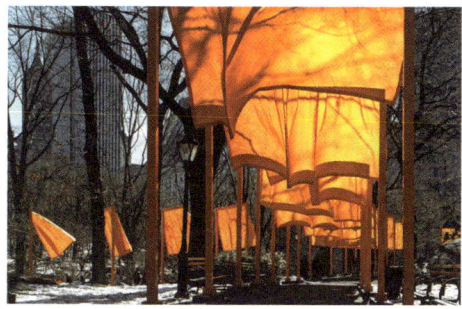

5.2

Christo and Jeanne-Claude, *The Gates, Central Park, New York City*, 1979–2005. Photo: Wolfgang Volz. © 2005 Christo and Jeanne-Claude.

"Do you know," Christo once said, "that I don't have any artworks that exist? They all go away when they're finished. Only the preparatory drawings, and collages are left, giving my works an almost legendary character. I think it takes much greater courage to create things to be gone than to create things that will remain."

Through these artists, I've learned to take into account absolutely everything that affects the art experience, to the point that I'm likely to ask a student who has failed to prepare their painting surface properly, "So what does that warped stretcher signify?"—or rail about museum wall text and artists' statements that predigest the art for viewers, or become annoyed when space and light artists like Doug Wheeler and James Turrell require that I don Tyvek booties so I won't make tracks on their pristine surfaces—and then expect me to separate my displeasure at having to wear these ugly things from the transcendent experience I'm supposed to be having.

The question is always, "How does the medium match the message?"—which can extend not only to issues of placement, promotion, and timing, but sponsorship. "Where does the money come from and how might it affect the outcome?" is an inquiry to make not only of politicians, but artists. It was Christo and Jeanne-Claude who first brought the issue of sponsorship to my attention. To ensure total artistic freedom, their gigantic projects were always self-funded through the sale of Christo's drawings and other smaller artworks. Consequently, there were no volunteers—all workers were paid—and no engagement with donations, grants, sponsorships, licensing deals, or commissions. Well, almost never. There was one commission for which I, ironically, was responsible when, as art consultant for *Time*, I tapped Christo to create the cover for the magazine's 1988 Planet of the Year issue about the environment, and his globe, suffocating in its wrapping of plastic and twine, became *Time*'s symbol for the environment for many years after. The couple hesitated when I first presented the idea ("Christo doesn't do commissions," Jeanne-Claude told me sternly) but ultimately ended up seeing it not as a conflict but as something like a collaboration—especially as the contract we worked out, in a long but genial *pas de deux* between Jeanne-Claude and *Time*'s lawyer, assured them total control over the final image.

Since the earliest of times, art and patronage have been intertwined—it was with art that popes and kings enhanced their prestige and celebrated their conquests. Over the centuries, however, the tables have gradually turned to the point that now many contemporary artists are making work that's actively hostile to capitalism. Yet, more often than not, this protest art is funded by galleries, museums, and other arts organizations that remain deeply embedded in the system, backed by individuals and corporations which, like the royalty of yore, use art to polish their images. Is there integrity in criticizing corporate power when you're also profiting from it? Can your motives be believed?

Persisting in issues of sponsorship caused controversy when, in 2014, I blogged about African American artist Kara Walker's gigantic sculpture composed of polystyrene and eighty tons of sugar, located in the defunct Domino sugar factory in Brooklyn and commissioned by Creative Time, a nonprofit that supports "innovative, site-specific, socially engaged artworks in the public realm." Resting at seventy-five feet long and thirty-five feet high, it was a work of spectacular beauty. Sparkling with a surface of white sugar, this massive crouching Sphinx-like female figure conflated two white Jim Crow parodies of Black women: the big-assed, sexually available Jezebel, with her vulva hanging out for the taking, and her opposite, the maternal, large-breasted but desexualized Mammy, who sublimates her own needs to fulfill those of her white charges. With gentle, undulating curves like those of a Brancusi, the sculpture loomed like a symbol of purity in the vast darkness and decay of the derelict factory's interior.

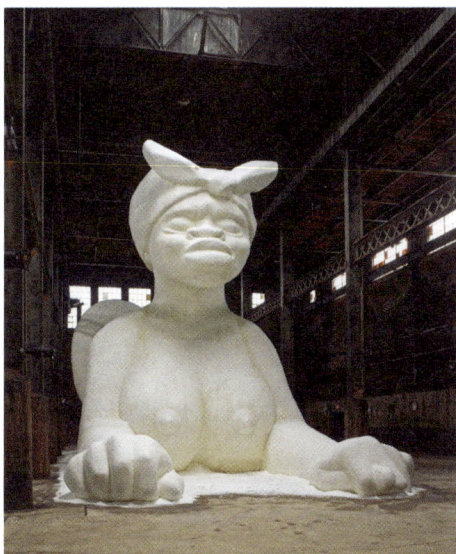

5.3

Kara Walker, *A Subtlety, or the Marvelous Sugar Baby, an Homage to the unpaid and overworked Artisans who have refined our Sweet tastes from the cane fields to the Kitchens of the New World on the Occasion of the demolition of the Domino Sugar Refining Plant*, Domino Sugar Refinery, Brooklyn, NY, 2014. Photo: Jason Wyche. © 2014 Kara Walker.

In the work's title, the artist referenced the history of the sugar trade and its dependence on slavery: *A Subtlety or The Marvelous Sugar Baby, an Homage to the unpaid and overworked Artisans who have refined our Sweet tastes from the cane fields to the Kitchens of the New World on the Occasion of the demolition of the Domino Sugar Refining Plant.*

Walker's installation, however, was sponsored and the sugar donated by Domino Foods, which, my research indicated, is owned by the Fanjul family whose "Big Sugar" empire is overseen by siblings who have been dubbed the "Koch Brothers of South Florida." The Fanjuls have been accused of brutal working conditions in what amounts to modern-day slave labor, such as harvesters being forced to work at gunpoint—and if that weren't enough, Pepe Fanjul's longtime executive assistant, Chloe Black, who has been a fundraiser for Marco Rubio and Donald Trump, is the ex-wife of former KKK leader David Duke, and the current wife of Don Black, a former KKK grand wizard and member of the American Nazi Party who now runs the white supremacist website StormFront.org.

My post generated significant pushback on social media from artist peers who seemed most worried that my criticism of Walker might ultimately put them in the line of fire. As one artist put it in a comment on my Facebook page, "As you say, she could have called this history out more explicitly, but she's not an investigative journalist, she's an artist. So many artists, including myself, make giant public projects funded by municipal or private money that if traced may unearth uncomfortable truths." She continues, "Why does Kara Walker have to be more politically pure than say, Anish Kapoor, or Urs Fischer, or Jeff Koons? Or me?" This from an artist who has since become active in progressive politics in the city of New York, yet was one of many who were unable, or unwilling, to grasp the irony of a Black artist and the history of slavery being used to "whitewash" the current egregious labor practices of Domino, whose logo was splashed everywhere—not to mention that the whole project acted as an advertisement for a future $3 billion luxury development on the site by another sponsor, Two Trees Management, owned by the family of Creative Time board member Jed Walentas, who worked for Trump before taking over his father's real estate business. (Random fact: before the 2017 opening of the development's first residential building, Two Trees received 87,000 applications for 104 affordable units.)

This is a long way of explaining why, when Banksy came along, I may have been more predisposed than many to look beyond the painting on the wall for qualities that could expand the conversation about what characterizes art in these times, as well as its value, purpose—and integrity.

My first inkling that perhaps Banksy was thinking along some of these lines was when I looked for his website after the last day of his 2013 New York sojourn to find it . . . gone. At first, I was distressed, as I was just beginning to think about writing about Banksy's time in New York, and now there was no dependable reference. However, I got over my dismay quickly—in fact, laughed—when I thought of it in the context of street art, which pops up suddenly and might be obliterated by the next time you pass by. I saw the internet, as Banksy uses it, as an extension of the street—where there are no gatekeepers, no admission fees, and the possibility of reaching people from many backgrounds, cultures, and viewpoints.

Banksy's mode of communication blends the old and the new, the intimacy and immediacy of street art with the wide reach of technology. Where modern marketers haven't evolved past the old "more is more" doctrine, plastering the world, both physical and virtual, with logos and slogans, Banksy lives up to his anti-advertising credo by making an art out of connecting with his audience through a minimum of cryptic messages, strategically timed. Banksy's most recent major projects, his *Dismaland* theme park (2015) and *The Walled Off Hotel* in the West Bank (2017 and ongoing), were developed in complete secrecy to spring up suddenly, like his street art, with no fanfare whatsoever, not even an advance press release. Earlier, Banksy's month-long New York City "artist residency," which turned into what was no doubt the world's largest scavenger hunt, got the internet buzzing with rumors when, in mid-September, he reduced his website to a single page showing a stenciled silhouette of a man holding an aerosol paint can as he pukes up a stream of flowers. The image was accompanied by only four words—"BETTER OUT THAN IN"—and the date, "October 2013."

Silence followed until October 1 when the project was initially revealed not by Banksy but by a fan's twittered discovery of a spray painting in New York's Chinatown, an image of a boy standing on another's back to reach for a picture of a can of aerosol paint on a sign that read, "Graffiti is a crime." Shortly after, Banksy confirmed it was his painting with a photo on his site, where the initial page had been replaced with one that read: "BETTER OUT THAN IN, An Artists

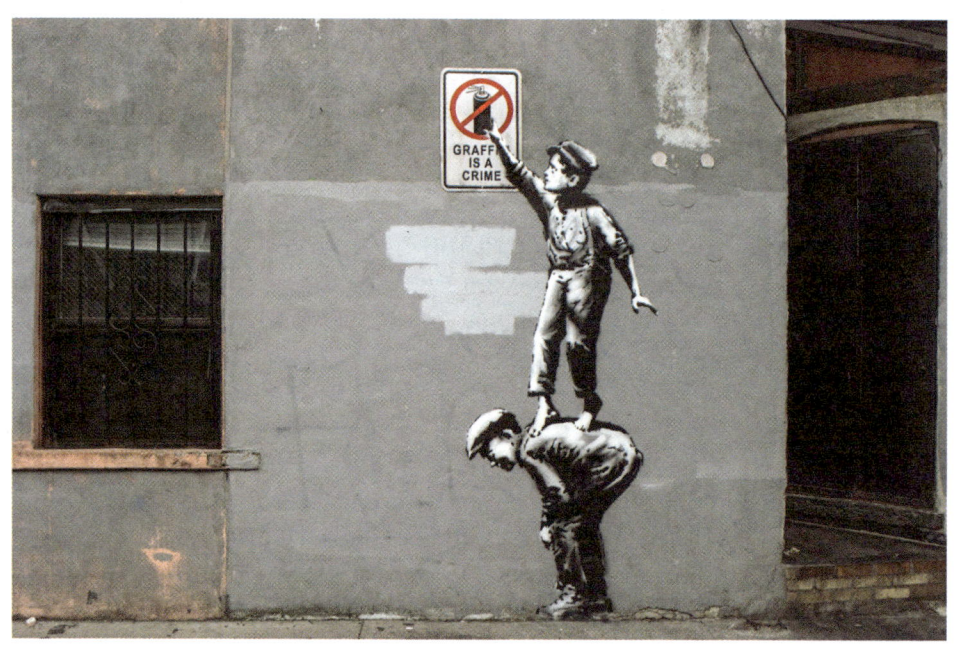

5.4
Banksy, *Graffiti Is a Crime*, 2013, spray painting,
New York, courtesy of Pest Control Office.

Residence On The Streets Of New York." The image was accompanied by a toll-free phone number with which one could access a museum-style audio guide. Those who called heard the following message, delivered by a smooth male voice with an American accent:

> Hello, and welcome to lower Manhattan. Before you, you will see a spray art by the artist Band-sky *[purposefully mispronounced]*—or maybe not. It's probably been painted over by now. If, however, you can still make it out, you're looking at a type of picture called "graffiti," from the Latin "graffito," which means graffiti with an "o." The children in this case represent youth, and the sign represents, well, signs. Now, let us pause for a moment to consider the deeper meaning of this work. Okay, that's long enough. This piece is typical of Band-sky's output, relying as it does on life-size characters viewed at a level perspective in monochrome. This effect is achieved by spraying automotive spray paint through an intricately cut shape in a piece of cardboard. Or to give it its proper term, "cheating." What exactly is the artist trying to say here? Is this a response to the primal urge to take the tools of our oppression and turn them into mere playthings? Or perhaps it is a postmodern comment on how the signifiers of objects have become as real as the objects themselves. Are you kidding me? Who writes this stuff? (Sound of papers rustling) Anyway, you decide. Really, please do. I have no idea.

For the next thirty days, Banksy rolled out at least one work per day somewhere in the five boroughs, sometimes with a hotline number and sometimes not, sometimes with a location hint and sometimes not—a mishmash of predictability and unpredictability and art which, along with wall stencils, included installations on trucks, his fiberglass Ronald McDonald, theatrical constructions, the altered painting at Housing Works, a stall in Central Park where passersby could purchase an authentic Banksy for sixty dollars, an online video, and more. The painted artworks' fate, however, was never in Banksy's control. Some, like the Chinatown piece, didn't last a day before being painted over, others were enshrined in Plexiglas, a few removed and shipped off to be sold at auction, while the last one landed in police custody, never to be heard of again. And with the website gone, documentation remained entirely in the hands of the media and the general public, who "completed" the work with uploaded photos and videos to the internet. The online magazine *Hyperallergic* did a count on Day 31: "'Banksy' on Twitter: 336,000, #banksy on Instagram: 42,110." The 2014 film *Banksy Does New York*, produced by HBO, is almost entirely a deftly edited collage of uploaded personal video footage, an innovative format that captures the spirit of the month-long chase Banksy instigated.

A commenter on *Hyperallergic* asked if there was any critical discussion about the artworks' political content—to which the editor, Hrag Vartanian, answered: "I think there were genuine conversations that happened, and I witnessed them repeatedly. Will it change art discourse? Hmmm . . . not sure. I do think it has changed the perception of street art in NYC, that's for sure. And in a city that has had a knee-jerk response to street art for so long—and once subscribed (almost religiously) to the 'broken windows' theory—this is welcome news."

> *Banksy:* I've learnt from experience that a painting isn't finished when you put down your brush—that's when it starts. The public reaction is what supplies meaning and value. Art comes alive in the arguments you have about it.

And, of course, there was no public sponsorship of the month-long event. Clearly, like Christo and Jeanne-Claude, by insisting on independently funding his work, Banksy is ahead of his time. As I'm writing, in July 2019, Warren B. Kanders, the vice chairman of the board at the Whitney Museum of American Art, stepped down after months of protest over his company's sale of tear gas, allegedly used against migrants at the Mexican border. His resignation came after eight artists withdrew from the museum's prestigious biennial exhibition, which has increasingly been characterized by political content addressing social inequity. There will be more dissent to come. For years we walked, without thinking, past those lists of individuals and corporations who made this or that exhibition possible, or the names of patrons engraved in brass or marble at the entrance of a cultural institution. Now each is under question.

So, while Christo supported his huge projects through the sale of his art, we can only guess how Banksy, who has no work publicly available, bankrolls efforts as large as *Dismaland* and *The Walled Off Hotel* in the West Bank, but we do know that no sponsors are using his work to advertise themselves. At *Dismaland*, the absence of familiar brands—no Coke, no Doritos, no pressure to buy—made for a surprisingly refreshing ambiance. Instead, at the *Dismaland* gift shop (through which you had to exit, of course) a faction called Special Control Group was selling a £6 packet of ad hack tools, said to be efficient at opening a third of the planet's bus stop advertising spaces, presumably so buyers could replace the ads with their own. More than two thousand were sold.

Similarly, at *The Walled Off Hotel*, the only labels guests are likely to see are on the bottles of beer served in the café. In an act simultaneously respectful and disrespectful, a mad stroke of fresh-looking white paint, complete with drip, obliterates the logo on the shiny black, baby grand, state-of-the-art player piano that occupies the café's center. It's the only new-looking object in the hotel and clearly the most expensive—comparable models go for upward of $25,000. No doubt Steinway or Yamaha, the two brands that make these technical wonders, would have been delighted to donate one and get the full benefit of exposure. Instead, the painted stroke defiantly rejects corporate patronage while, ironically, because it's Banksy, making this object, if it were ever resold, worth at least ten times more.

Banksy: Nobody ever listened to me until they didn't know who I was.

Of course, just as Banksy refuses to identify the piano, he refuses to identify himself. To me, Banksy's anonymity constitutes a work of conceptual art on its own. I refer to "him" throughout this book because it would be grammatically unwieldy to do otherwise, but do I really know who or what I'm referring to? Banksy is a concept that could represent one person, or twenty, or a hundred. The guy who came up through Bristol's underground scene and hung out with the band Massive Attack could have moved on and been replaced by someone else, or many someone elses, for all we know. The original could now be your dentist, or your kid's teacher, or the guy who sells you aerosol paint in the hardware store. By being anonymous, Banksy occupies a much bigger space than an identifiable human. Because he can't be pinned down, he's a subversive presence who hovers everywhere, could be anywhere, even right HERE.

Banksy: I don't know why people are so keen to put the details of their private life in public; they forget that invisibility is a superpower.

Do I want to know the full story, to meet him, her, or them? No more than I wanted, as a kid, for Santa Claus to be revealed. Do I want to know how he goes about pulling off these seemingly impossible stunts? No more than I wanted to know how Santa got all that stuff down the chimney. By being anonymous, Banksy becomes an entity we can project our fantasies on—bigger than life and the embodiment of the altruism he projects. I really really really don't want to find out that he's Damien Hirst.

Banksy: I have no interest in ever coming out. I figure there are enough self-opinionated assholes trying to get their ugly little faces in front of you as it is. You ask a lot of kids today what they want to be when they grow up, and they say, "I want to be famous." You ask them for what reason and they don't know or care.

I think Andy Warhol got it wrong: in the future, so many people are going to become famous that one day everybody will end up being anonymous for 15 minutes. I'm just trying to make the pictures look good; I'm not into trying to make myself look good. I'm not into fashion. The pictures generally look better than I do when we're out on the street together. Plus, I obviously have issues with the cops. And besides, it's a pretty safe bet that the reality of me would be a crushing disappointment to a couple of 15-year-old kids out there.

Like the French electronic music duo Daft Punk, who have performed disguised in helmets since the 1990s, Banksy will never grow old—nor can he/she/they get caught in the web of identity politics. But the most important aspect of anonymity is that we have no choice but to concentrate on the message rather than the messenger.

Biographical criticism is the norm, and I have unwittingly engaged in it, but writing about an anonymous artist has shown me its limitations. Not that the thoughts of artists cannot be stimulating and significant (I wouldn't have formed any of these ideas had I not read Kandinsky's *On the Spiritual in Art*, Irwin's *Notes toward a Conditional Art,* or Gerhard Richter's *Writings*), but it can be limiting when biography becomes the vehicle through which to explain the art. Like the anticipation engendered by prepublicity, biography overshadows the work itself to become the frame through which we see it, thereby short-circuiting our own aesthetic reactions. For example, note how nearly impossible it is to look at a Van Gogh or Basquiat without thoughts of their tortured lives creeping in. I've also come to realize that many artists, including me, do not completely understand what their work can mean to others. In his *New York Times* obituary, pop art icon Roy Lichtenstein was quoted as saying "I don't think artists like myself have the faintest idea what we're doing."

Hopefully, we're more complex than the objective particulars of our existence. It's not the story of the artist's life but the degree to which their art can focus our own experience that excites us.

While many of my artist friends are convinced that Banksy is a collective, one insists it's not likely because, she says, the sensibility and sense of humor are too particular for a group to carry off. That made me think of the Guerrilla Girls, the game-changing collective of anonymous feminist artists who formed to combat sexism and racism in the art world, after noting that, of the 169 artists in MoMA's 1983 International Survey of Painting and Sculpture, all were white and only 13 were women. In public appearances the Guerrilla Girls disguise themselves with big hairy gorilla masks (giving them what they call "mask-ulinity" to avoid the stereotype of female sexiness) and adopt pseudonyms based on the names of famous deceased female artists, like Frida Kahlo, Alice Neel, and Georgia O'Keeffe. Their anonymity protects them from professional backlash and gives courage to a gender not generally reared to speak out. As one said, "You'd be surprised what comes out of your mouth when you wear a mask."

Along with staging interventions at arts institutions, the Guerrilla Girls produce posters, books, and billboards posing such (now famous) questions as "Do women have to be naked to get into the Met Museum?" and "When sexism and racism are no longer fashionable, what will your collection be worth?" and listing "The advantages of being a woman artist: working without the pressure of success, knowing your career might pick up after you're eighty, not having to undergo the embarrassment of being called a genius," etc. Although over the past forty or so years their fluctuating membership has grown beyond the initial seven, the Guerrilla Girls' style and arch humor has retained all of its original character. Of course success breeds success, so it's an inevitable irony that the Guerrilla Girls are now collected and invited to exhibit by the very museums that have been the targets of their protests. The question of whether their effectiveness is enhanced or compromised by collaboration with the institutions they critique would constitute another entire chapter. You can probably guess where I stand.

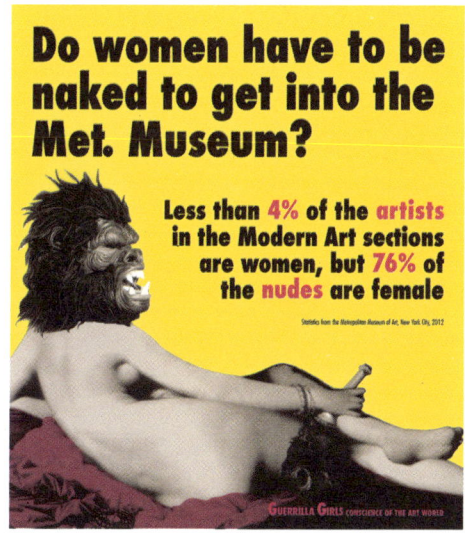

5.5

Guerrilla Girls, *Do women have to be naked to get into the Met. Museum?*, 2012, paper poster, courtesy of guerrillagirls.com.

The fact that Jane Austen's books, in her lifetime, were published not under her name but "By a Lady" (following the custom of the day when, for a woman of a certain class, having a full-time occupation was seen as unfeminine) made a great impression on the pseudonymous best-selling novelist Elena Ferrante, who said in the *Paris Review*:

> I'm still very interested in testifying against the self-promotion obsessively imposed by the media. This demand for self-promotion diminishes the actual work of art, whatever that art may be, and it has become universal. The media simply can't discuss a work of literature without pointing to some writer-hero. And yet there is no work of literature that is not the fruit of tradition, of many skills, of a sort of collective intelligence. We wrongfully diminish this collective intelligence when we insist on there being a single protagonist behind every work of art.

I've never forgotten the 2001 exhibition "Vermeer and the Delft School" at the Metropolitan Museum in New York, where Vermeer's paintings were exhibited along with those of fellow painters of his time, whose subject matter and approach to space, light, and composition were remarkably (or unremarkably, as the case may be) similar. Yet despite the parallels, the artists all having developed with the same influences, Vermeer's work popped out, obviously exceptional. Still, one wonders, would his achievement have been possible without the others? Even if art is made in opposition to the milieu, the effect remains.

Therefore, when some insist Banksy is simply copying his French street art predecessor Blek le Rat who, in the early 1980s, was one of the first to use stencils in graffiti and had a rat as his tag ("Every time I think I've painted something slightly original," Banksy is widely quoted as saying, "I find out that Blek le Rat has done it as well, only 20 years earlier"), I think many other graffitists of his time saw Blek le Rat too, but they didn't turn out to be Banksy. Another acknowledged influence is antiwar activist/artist Peter Kennard, whose photomontages, such as *Haywain with Cruise Missiles* (1980), where he inserted a cluster of American weapons into Constable's revered pastoral painting *The Hay Wain* (1821), preceded Banksy's similar corruptions of traditional paintings. And then there's Robert Del Naja, known as 3D, graffitist and founding member of the band Massive Attack, and the entire fertile music/graffiti scene in Bristol in the late 1980s to early '90s, which was inspired on all levels by a fusion of punk and West Indian cultures.

Truly missing the forest for the trees, art writers tend to see Banksy's spray paintings as if in a vacuum. Perhaps because they're so accustomed to viewing images one by one on a wall, or encountering conceptual art within the container of the gallery or museum, critics have been rendered incapable of considering the randomness of the street, the exchange on social media, and the events Banksy's work provokes as part of the art. In New York, critics didn't consider his website and "audio guides" intrinsic to the artworks, or view the entire event for what it clearly was: a month-long performance.

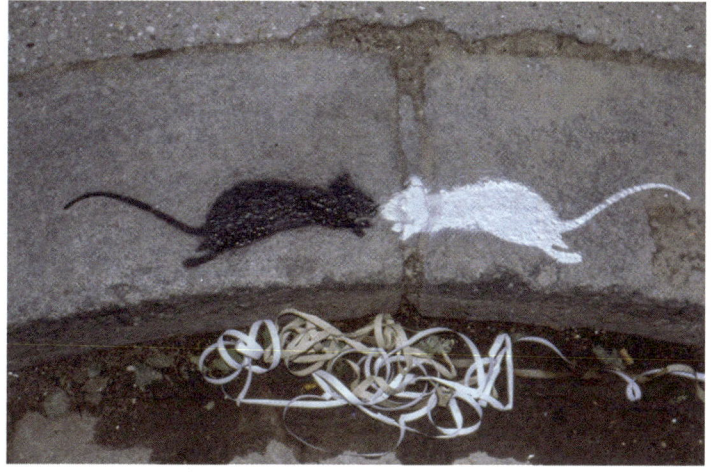

5.6
Blek le Rat, *Deux rats de Blek*, 1983, wall painting, Paris. Photo: Rosine Klatzmann.

5.7 *following pages*
Peter Kennard, *Haywain with Cruise Missiles*, 1980, photomontage, courtesy of the artist.

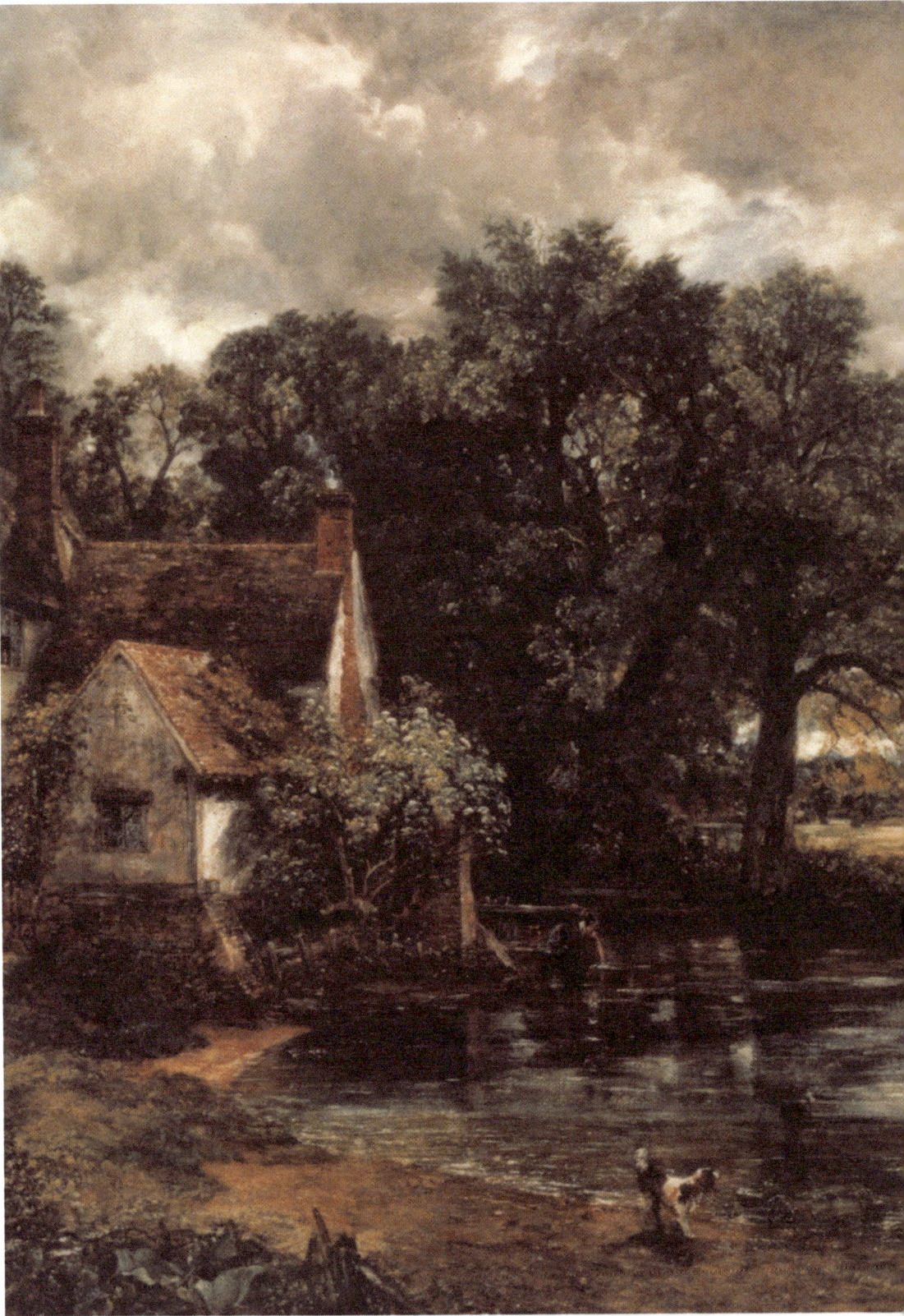

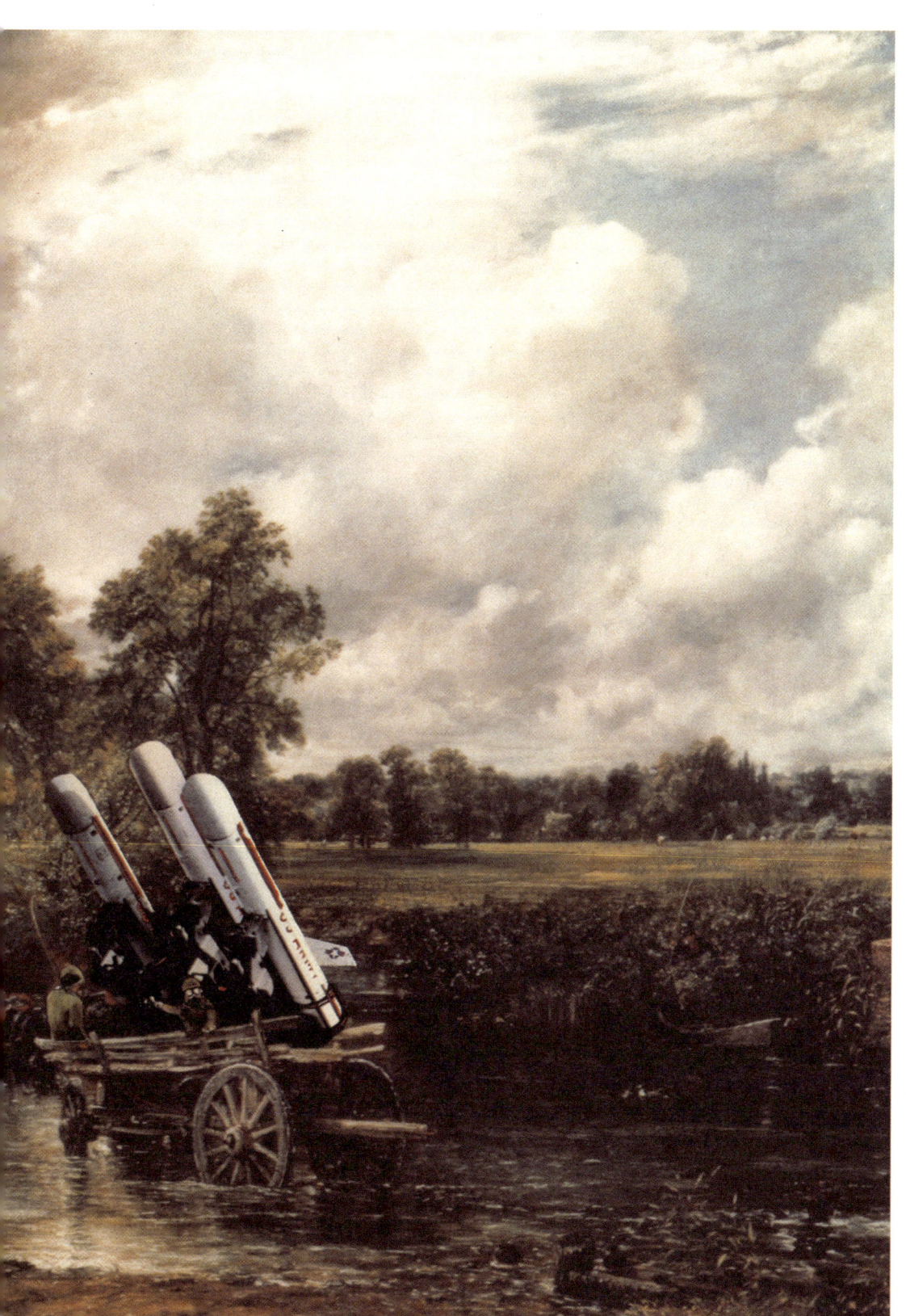

Like our critic buddy Jonathan Jones, critic Cal Revely-Calder insists that art must be contemplative. In one of several Banksy-bashing articles, Revely-Calder writes, "simplicity is desirable in political tracts, but not in a medium that has the capacity to deal in complexity instead." Is it possible that Jones and Revely-Calder have never heard of pop art, minimalism, or conceptual art? Without realizing it, they've been caught in Banksy's snare, wherein he drives art writers so crazy they ditch all requisites of professionalism in order to prove their intellectual superiority. In his 2019 article entitled "Overpriced, Obvious and Ubiquitous: What Is the Point of Banksy?" about Banksy's painting of a refugee child on a wall in Venice, Revely-Calder, winner of the 2017 *Frieze* writer's prize and 2014 *Guardian* Student Critic of the Year, consults James Elkins, E. C. Chadbourne Chair of art history, theory, and criticism at the School of the Art Institute of Chicago and author of several well-known books, including one entitled *What Is Art?* Revely-Calder asks Elkins, who "doesn't follow Banksy, why he thinks other people do." Really? Why would you seek out the opinion of someone who doesn't know the subject? And why would he be willing to comply? True to form, not following Banksy hardly stood in the way of Elkins's eagerness to answer: "The admiration in the press is widespread," he suggests, "because his works are political and social provocations, so they relieve the critics of the obligation to consider the works' intrinsic interest"—thereby revealing that, because he doesn't follow Banksy, Elkins doesn't know that "admiration in the press" for Banksy is hardly a thing and that the political and social implications of his work are rarely addressed—indeed, the very reason I've been compelled to write this book.

Another phenomenon Banksy provokes from otherwise responsible writers is their comfort with making negative judgments on the basis of a photo. I can't imagine Revely-Calder or another critic writing some four thousand words to disparage an artwork by any other artist that they'd only seen reduced to a square on a computer. Street art is all about context: the wall, the neighborhood, and, in this case, the Venice Biennale which, Revely-Calder confirmed in an email, he did not attend. In fact, I'm wondering if he's ever been to Venice, as he describes the wall Banksy painted on as "drab," when so much of Venice's charm lies in the obvious age of its walls, the patched layers of mortar and brick that reveal its history. In this case, the life-size black-and-white stenciled image of a refugee child signaling for rescue with a flare is carefully placed to merge with the random abstraction created by the natural wearing away of the wall. The gestural trail of the neon pink flare both contrasts and harmonizes with the aura of antiquity to make for a composition that appears simultaneously ancient and new.

As I write, Jonathan Jones is conveniently going apeshit over another poll, this reported in the tabloid *Sun*, where Banksy comes in as "Brits' favourite painter of all time . . . beating greats such as Leonardo da Vinci, Vincent van Gogh, Rembrandt, and Monet"—causing Jones to categorically state that "A meaningful comparison between Banksy and Van Gogh can only be made a century or so from now when he is part of history. Will his works endure as Van Gogh's do? That is the only test of greatness in art. And it is one Banksy is unlikely to meet simply because his art is so pointed and current."

Well, for one thing, if humans keep going as they are, who knows if anyone will even be around in a hundred years to make the call—but if they are, hopefully they'll be smart enough to distinguish between apples and oranges. Is it not possible that there exists both art that makes us look inward, which alters how we perceive ourselves, and art that causes us to look outward, changing how we perceive the world?

Regardless, it seems wacky to attempt to second-guess posterity's judgment—especially when applying criteria left over from the last century. Hopefully, art is a living concept whose limits we're constantly expanding. If not, why bother to make it?

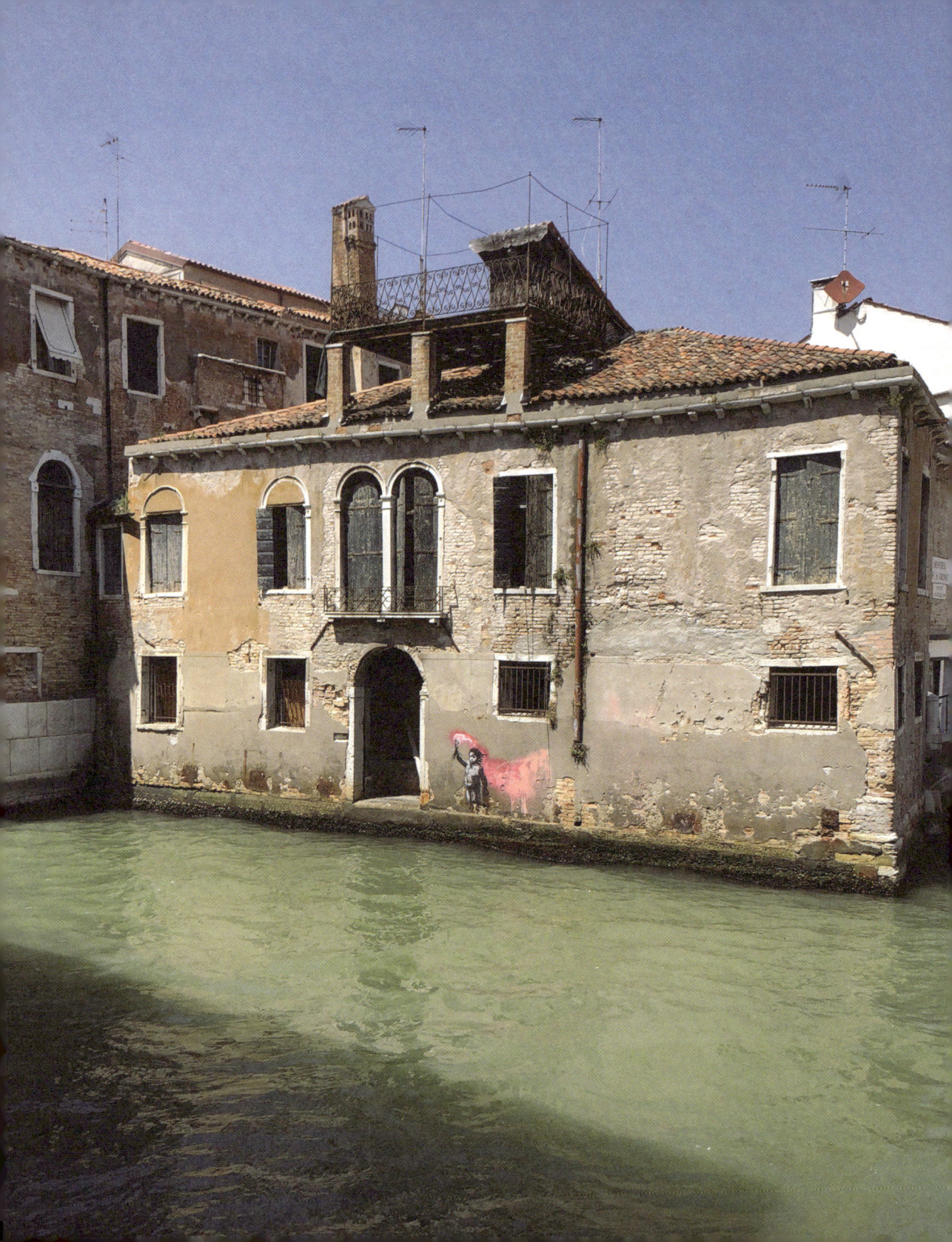

5.8
Banksy, spray painting, Venice, 2019.
Photo: Christopher Natrop.

B anksy and the Art Market

What strip mining is to nature the art market has become to culture.
Art critic Robert Hughes

Sotheby's, London, October 5, 2018: It was the shred that was seen around the world. Seconds after the auctioneer banged his gavel announcing the sale of Banksy's painting *Girl with Balloon* for more than $1.4 million ($700,000 over its original estimate), an alarm beeped and a stunned audience watched as the canvas began to self-destruct. Passing through a shredder hidden in its heavy gilded frame, the image of the little girl came out from the bottom in long, vertical strips like linguine, only to stop before devouring the heart-shaped balloon. Sotheby's handlers quickly hustled the half-shredded artwork out of sight, and shortly after, Banksy posted a photo on Instagram of the painting in mid-shred with the caption "Going, going, gone."

The auction house recovered gracefully, claiming they'd been "Banksy-ed." "He is arguably the greatest British street artist," said Alex Branczik, head of Sotheby's contemporary art for Europe, "and tonight we saw a little piece of Banksy genius," while adding that the auction house was "not in on the ruse."

Sotheby's press release stated that this widely recognizable image was not a multiple but a unique work, made with stencil and spray paint on canvas mounted on board, signed by the artist and fully authenticated by his management company, Pest Control. According to Sotheby's, the consignor acquired the painting directly from the artist following the Los Angeles warehouse exhibition Banksy had organized in 2006, and the gold frame was original.

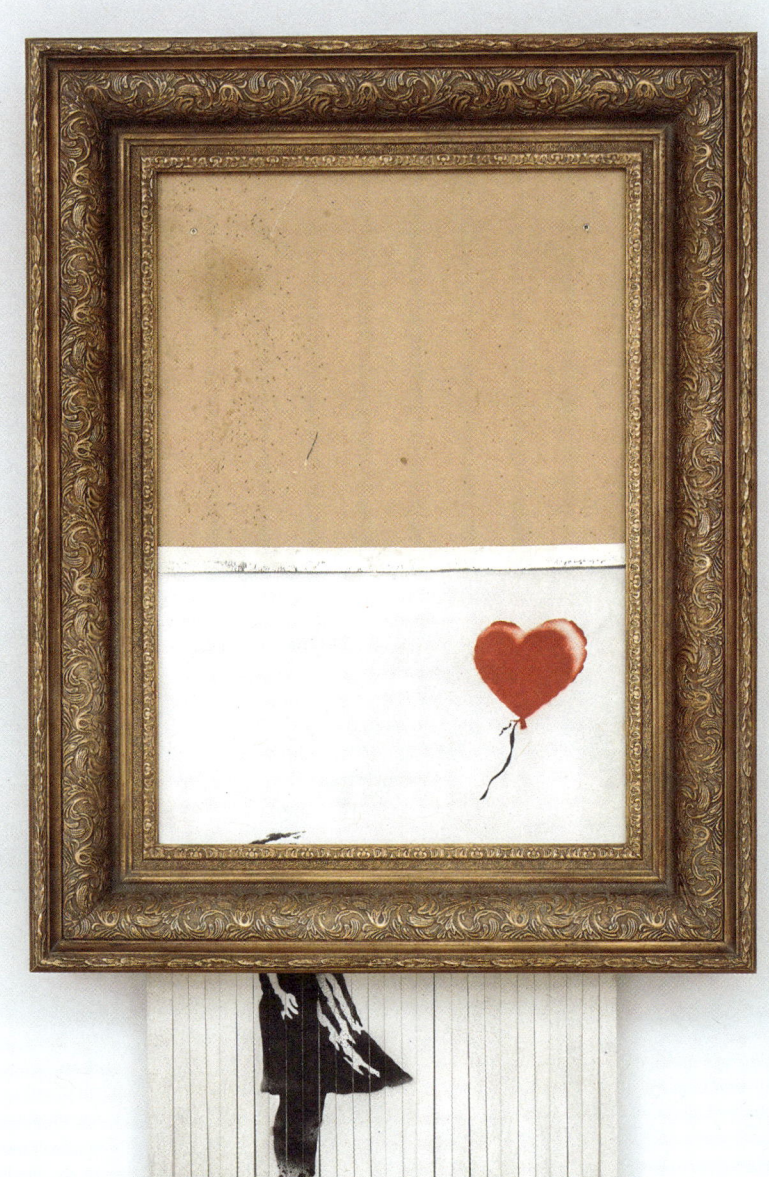

6.1

Banksy, *Love Is in the Bin*, 2018, paint and acrylic
on canvas, mounted on board. Framed by the artist
with remotely controlled shredding mechanism
hidden in the frame and integral to the work,
London. Courtesy of Sotheby's.

The act was a tour de force. Even critic Jerry Saltz temporarily suspended his animus toward Banksy to post on Facebook and Twitter: "Banksy pranked the insidious auction world and disrupted the flow of capital—if only for an evening. I'm not a Banksy fan but this made me want to dance barefoot with him."

Saltz's remark reflected the attitude of artists and writers who feel that the art world has been stolen from them, co-opted by the auction houses, art fairs, and billionaire collectors who have found the unregulated and generally opaque market convenient for storing assets, money laundering, speculation, and social climbing. There are no more cultural movements; investors follow trends, not ideas. No longer appreciated for its intellectual and aesthetic value, art has become little more than a commodity, with money defining its worth, while we, the artists, participate in neither its meaning nor its profit. The middlemen are the ones making out—art advisors, auction houses, investors—because the more times an artwork changes hands, the more its value increases, leaving artists at the bottom of the hierarchy. Except in Australia and the United Kingdom, where they're supposed to receive 5 percent of the auction take, visual artists, unlike writers and musicians, don't earn future royalties but see returns only from the original sale. And with speculators cutting so much of his work out of the walls for which it was intended and putting it up for auction, Banksy doesn't even see that percentage. No wonder he was moved to make a statement.

By the next morning, however, Saltz had retracted his praise (one Facebook commenter noted, "It isn't even noon"). Clearly having decided that Sotheby's was in on the prank, Saltz tweeted a photo of himself behind a Sotheby's podium, giving the middle finger with both hands: "Good morning, Sotheby's. Did you enjoy doing your little Banksy dance? Con? The market is so dumb that it only buys what others in the market have already bought—only at higher prices. This world should explode."

Banksy, too, released a statement saying there was "categorically no collusion" with Sotheby's and he "was surprised as anyone when the painting made it past their security systems." The auction house, meanwhile, stressed it had "no prior knowledge of this event and were not in any way involved." Regardless, media speculation over Sotheby's possible complicity continued for the next week— the artwork was the last in the auction lineup; it was hung on a wall instead of being propped on an easel; auction houses always take works apart and examine the frames (actually not so if it's designated, as this one was, an "artist's frame," meaning an integral part of the art). Meanwhile, I was wondering how this kind of publicity could possibly benefit Sotheby's, whose first consideration must be their reputation as careful handlers of artworks worth millions. Could it be counted on that a billionaire prince in Abu Dhabi would get the joke?

Finally Sotheby's put out another statement announcing that the partially shredded piece was now to be considered a brand-new artwork, "the first artwork in history to have been created live during an auction," and authorized by the artist, who christened it with a new name: *Love Is in the Bin*. Sotheby's also confirmed that the altered work had been sold at the original price to the anonymous female European buyer, who later placed it on longtime loan to Stuttgart's Staatsgalerie to hang with its collection of masterworks. Banksy released a video on Instagram showing how he had inserted the machine into the frame, saying, "A few years ago, I secretly built a shredder into a painting, in case it was ever put up for auction." Explaining that a malfunction had thwarted his intention for the painting to be shredded completely, he posted footage of the machine working perfectly in "rehearsals" and proving, at least to PBS, that "he is a master manipulator and that his word cannot be trusted." Experts estimate that since becoming *Love Is in the Bin*, the artwork's worth has now doubled.

Later, when *The Art Newspaper* interviewed representatives at Sotheby's, Branczik revealed that two stipulations of the consignment were that the work be placed in the evening sale and hung in the room for the auction. According to Branczik, such conditions did not raise suspicions: "People often say, I will only give you this if you put it in an evening sale. Then there are people who want their works hung in the room because they believe that the assembled crowd are likely to bid more. And that was what was quoted to us." It was Branczik's decision to allocate the Banksy in the last lot. He also said that Sotheby's request to Banksy's management organization, Pest Control, to remove the frame was denied. "Pest Control said very clearly: the frame is integral to the artwork, which it was, just not in the sort of way that we thought. We also had a third-party conservator look at the work." So how did the conservator not spot the slit at the bottom and question the frame's double thickness and apparent weight? "You address what you see, it was more like a sculpture," Branczik said. "If it says the frame is integral, you don't rip it apart." Oliver Barker, the auctioneer for the night, pointed out that Banksy often employs misshapen frames in his works, "and that's part of the joke." He added: "The accusation that we were somehow negligent in the way this was catalogued does not stand up. We did everything. Going forward, are we going to question a frame like this? Absolutely."

Further, the auctioneers may have realized that in Banksy's case, the gold frame is not just a frame but a constant motif throughout his work, a symbol, like the doctor's coat in Milgram's experiment, which lends substance and legitimacy—deserved or not. Gold frames appear on the walls throughout Banksy's West Bank hotel, *The Walled Off*, surrounding scenes of nature covered with gridded protective wire, paintings of refugees' life jackets washed up on the shore, or just stenciled notations of what could be there: "NAVAL BATTLE," "DOG," "TWO DOGS," "FRUIT." Banksy's best use of the gold frame has to be in his 2006 print made in response to the high prices his works were then commanding at Sotheby's. The image is an ink drawing based on a photo from the historic 1987 Christie's sale where, at $39.9 million (which seems like nothing now), Van Gogh's *Sunflowers* broke the record for the most expensive painting ever sold at auction at that point. In Banksy's iteration, the Dutch master's painting, on the easel in its gold frame, has been replaced with crudely hand-lettered text saying, "I CAN'T BELIEVE YOU MORONS ACTUALLY BUY THIS SHIT." In double irony, Banksy placed the print in a heavy, ornate gold frame—and in triple irony, the print now sells for tens of thousands at auction.

Banksy's video of his construction of the shredding frame was accompanied by the quote, "The urge to destroy is also a creative urge." (Banksy attributes the quotation, as many have, to Picasso, but it actually originated with a leading anarchist theorist of the nineteenth century, Mikhail Bakunin.) And certainly Banksy isn't the first artist to incorporate destruction in art-making. In a Dadaesque moment in 1953, Robert Rauschenberg famously erased a drawing by Willem de Kooning. Eight years later the pop artist was among bystanders invited to shoot a .22 caliber rifle at a painting by the artist Niki de Saint Phalle, puncturing bags of paint that then ran down the canvas surface. MoMA proudly owns a fragment of what Jean Tinguely called a "self-constructing and self-destroying work of art," composed of bicycle wheels, motors, a piano, an addressograph, a go-cart, a bathtub, and other cast-off objects. Twenty-three feet long, twenty-seven feet high, and painted white, the machine was set in motion on March 18, 1960, before an audience in the museum's sculpture garden. During its brief operation, a meteorological trial balloon inflated and

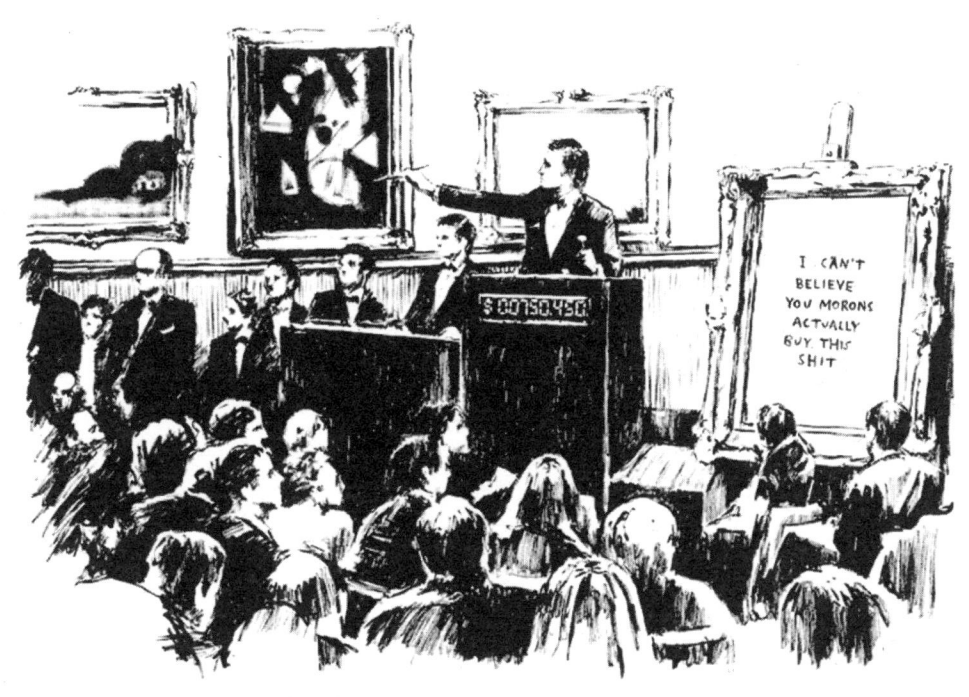

6.2

Banksy, *Morons*, 2007, screen print,
courtesy of Pest Control Office.

burst, colored smoke was discharged, paintings were made and destroyed, and bottles crashed to the ground. A player piano, metal drums, a radio broadcast, a recording of the artist explaining his work, and a competing shrill voice correcting him provided the cacophonic sound track to the machine's self-destruction—until it was stopped short by the fire department.

Along with Sotheby's involvement, Banksy's motives were also widely hypothesized. The art world piled on in its usual anti-Banksy style, with Ben Davis of *Artnet* one of the few outliers. In an article entitled "Can We Just Admit That Banksy's Art-Shredding Stunt Is Actually Really Good?," Davis allowed that "It's OK to let yourself like this confounding bit of auction theater." Otherwise, *Frieze* called it "a tiresome bit of attention-seeking," while Andrea K. Scott in the *New Yorker* labeled the self-destructing artwork "an empty gesture." Sarah Rose Sharp at *Hyperallergic* said, "Feels a bit like a publicity stunt by an artist who, in spite of his tendency to subvert art-world conventions, has nonetheless done very good business by his place in the spotlight. Cheers to Banksy, for another headline-stealing prank, thus taking the art world to the bank once more!"

Sharp implies that Banksy stands to gain financially from any increase in the value of his works at auction, part of what's known as the "secondary market," where artwork is sourced for resale from collectors or dealers rather than directly from the artist. What Sharp is not taking into consideration is that to benefit from a hike in prices in the secondary market, an artist must first have a primary market—something to sell, available new work. At the time of this writing, in fall of 2019, Banksy has a "primary market"—only if one is willing to travel to the West Bank, where guests at *The Walled Off Hotel* can buy from a narrow selection of prints and small sculptures, priced at approximately $150 to $300, with the profit going to the Palestinian-owned hotel or to benefit local causes. Otherwise, you're out of luck.

Banksy split with his longtime photographer and dealer, Steve Lazarides, in 2008, and sold prints through a London-based collective of street artists, Pictures on Walls (POW), until they closed at the end of 2017—after, as POW put it in its final announcement, "disaster struck—and many of our artists became successful. Street Art was welcomed into mainstream culture with a benign shrug and the art we produced became another tradeable commodity. Despite attempts at price fixing regrettably some POW prints have become worth tens of thousands of pounds. Either unable or unwilling to become part of the art market we once so self-righteously denounced—we called it quits."

The problem for Banksy, who's still at the low end of the stratospheric art market scale—as well as for German painter Gerhard Richter, at this point the world's top-selling living artist, with paintings going for tens of millions—is that the moment they try to offer something at an amount at least some genuine art enthusiasts might be able to afford, it gets snapped up by speculators known as "flippers," to be resold at higher and higher prices. Richter has called the art market as "absurd as the banking crisis" and "daft."

So when POW called it quits, Banksy did too, stopping all public sales, and now, how he makes the money to fund such elaborate projects as *Dismaland* and *The Walled Off Hotel* is as much a mystery as his identity. It's anyone's guess, and they do guess! What's fun—or depressing, depending on how you look at it—is to compare estimates of his net worth on the internet, where Banksy can be depended upon to be the catalyst that reveals just how reliable the media's facts are. *Forbes*, which advertises itself as "a leading source for reliable business news and financial information," wrote with assurance in 2013, "He is estimated to have a net worth upwards of $20 million." In 2014, *MSN* (*Microsoft News*) reported, "Most commonly, it is suggested that he has amassed a fortune of more than $20 million. However, it's not clear who originally made that estimate and the artist himself certainly isn't talking about it." Jump to 2019 when, according to websites like *Celebrity Net Worth* and *The Richest*, Banksy's estimated net worth has soared to $50 million (£38 million), "given that his work now sells for millions of dollars" with *The Richest* listing as "assets" the amounts Banksy's work sold for at auction, even though none of that money went to him.

However, what hardly anyone mentions is that along with being arguably the world's most famous living artist, Banksy is also the most ripped off. No doubt far eclipsing the money he purportedly gains is the fortune others make from stealing, reselling, copying, and exhibiting his work. A current search for Banksy on Etsy gets 3,588,000 results, ranging from prints to T-shirts, and on eBay, nearly the same (and surely greatly multiplied by the time you read this). Even Walmart is in on the act—the ultimate irony was when the capitalist behemoth put on sale a copy of Banksy's *Destroy Capitalism* print, now out of stock. But not to worry, there are more on Overstock.com on archival grade canvas for a sale price of $74.24, with free shipping. Showing true gall, directly next door to *The Walled Off Hotel* in Bethlehem is a shop specializing in Banksy souvenirs

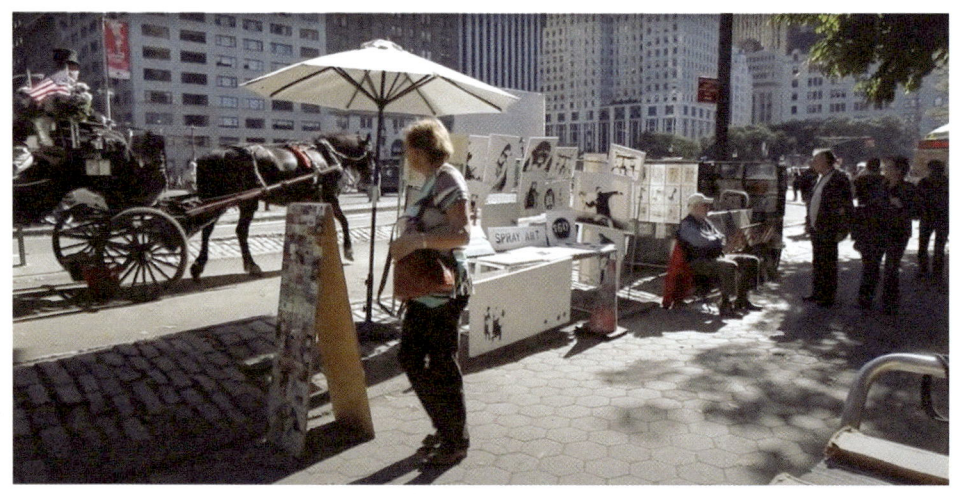

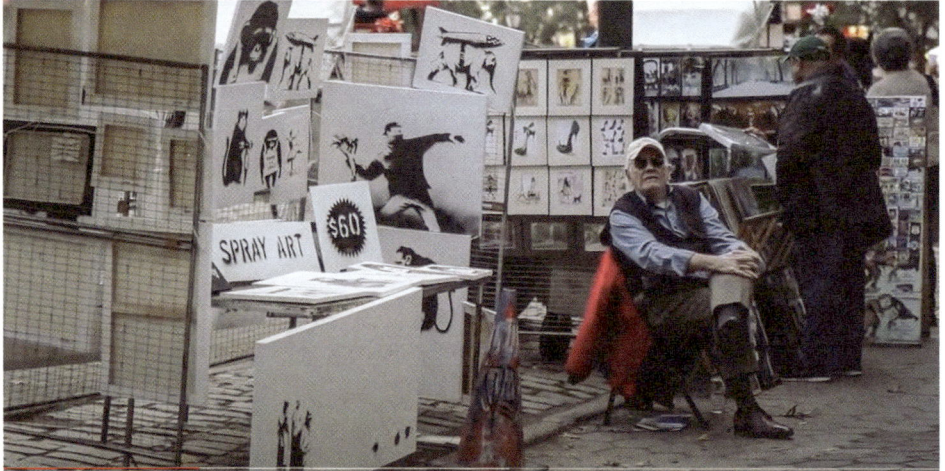

6.3
Banksy, *Art Sale*, 2013, Central Park,
New York. Screenshot: author.

with T-shirts made in California, as opposed to those in the hotel bookstore with labels proudly indicating their Palestinian provenance.

In the visual art equivalent of virtuoso Joshua Bell playing his $3.5 million violin in a Washington, DC, Metro station, Banksy, on a busy tourist Saturday that was Day 13 of his 2013 New York "residency," set up a stall offering "SPRAY ART" among other vendors at the edge of New York's Central Park. Documented by Banksy in a video released later, a white-haired man, uninterrupted by customers, eats his lunch and occasionally yawns, while overseeing the offering of authentic Banksy prints—iconic images such as *Flower Thrower* and *Kids on Gun Hill*—at sixty dollars a pop. He makes his first sale midafternoon to a woman who buys two small canvases for her children after negotiating a 50 percent discount. A bit later, a woman from New Zealand is seen buying two of the paintings, and after an hour and a half, a man from Chicago buys four, saying he has a new home and needs something for the walls. With each sale, the vendor gives the buyer a hug or kiss. It was later reported that the savvy New Zealand woman who bought the two prints, after suspecting they might be authentic and accepting the vendor's confirmation, sold them and used the proceeds to buy her dream home.

The *Guardian*, who called it a "publicity stunt," estimated that the entire stall was holding over $1 million worth of canvases, while Banksy took in just $420 for $225,000 worth of art. Although numerous articles used the story to make the case that, like the Joshua Bell performance, we don't recognize great art unless it's placed in a context that will point to it—really, where Banksy is concerned, it just proves that the world is so saturated with Banksy knock-offs that the real thing gets lost in the morass.

So how do you determine if the artwork you're buying is genuine? The problem is so endemic that in 2009, Banksy set up a service to handle such requests: Pest Control, the link to which can be found (at least at the time of this writing) on his website. Accompanied by a drawing of a little rat with a broom, the description reads thus:

> Pest Control is a handling service acting on behalf of the artist BANKSY.
>
> We answer enquiries and determine whether he was responsible for making a certain piece of artwork and issue paperwork if this is the case. This process does not make a profit and has been set up to prevent innocent people from becoming victims of fraud.

Please be aware that because many Banksy pieces are created in an advanced state of intoxication, the authentication process can be lengthy and challenging. Pest Control deals only with legitimate works of art and has no involvement with any kind of illegal activity.

SALES: Pest Control is now the sole point of sale for new work by Banksy, of which there is currently something/nothing available.

Banksy is not represented by any other gallery or institution. All enquiries and complaints should be directed to the address below.

customerservice@pestcontroloffice.com

As it happens, the verification process is a work of art in itself. Essentially, you submit images of the artwork and if it's deemed genuine, for a small fee you receive a certificate of authenticity, which includes a torn half of a "Di faced tenner" banknote.* The torn bill includes a handwritten ID number that matches the other half of the note held by Pest Control, requiring the holder to match both the tear and the number. And, as we should by now expect from Banksy, this method of authentication has a history. In medieval times, a "chirograph" was a legal document written in copies on a single piece of parchment with "chirographum" or another word written across the middle and then cut or torn through to separate the parts, so that each holder of a portion could prove it matched the others.

Having a zillion knock-offs in your name is the downside of being an anonymous artist, and for Banksy, it also means that there are Banksy exhibitions all over the world, raking in admission fees of six to forty dollars from tens of thousands of visitors, from which the artist receives no income—nor has he control over what's exhibited or promoted, even to confirm that the work is indeed genuine. As of this writing in late 2019, Banksy cites on his website exhibitions in twenty-two international cities from Melbourne to Miami to Moscow that occurred between 2016 and 2019 under the heading "FAKE" with the warning "PRODUCT RECALL—Art of Banksy: Members of the public should be aware

---

* This "Di faced tenner" is one of 100,000 counterfeit £10 notes created by Banksy in 2004 where he replaced the visage of Queen Elizabeth with that of Lady Diana (D-faced, get it?) to drop on crowds at the Notting Hill Carnival and the Reading music festival. Issued by the "Banksy of England," the currency reads, "Trust No One," and features Charles Darwin on the other side. *Artnet News* reported in 2019 that the British Museum accepted one of the notes for its collection of coins and metals.

there has been a recent spate of Banksy exhibitions none of which are consensual. They've been organised entirely without the artist's knowledge or involvement. Please treat them accordingly."

The artwork in these exhibitions has been borrowed from collectors or, in the case of the predominant organizer, Banksy's former dealer, Steve Lazarides, from his own holdings. For the Toronto iteration of "The Art of Banksy," Lazarides even hired artists to recreate (i.e., copy) some of Banksy's well-known paintings on slabs made to look as if they'd been cut out of walls. Rather than hide the fact that these presentations are unsanctioned by the artist, Lazarides advertises and appears to take pride in the "unauthorized" aspect, presenting himself as some kind of punk outlaw vandal, akin to a street artist, instead of an operator taking financial advantage of his old friend with whom, he told a Toronto publication, he'd "been at loggerheads for years."

Lazarides is also no doubt smart enough to know that such technicalities will be lost on most of those who buy tickets. Recently I met an octogenarian Banksy fan who was going on rapturously about a Banksy exhibition he saw in Amsterdam; I didn't have the heart to tell him Banksy had nothing to do with it. And in the West Bank, a Palestinian artist told me he felt that Banksy was being two-faced, putting on an exhibition in Tel Aviv just as he was opening his hotel in Palestinian Bethlehem; I had to explain that the two events were not only unrelated, as far as Banksy was concerned, but could be seen as a calculated attempt by Lazarides to undermine Banksy's credibility with the Palestinians.

Nor do journalists always get it, as in the *Euronews* coverage of a four-and-a-half-month exhibition in Lisbon, entitled "Banksy: Genius or Vandal?": "The anonymous artist includes his distinctive stencilling technique, sculptors [sic], videos and photographs. This exhibition has already been to Moscow and Madrid attracting more than 600,000 people." But perhaps even worse is the Lisbon exhibition "curator" Alexander Nachkebiya's interpretation of Banksy as in, "He is a messenger, he is not somebody who can solve anything, he is not somebody who has the power to solve a problem, he is just showing us the problem, he is a messenger that gives us the message of guys. We have to stop somehow and think about it and then do something about it." Yikes! Then again, having an exhibition of one's work promoted, as Lazarides did in Toronto, as containing "$35 million worth of art" might not go down well either. When have you seen a Picasso exhibition (or any other) that announces itself with dollar signs?

On top of everything is the issue of exiting through a gift shop rife with Banksy knock-offs. Live Nation, the mega-concert promoters who teamed up with Lazarides, were quoted as saying that what Banksy paints in a public place is considered in the "public domain." I read a couple of articles reporting that Banksy tried to stop such sales in Italy, but to continue with litigation would have required that he reveal himself and show that such facsimiles were damaging to current sales of his work, meaning that he'd have to produce works to sell in order to prove losses. Not so, say my legal consultants, who explain that in the United States copyrights can be registered pseudonymously and even anonymously, and that painting something on a building without permission doesn't place the work in the public domain. In fact, in the United States (and presumably elsewhere, as in Europe, where intellectual property is even more stringently protected), reproducing an artist's work in any form without their permission is illegal. So when there is an exhibition of an artist's works owned privately or even borrowed from institutions, it cannot be promoted in any way with visual reproductions of the work—no press releases with images, no catalogs, no advertising, no reproductions in accompanying reviews—and certainly no tchotchkes or banners with their name lining city streets.

In a rare instance of a journalist questioning the blatant rights issues, Kate Taylor wrote in Toronto's *Globe and Mail*: "The unwary consumer who decided to spend $35 to enter the Banksy exhibition making its North American premiere in a Toronto warehouse will see lots of the prints that the anonymous British street artist has sold to underwrite his graffiti activism. One is *Festival*, a bitter image that shows music fans lining up to buy $30 T-shirts bearing the slogan Destroy Capitalism. The irony of this exploitative show unauthorized by the artist is enough to make a critic gag."

Banksy is famously quoted as saying, "Copyright is for losers," but this is not exactly the same as tacit approval of those who take advantage. Nor should his Sotheby's auction caper be considered anything less than a serious rebuke to the rapacious nature of the market. My favorite arts journalist, Lee Rosenbaum, in her *CultureGrrl* blog, wrote: "The event, however risible, is not something that Sotheby's can responsibly make light of: If the auction house winks at vandalism of consigned property, how can it take a strong stance against others who might decide to physically attack works on its premises? . . . That said, the opposite course of action would be equally unpalatable: If the auction house were to seek civil damages and/or press criminal charges against Banksy (and/or whoever activated the frame's mechanism) for what might be interpreted as an illegal act, much of the artworld would surely take umbrage. . . . However you look at it, this high-profile 'prank' was a lose-lose for Sotheby's."

Rosenbaum also cites Tinguely's art explosion at MoMA as a possible inspiration, quoting the late art critic Dore Ashton's firsthand account of the event, which frames it as a defiantly anti-establishment act: Tinguely's performance "was sufficiently iconoclastic . . . this is an institution and us old anarchists, we're against institutions, right?"

In the same spirit, I see Banksy's intervention as a warning to the auction houses not to be so eager to accept his works for auction.

The next one just might blow up.

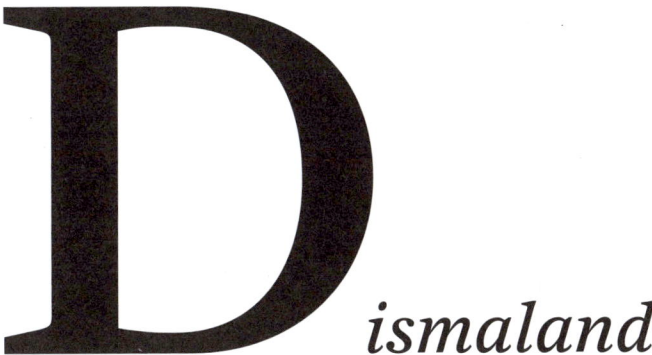

Dismaland

Art is not a mirror held up to reality, but a hammer with which to shape it.
Banksy quoting Bertolt Brecht in the *Dismaland* catalog

Banksy's unofficial entry in the 2019 Venice Biennale probably garnered more attention in the media than the international art exhibition itself. In his video, Banksy (we presume) is hiding behind a newspaper, while sitting at a stand in the famous Piazza San Marco, where rows of vendors hawk paintings of Venice's picturesque buildings and canals. But, of course, the paintings Banksy has on offer are hardly traditional—each of his nine gold-framed paintings contains a portion of an image which, when seen together, portrays a massive cruise ship. The small, hand-lettered placard that reads, "Venice in oil," can be seen as referring not only to the paintings but to the pollution the cruise industry causes in Venice and around the world.

7.1 *following pages*
Banksy, *Venice in Oil*, 2019, installation, Venice, Italy, courtesy of Pest Control Office.

7.2 *following pages*
Dismaland overview, 2015, photograph, Weston-super-Mare, England, courtesy of Pest Control Office.

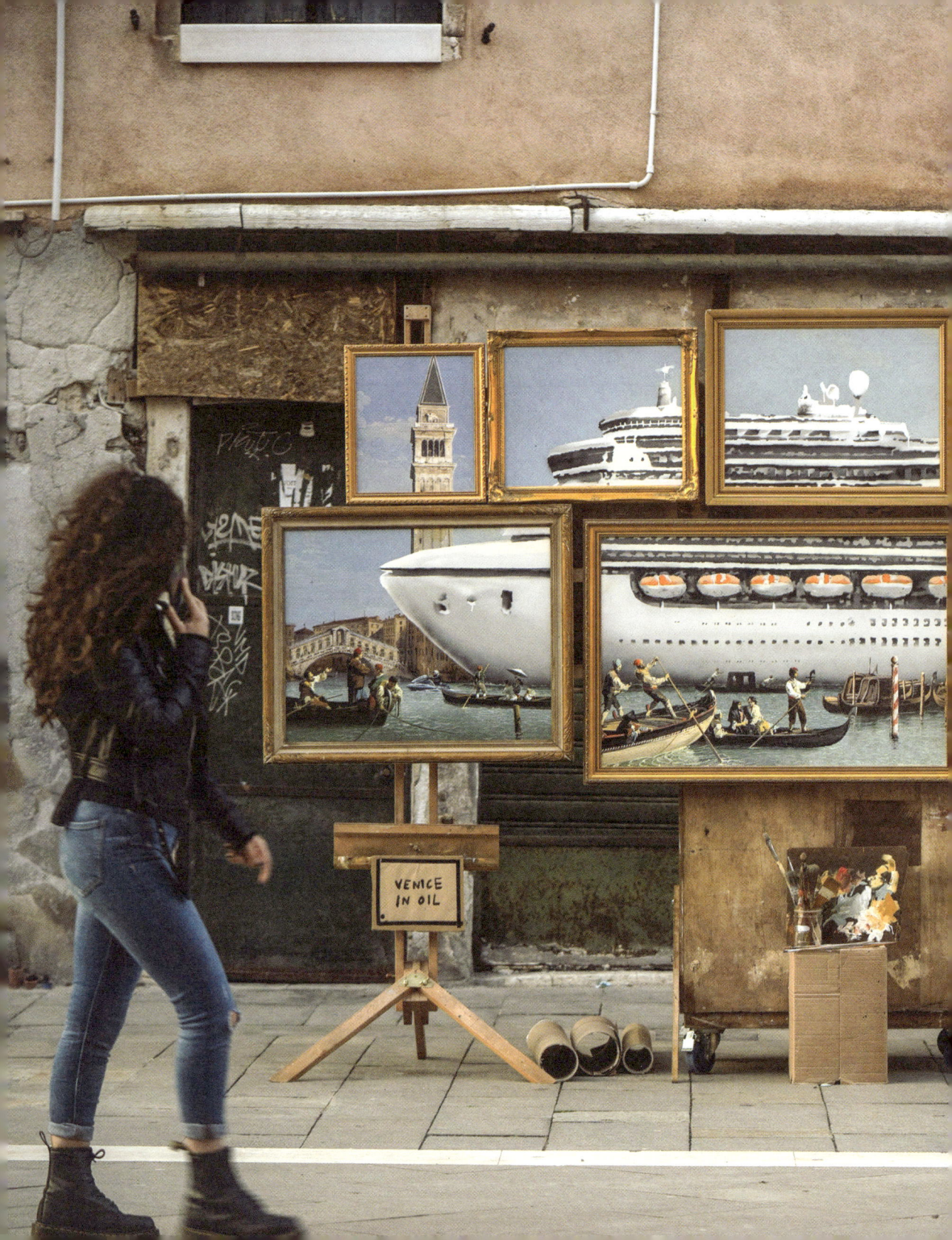

VENICE
IN OIL

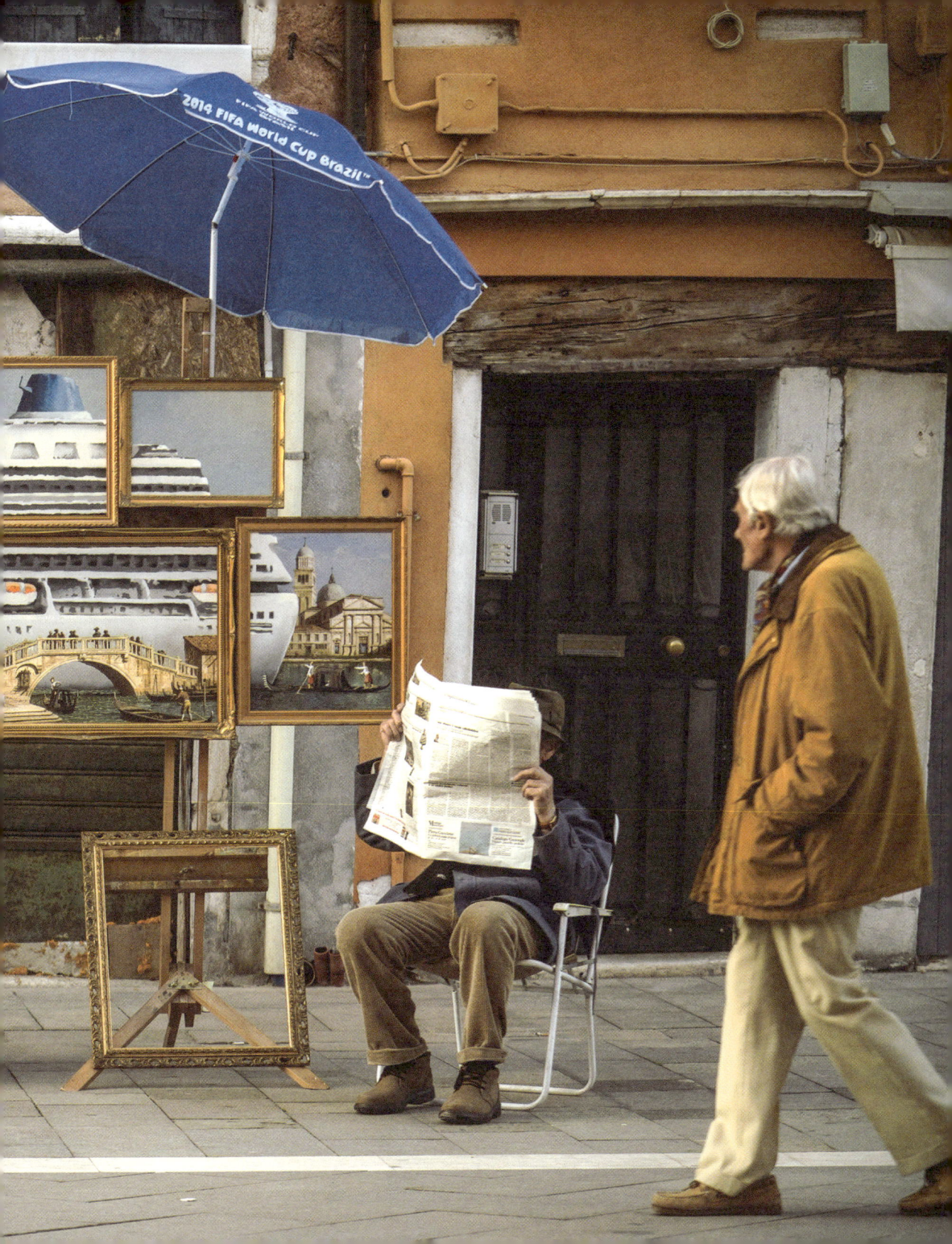

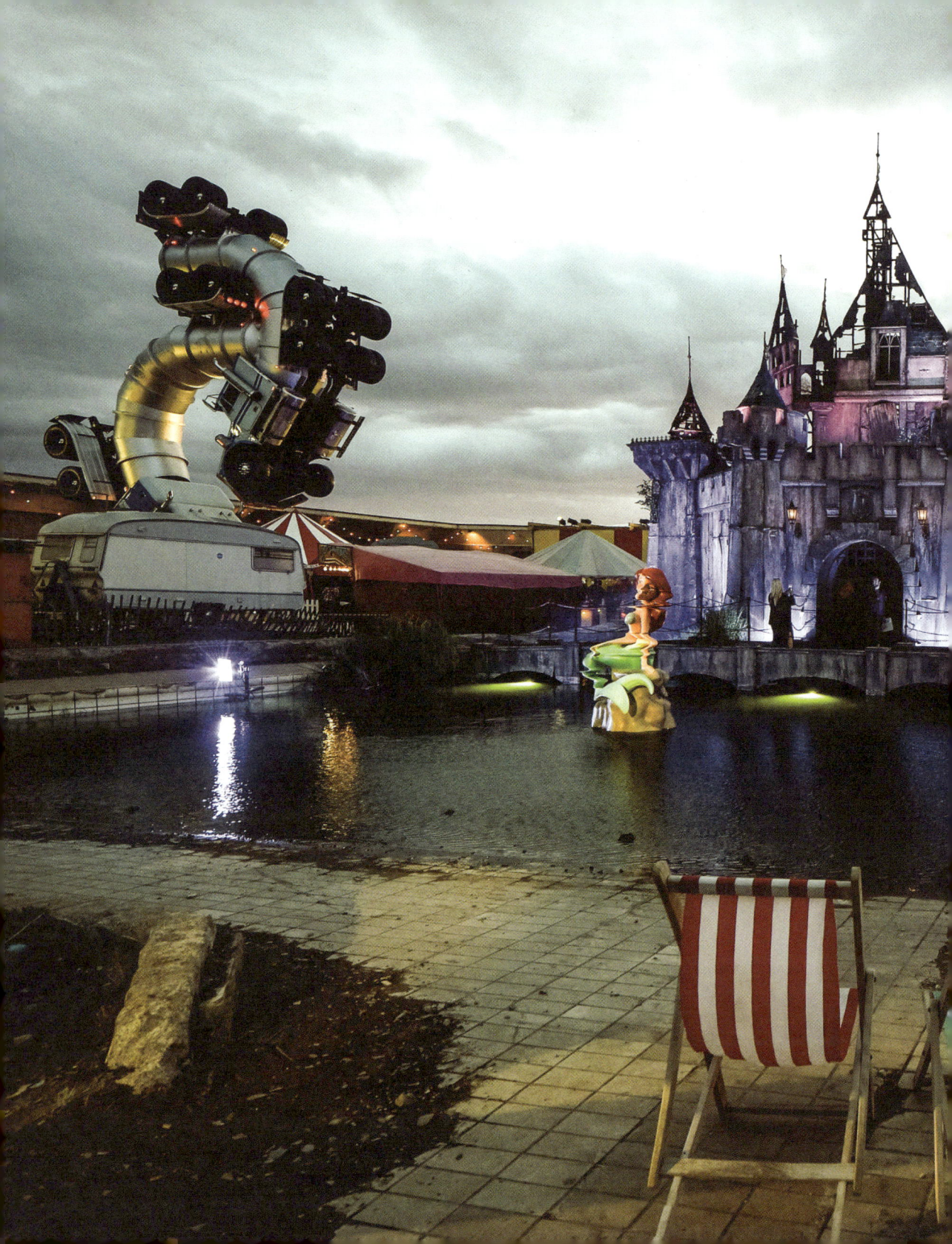

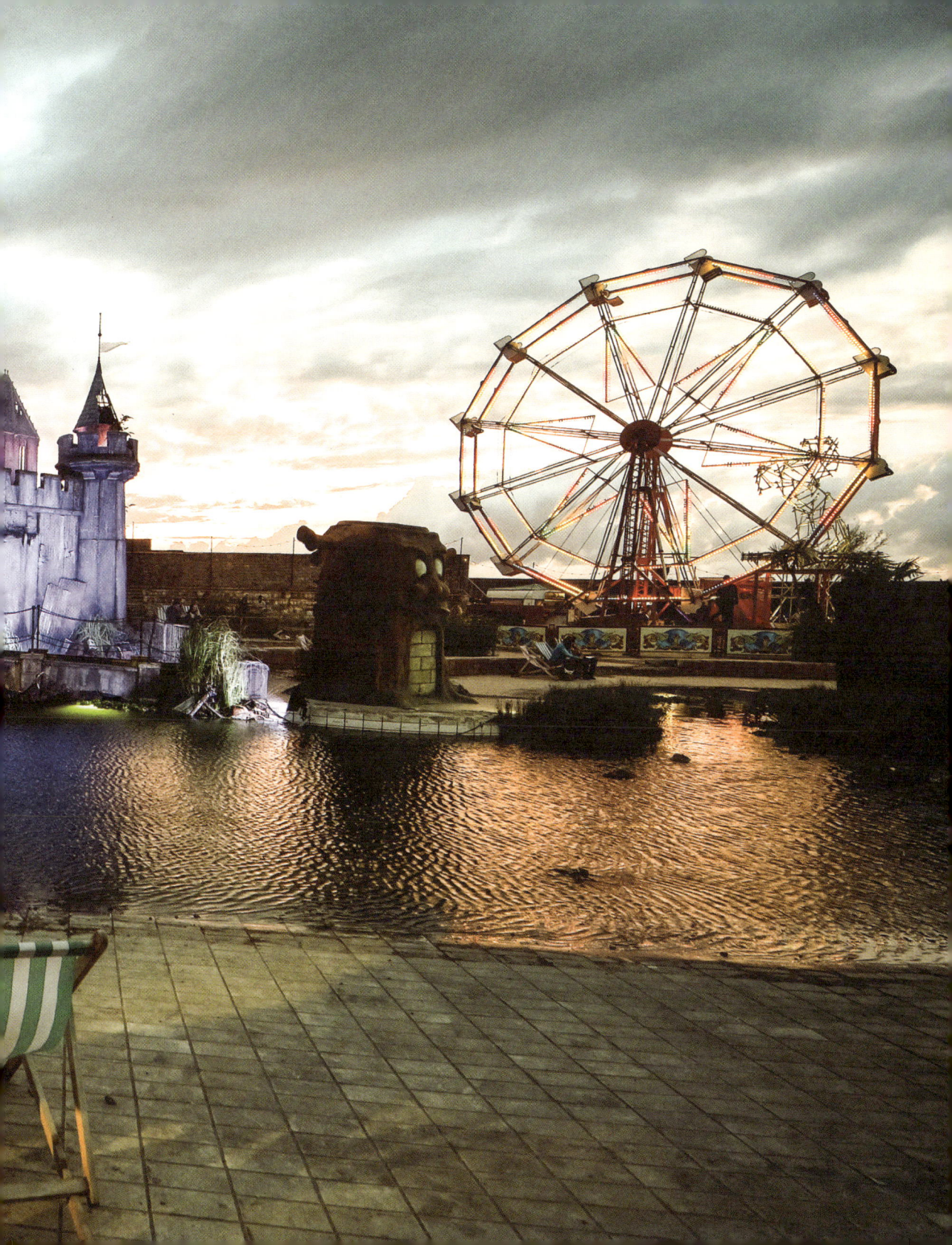

A *Forbes* article entitled "Cruise Ship Pollution Is Causing Serious Health and Environmental Problems" reports that "over 50,000 Europeans die prematurely every year as a result of shipping-based pollution," and that cities and environmental groups are "implementing emissions tests and issuing fines to the offending cruise lines." But who gets ticketed in Venice? The artist flacking his "oils"—next seen carting away his canvases after being confronted by the *polizia* for not having a permit.

Banksy captioned his Instagram video "Setting out my stall in the Venice Biennale. Despite being the largest and most prestigious art event in the world, for some reason I've never been invited."

However, I don't think this was the first time Banksy mounted a response to the Venice Biennale. In fact, although neither he nor others have made the connection outright, it could be said that he staged his own. In 2015 the theme in Venice was "All the World's Futures," and the intention, as described by the curator, was to explore "the aura, effects, affects, and spectres of capital[ism]." What a concept! Spend €13M ($14.8 million) to mount an international art fair spotlighting the dire consequences of capitalism for an audience of billionaire collectors whose superyachts crowd a harbor bordered by ancient palaces and five-star hotels. To add insult to injury, entertainment included daily seven-hour readings of Karl Marx's *Das Kapital*. I attended that Biennale (paying the daily €35 entrance fee), and can attest that there was no sense of irony to be found.

So what does Banksy do? Invites fifty-eight artists from seventeen countries (among them Britain and the United States, as well as Australia, Finland, Germany, Spain, Lithuania, Saudi Arabia, Portugal, Egypt, Iran, Syria, Israel, and the Palestinian territories) to address the failure of capitalism in a pop-up 2.5-acre theme park "unsuitable for children." Fittingly named *Dismaland*, it was open for five weeks, August 22 to September 27, 2015, during the run of the Biennale. Billed as a "festival of art, amusements and entry-level anarchism," this dystopian Disneyland included ten new works by Banksy in addition to weekly concerts, films, miniature golf (or rather miniature "Gulf" with an appropriate oil spill), a whacked-out Cinderella's castle, games that were impossible to win, a carousel invoking the horse meat scandal, remote-control boats overflowing with refugees, disgruntled park guides, vegetarian food stands, and an art gallery that included among the works a postapocalyptic miniature model village by Jimmy Cauty (whose 1990s pop band KLF once infamously burned a million pounds in the name of art), Damien Hirst's beach ball dangerously hovering over knife blades, and Jenny Holzer's LED signboards spelling out her famous *Truisms*, such as "Abuse of power comes as no surprise." (Random note: Holzer was the first female artist to represent the United States at the Venice Biennale, and won the Golden Lion award for best pavilion in 1990.)

Dismaland's preparation was shrouded in secrecy. Residents in Weston-super-Mare, a seaside resort town in Somerset near Bristol, were led to believe the project at the abandoned Tropicana swim park was a film set for a Hollywood crime thriller to be called "Grey Fox," with signs saying "Grey Fox Productions" posted at the entrances. My scrutiny of Banksy thus far led me to surmise that this choice of title wasn't arbitrary, but would have some sinister connotation related to his theme. Sure enough, a search revealed that "Grey Fox" is the code name for the most secret of secret military units of the American Special Forces. According to the *Mirror* in 2011, it refers to the "shadowy group of Seals, Delta troops and CIA" who played a crucial role in the capture of Saddam Hussein in 2003, a "kill squad" that later took up "secret positions throughout Asia and the Middle East to track down and 'eliminate' key al-Qaeda members" following Bin Laden's assassination in Pakistan. Banksy does not disappoint.

The place Banksy chose to carry out his covert operation was one that had been neglected for years. As with his placement of a hotel in an out-of-the-way corner of Bethlehem in the conflict-torn West Bank, instead of siting his projects where they will attract the most visitors, Banksy often chooses undervalued locations and brings the audience to them, thereby contributing significantly to the economy. Weston-super-Mare's decline was represented by that of the Tropicana, which Banksy mentioned in interviews he'd frequented as a child, and he had the inspiration for *Dismaland* only seven months before its opening after peering through a crack in the park's surrounding wall. In its heyday, the 1937 Art Deco park was known for fountains, fruit-themed water slides, and beauty pageants, as well as boasting the largest outdoor pool and highest diving board in all of Europe. But like many coastal cities in the United Kingdom, Weston-super-Mare suffered economic decline with the rise of package tours to Europe and the closing of express holiday train lines. The Tropicana was shuttered in 2000, prompting proposals that it be demolished, and it's possible that Banksy's intervention constituted an eleventh-hour attempt to save the site from developers. Since *Dismaland* closed, the location, which continues to attract tourists,

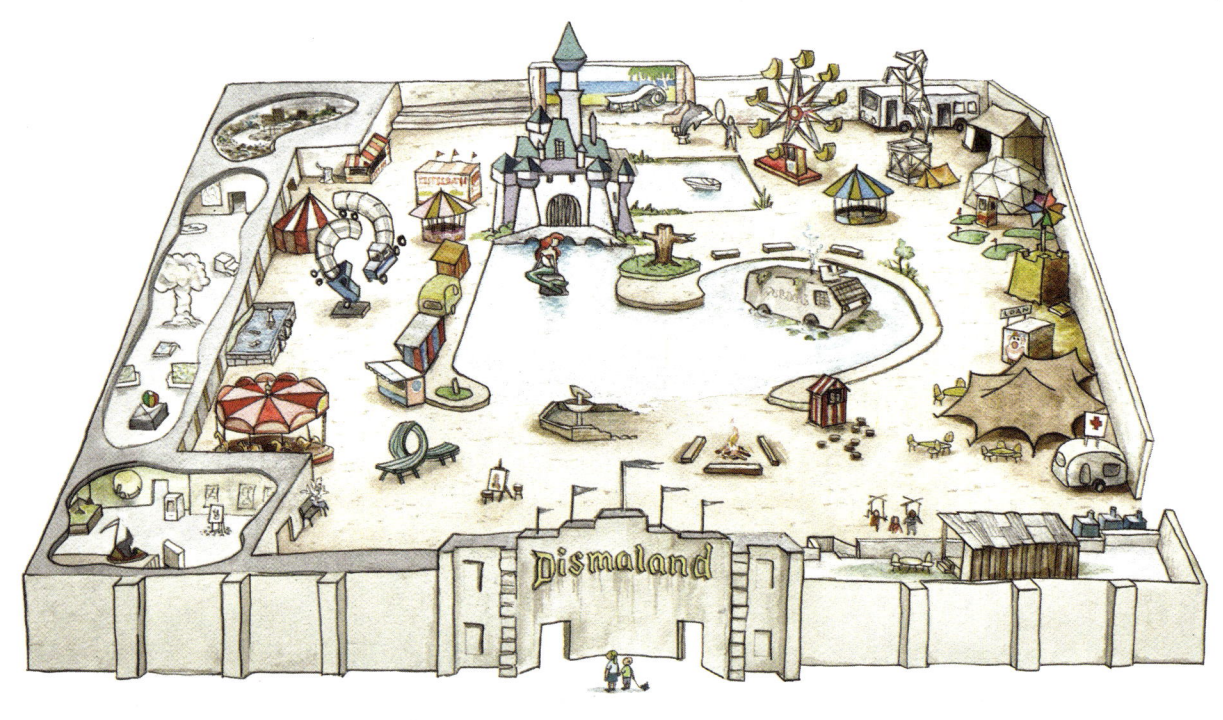

7.3

Banksy, *Dismaland*, drawing, 2015, courtesy of
Pest Control Office.

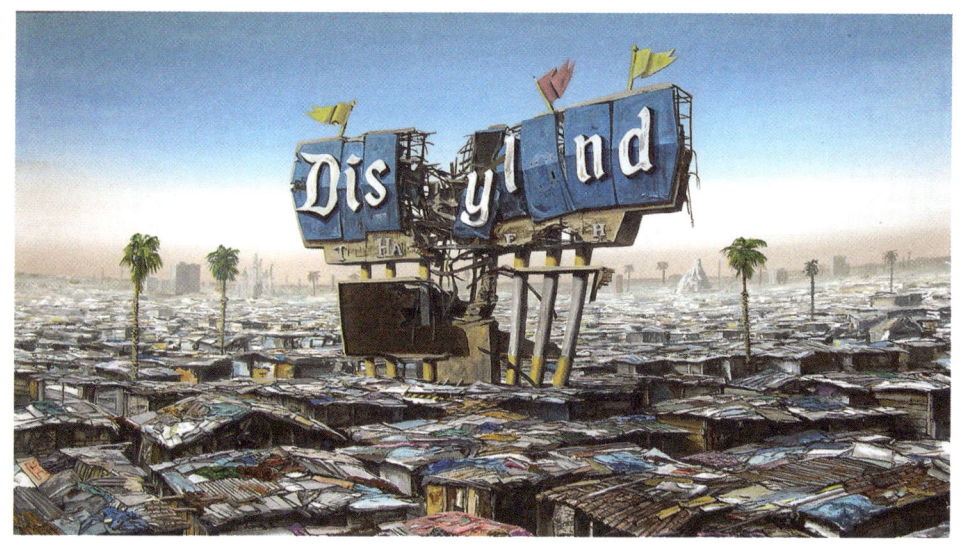

7.4

Jeff Gillette, *Disyland*, ca. 2011, oil and acrylic on canvas,
courtesy of the artist.

has been home to Funland, a conventional "family-friendly theme park" open in the summer months, along with multiuse indoor and outdoor event spaces, while the town looks into developing it as a creative and cultural hub.

Keeping such a huge project secret had to be a logistical nightmare, no doubt requiring bushels of nondisclosure agreements. The North Somerset Council, which owns the Tropicana, had to give its approval, but only four of its members knew the true nature of the project before it opened. The council's Conservative leader, Nigel Ashton, told the BBC, "I gave it a lot of deep thought . . . for about two and a half seconds. For a second, I thought, 'who is behind the wind up?' because you don't get that lucky. But how do you say no?" Advertisements followed in the local paper for "auditions" at the nearby Royal Hotel for a hundred or so runners and extras needed in the fictitious film's production, but none were told what their jobs really were until the day before *Dismaland* opened. Given distressed Mickey Mouse ears and shocking pink high-visibility vests with "Dismal" written across the back, park guides were instructed to subvert legendary English politeness by not only refusing to smile but being as grumpy and unhelpful as possible—even, or especially, to the celebrities who flocked there. Interviewed by a local journalist, one young woman recalled "meeting the comedian Jack Black, greeting him with a nonplussed stare and mouthing 'you what?' in his direction." Just like when I paid £1 for three ping-pong balls in a game called "Topple the Anvil," created by British artist and Turner Prize nominee David Shrigley, and after hurling the balls at the iron anvil which, clearly, did not topple, I said to my friend, "Well, I tried," to which the attendant growled, "Not hard enough."

Revealed just two days in advance with an announcement on the front page of the Weston *Mercury*, *Dismaland* opened to journalists. The next day, a Friday, free tickets were offered to two thousand local residents, and then every day afterward, for the next five weeks, five hundred tickets were made available to the general public at the door and four thousand more online for £3 (about $4.70), with two viewing sessions, 11 a.m. to 6 p.m. and 7 to 11 p.m. That Friday, however, the *Dismaland* website crashed after receiving more than six million hits, causing speculation on Twitter and elsewhere that the ticket website was another Banksy hoax. When the website was finally upgraded several days later, tickets for the allotted times sold out within hours. Intentional or not, frustration in buying tickets was the perfect introduction to "the UK's most disappointing new visitor attraction," which ultimately drew some 150,000 visitors.

Banksy first used the word "Dismaland" in a piece of graffiti with a Mickey Mouse figure that appeared in 2012 with the lines: "Welcome to Dismaland . . . Life isn't always a fairytale." The park's aesthetic tone is widely considered to have been influenced by California artist and *Dismaland* participant Jeff Gillette, who has been painting scenes of Disney characters juxtaposed with postapocalyptic landscapes, landfill sites, and slums in his *Slumscapes* for over twenty years. "I would like to think that I had a part in the inspiration for Banksy's satirization of the magic kingdom," Gillette admits in *Vice*, "but I've maintained, even to Banksy in an email, that I felt that we have 'similar sensibilities.' *Dismaland* itself had some strong similarities to the real Disneyland: long lines, and unhappy workers. It also had the excellence that Disney maintains in its productions and presentations." The *Dismaland* website included the small print: "The following are strictly prohibited in the Park—spray paint, marker pens, knives and legal representatives of the Walt Disney Corporation."

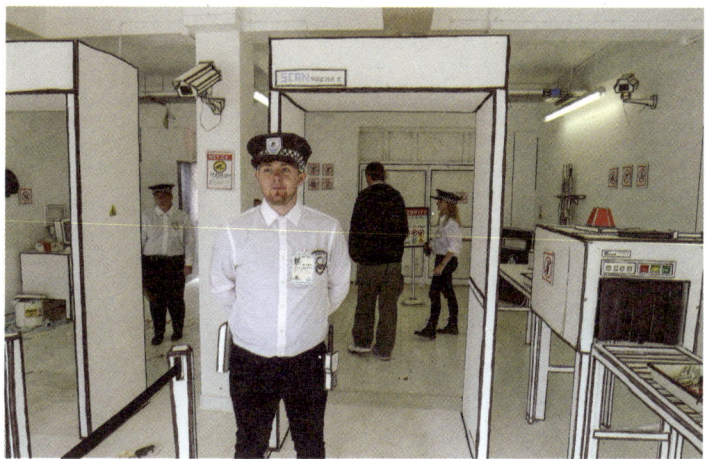

7.5
Bill Barminski, *Dismaland* installation,
2015. Photo: Mark Isbin.

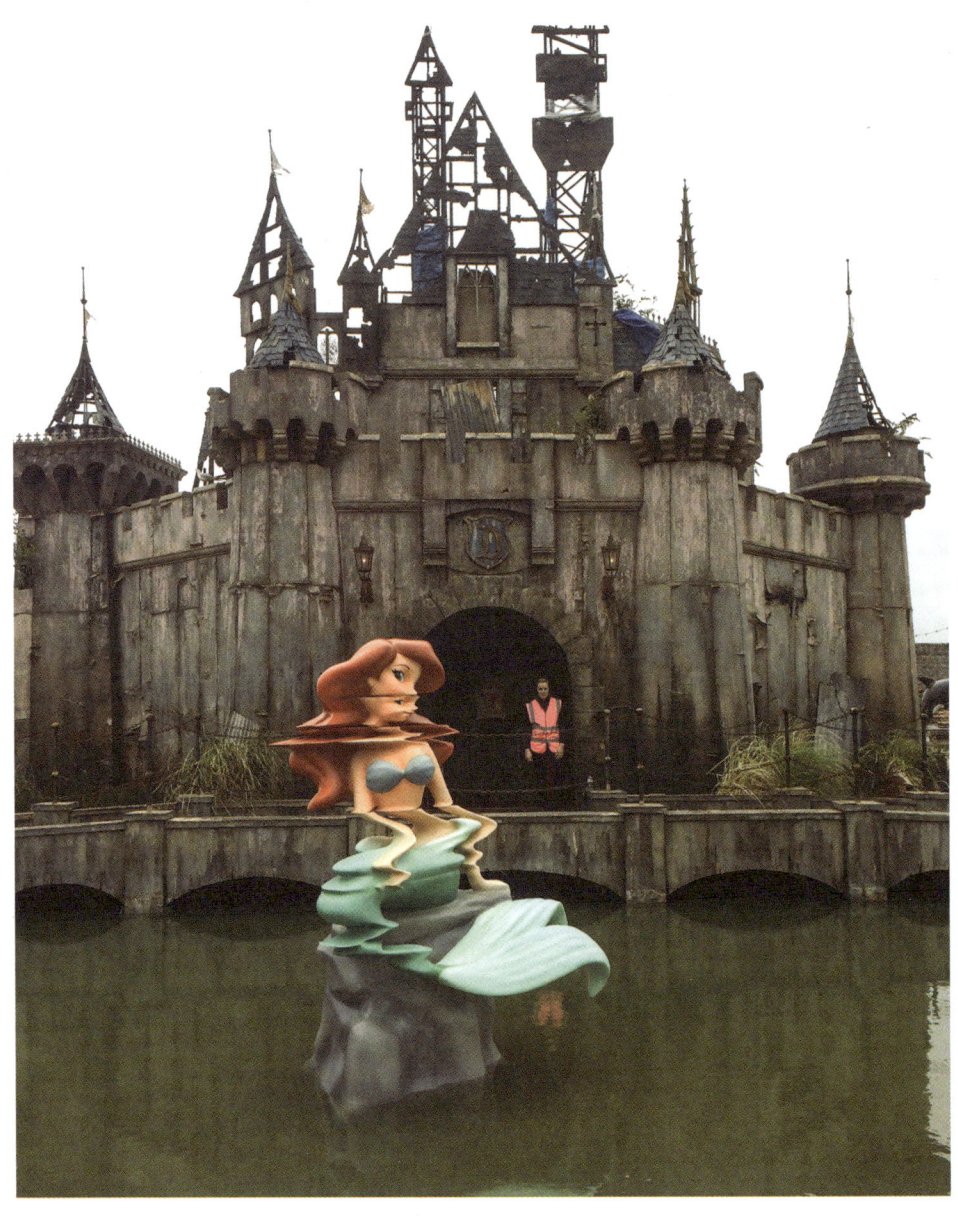

7.6
Banksy, *Little Mermaid*, in *Dismaland*, 2015.
Photo: Christopher Jobson.

I'd just returned to New York from a visit to England when I got the Google Alert announcing *Dismaland* and realized I'd have to go right back. Through Facebook I arranged to stay in London, sleeping on an inflatable mattress in the storeroom of an artist friend, and then he and I and another friend, a Bristol street artist who had returned to university to get his master's degree, met up for the nearly three-hour train trip east to Weston-super-Mare. Once at the station, *Dismaland* was easy to find. Like the stenciled directions used in World War II to conduct troops in unfamiliar urban locations, "Banksy" with an arrow was stenciled on the sidewalks at every corner.

To enter the concrete-walled park, visitors had to pass through an airport-style security checkpoint that was, of course, entirely fake, constructed of elaborately crafted cardboard and paint by California artist Bill Barminski. Here we were "scanned" by guards with cardboard instruments while they talked into cardboard walkie-talkies, with tables nearby of "seized" cardboard objects, and signs banning unicorns and other contraband. Continuing the mood of unreality, when we passed through the door into the park we were ordered by the unsmiling "guards" to "Enjoy!" Barminski, an adjunct professor in new media, digital art, and design at UCLA, was clearly the artist for the job. One of his previous works paired a large-scale video installation with a series of cardboard sculptures depicting some of popular culture's most subversive products: guns, spray paint, and skateboards. The video featured footage taken from a recent group exhibition at POW Gallery in London (the street artist collective of which Banksy was a part, mentioned in the last chapter), where Barminski filmed artists destroying their work using items from his cardboard arsenal. Barminski told the Weston *Mercury* that he had been invited five months earlier to create a security installation, without really knowing what it was for. When he got to Weston-super-Mare five days before the opening, Barminski realized, "This is not a small group show!"

After successfully negotiating "security," we entered through plain white doors into the park to join the other visitors wandering about in a visual cacophony that blended Hollywood fiction, symbols of governmental authority, and old-fashioned amusement park trappings into a decidedly punk vibe—accompanied by the woozy whine of piped-in Hawaiian luau music under gray English skies. Cinderella's crumbling castle loomed. Placed at its front was a sculpture of Disney's Little Mermaid, distorted as if seen through rippled water (a play, I thought,

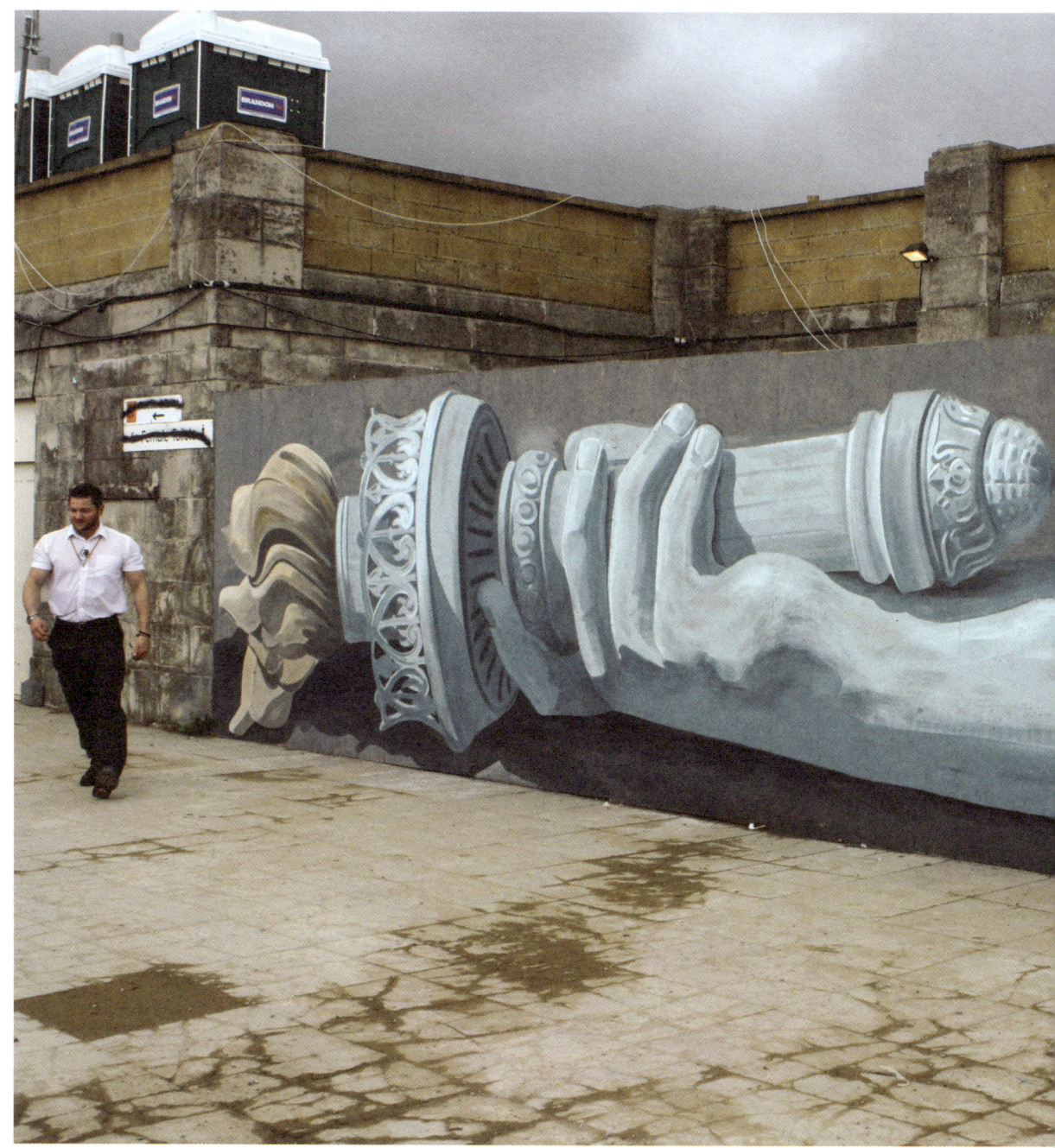

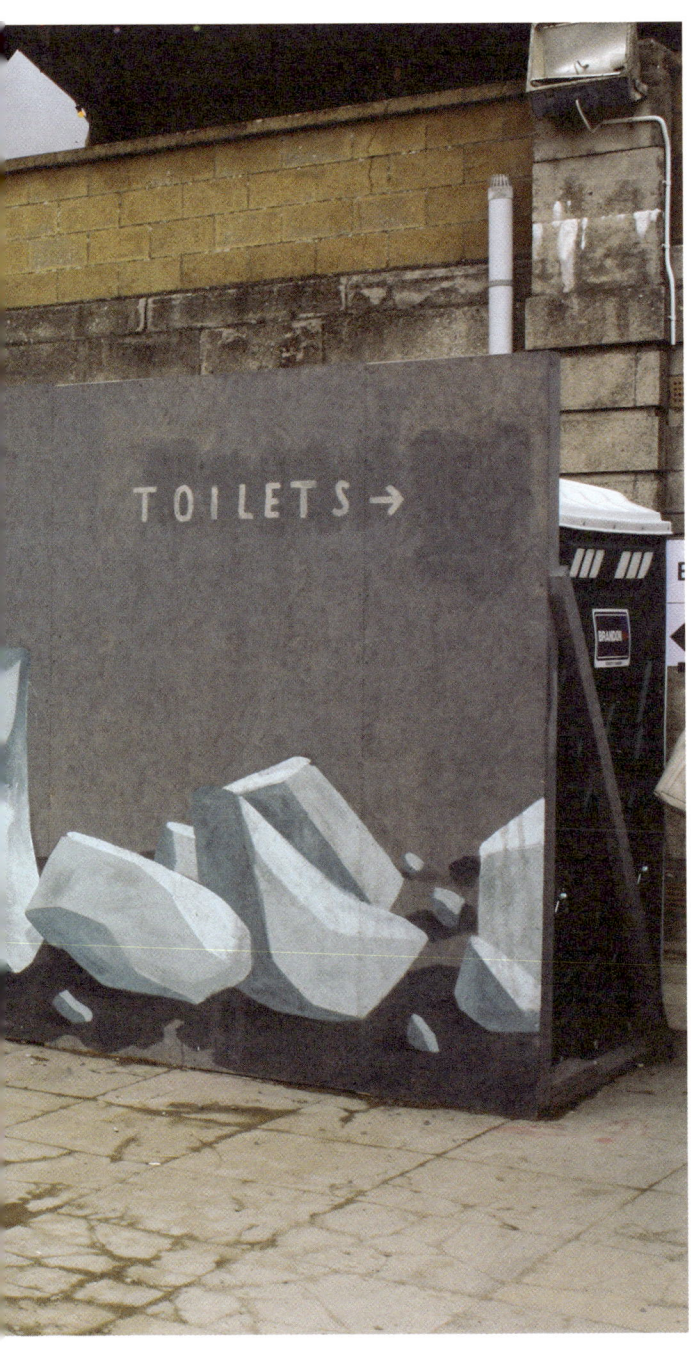

7.7
Escif, *American Piss* (*Peace*),
wall painting, *Dismaland*, 2015.
Photo: Sam Millen.

on the work of British sculptor Tony Cragg) and a police water cannon repurposed as a fountain. From the monumental pinwheel to a nausea-producing Ferris wheel that ran backward, to a replica of a life-size killer whale springing out of a toilet toward a kiddie pool, it was hard to take it all in—yet, in its seemingly haphazard way, it all made sense. This was incoherence made coherent through Banksy's very specific curatorial sensibility, with every artwork, sign, and piece of rubble in its right not-right place—a triumph of micromanaged angst that coalesced the artworks of fifty-nine artists, including himself, into a single immersive performance. British artist Darren Cullen, who created a pocket-money loans shop where children could use their allowances to borrow at an interest rate of 5,000 percent, told the *Guardian*, "It is just amazing having this much sarcasm in one place."

Our chum, critic Jonathan Jones of the *Guardian*, hated *Dismaland* of course, saying he found it "thin, threadbare and, to be honest, quite boring." But then I'm guessing Jones doesn't have an anarchic bone in his body. At least he went, which is more than can be said for most of the other critics who wrote disparaging reviews. For me, whose life has bridged punk clubs, political activism, and the art world, it felt like home. I remember, back in the day, taking my eldest son, Matt, then twelve, to New York's Irving Plaza past midnight to see a wasted Johnny Thunders perform, something for which I'd no doubt be arrested now, but life-altering for him (he soon after started a punk band, and later became a music journalist). Suddenly Matt didn't even mind dancing with his mom because, he said, "This is a place where you can't embarrass yourself." In a situation where there's no "right" way to do anything, you can't do anything wrong. Similarly at *Dismaland* there were no expectations, no way you were supposed to be, no experience you were supposed to be having—and with entrances marked "exit," sometimes you *had* to do it wrong. The absence of name brands and people endeavoring to sell you stuff was a relief in itself. It was fun, sometimes hilariously funny—not in a way that requires you to block out all the ills in the world, but to take them in and rise above it all. Or be angry, it's okay. The world is going to hell, so we might as well have a laugh.

And at that moment in 2015, the world did appear to be going to hell. With deadly terrorist attacks occurring in France and school shootings in the United States, *Dismaland* opened at a time when everything seemed to be splitting apart—literally, in the case of clamors for Brexit in the United Kingdom—along

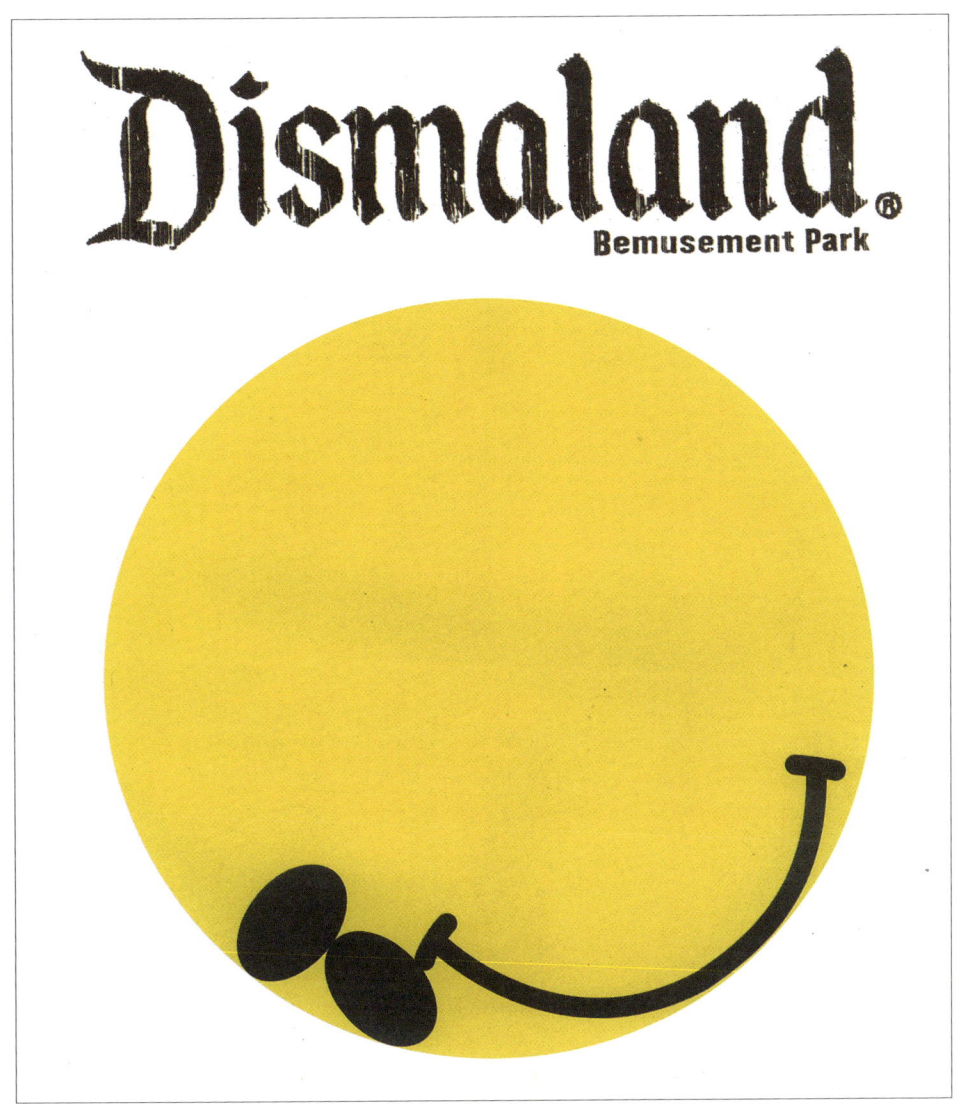

7.8

James Joyce, *Dismaland* program cover, 2015. Photo: author.

7.9 *following pages*

Banksy, Cinderella installation, *Dismaland*, 2015. Photo: Sam Millen.

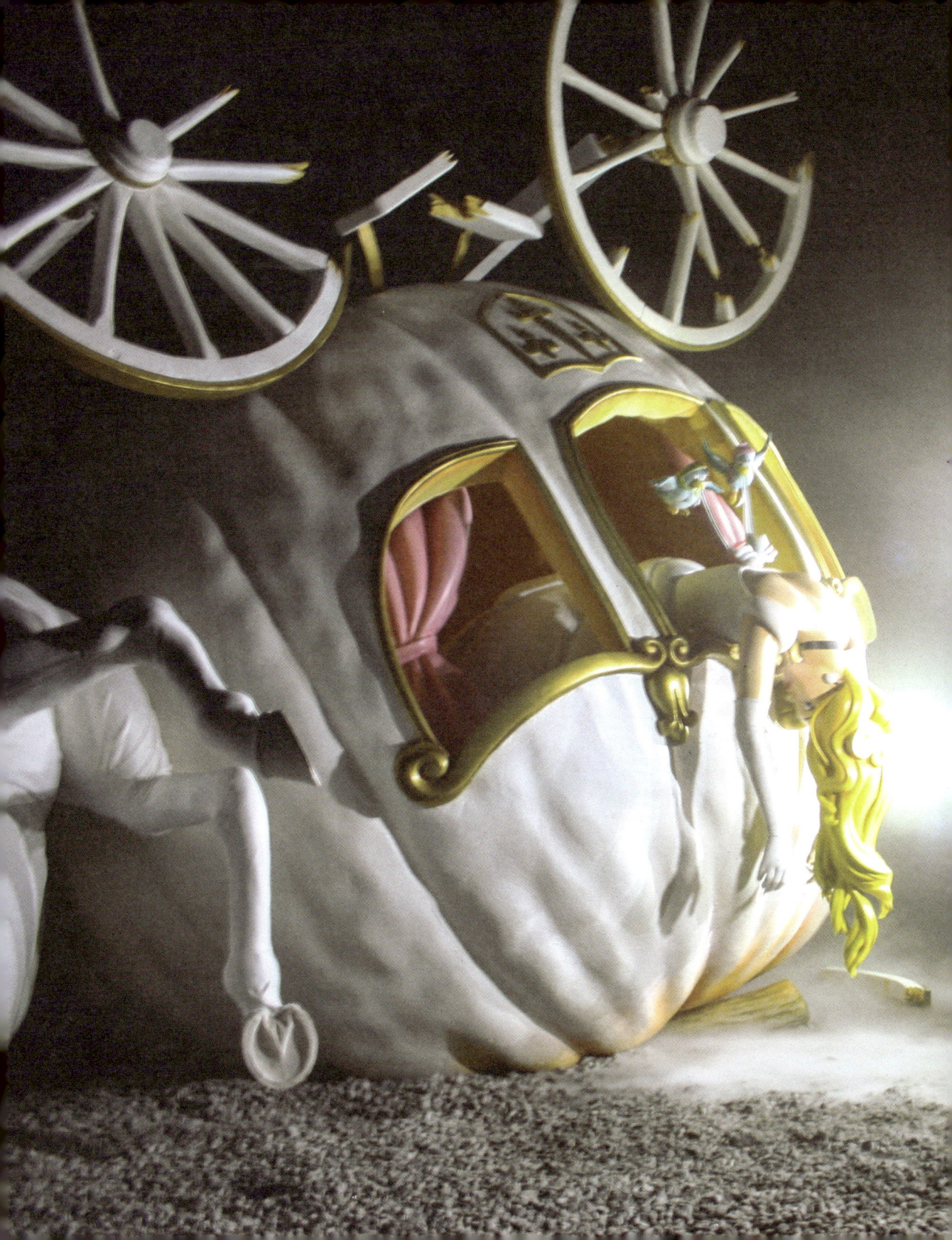

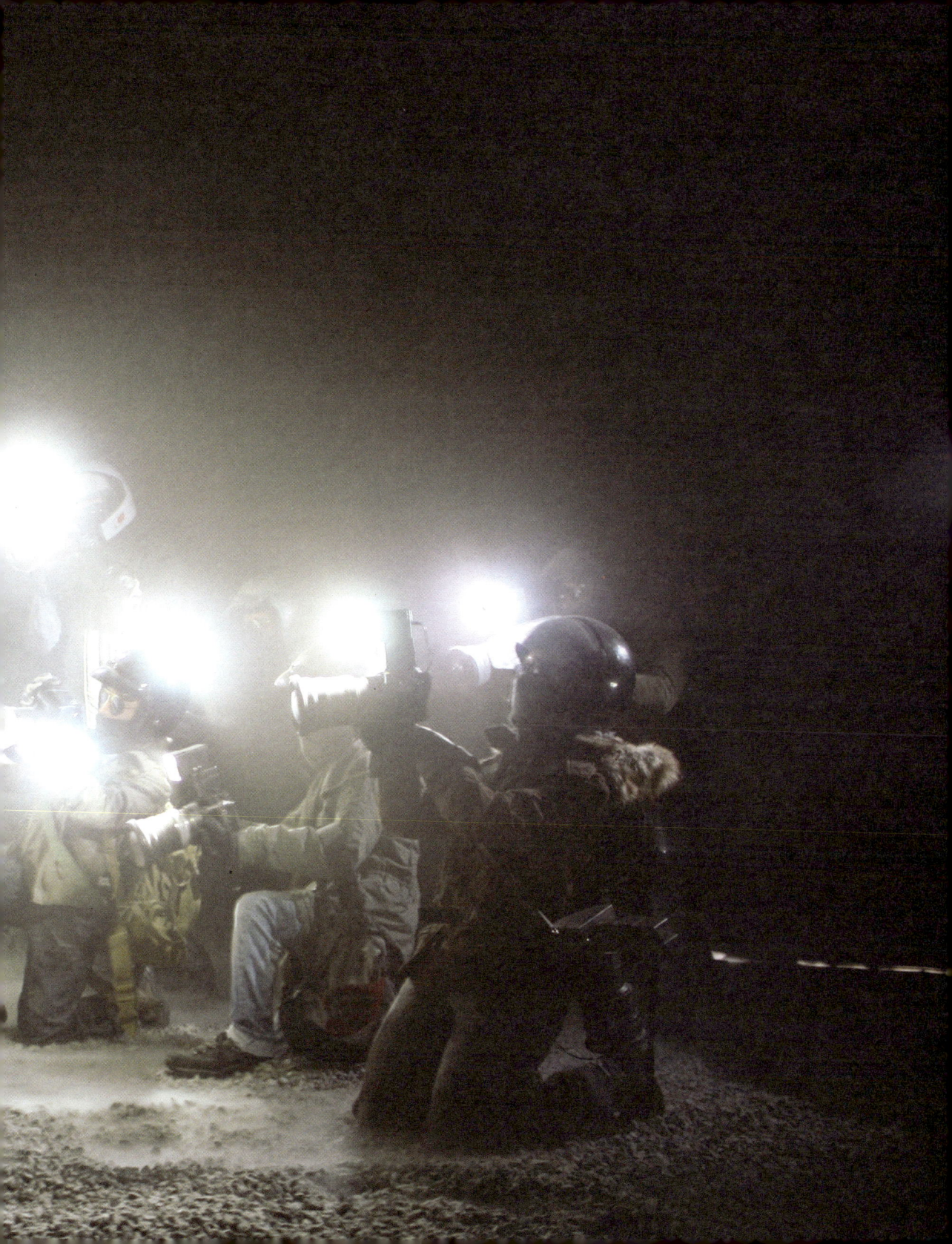

with populist movements emerging in Britain and the United States representing, in both countries, profoundly opposing visions from proto-fascism to socialism. Later, in his memoir, prime minister David Cameron wrote that "the rise of the far-left and hard-right parties in Europe [had] shown us that anti-establishment, divisive politics was the new normal"—as it was in the United States, with Donald Trump's ascendancy and the growing movement behind democratic socialist Bernie Sanders, and in the United Kingdom, with the tug of war over Brexit exemplified by Boris Johnson and Jeremy Corbyn. It was also the very moment when the English coast was thrust into the spotlight by the surge of Syrian refugees attempting to cross over from Europe. *Dismaland* brought together all of the anxiety and contradictions of the period. The topsy-turvy feeling shared by almost everyone was keenly personified in British artist James Joyce's "not so smiley face" animation in the *Dismaland* art gallery—a huge revolving yellow disk projected on the far wall, where the eyes and smile were loose elements like clothing in a laundromat drum dryer, rising up and falling to the bottom in haphazard configurations—randomly joined by the shadows of visitors who happened to pass in front of the projector.

Joyce told *Juxtapoz* magazine: "I got an email from Banksy's manager one night as I was going to bed, saying 'Can you confirm you're James Joyce, the artist? Banksy wants to talk to you.' I thought someone is taking the piss, but I wrote back and the next day he emailed me. He explained he really liked the work, and in particular, he really liked the collapsed yellow smiley face. . . . [So I] proposed a couple of paintings, but we started talking about making it move. It was gonna be a physical thing with all the bits falling around, but after I made test animations to show the idea he just said 'These are great! Let's just do this.'" Ultimately, Banksy told Joyce that his image summed up the whole event—to the extent that he chose it as one of several *Dismaland* logos reproduced on the program covers and on T-shirts in the gift shop (which, of course, we exited through).

Strangely enough, the one artwork that didn't resonate with me, which I actively disliked—no, okay, I hated—was Banksy's centerpiece, hidden within Cinderella's castle. The castle itself was a kind of masterpiece; with fire-ravaged skeletal turrets dominating the middle of the park, it clearly embodied the *Dismaland* concept and provided an essential visual anchor for the rest of the park's multifarious components. The offending work was at the end of a narrow dark hallway inside, a diorama that *Business Insider*, which devoted a short article

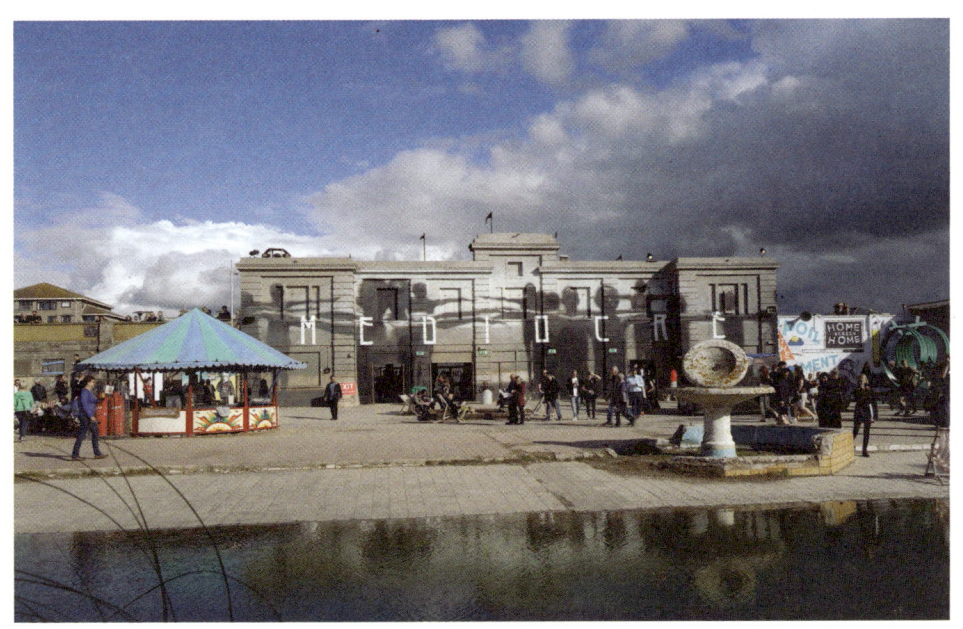

7.10
Axel Void, *Mediocre*, mural, *Dismaland*, 2015.
Photo: author.

to it, described as a "gut-wrenching Easter egg"—Princess Diana's tragic 1997 death recreated with life-size mannequins. Cinderella's body, hanging head first out of her overturned horse-drawn pumpkin carriage, was lit only by camera flashes from a bank of paparazzi representing those who, at the time, took photos instead of coming to Diana's aid—with the *Dismaland* spectators, flashing their own cameras, becoming unwitting accomplices in the reenactment. Visitors were invited to "Step inside the fairytale and see how it feels to be a real princess. Souvenir photos available."

There's only so much horrifying imagery most humans can take in before looking away and, in general, one of Banksy's greatest talents is that he doesn't bludgeon but uses surprise and wit to get us to pay attention to topics from which we might otherwise turn away. His work is characterized by a certain innocence, sometimes sarcastically feigned to be sure, but often genuine, as when he gets us to see events through the eyes of children. In this case, however, the inconsistency between the privileged life of the princess and its heartbreaking reality had long been obvious to anyone who was paying attention—which was almost everyone. It wasn't that I felt that Banksy's portrayal was "insensitive" or in "bad taste," as some of the critics quoted in *Business Insider* saw it, but that it was obvious and lugubrious, overwhelmingly so, and open to only one interpretation, leaving no room to breathe. But now, five years later, forced to wrestle with it in the context of *Dismaland* as a whole, I've reluctantly concluded that nothing else could have been inside that castle, that the diorama's extremity anchored the emotional experience of *Dismaland*, just as the castle anchored the physical space.

Another anchor was the backdrop provided by the stunning painting by Miami-based Haitian/Spanish artist Axel Void, which covered the long two-story interior façade facing the castle. Rendered in smoky blacks and grays, the building-size mural portrayed shadowy figures standing in rows with arms outstretched, suggesting ballet dancers in second position or, perhaps, detainees waiting to be patted down. Spelled out across the whole in Void's idiosyncratic lettering that looks at once technological and archaic was "MEDIOCRE"—rendered in a stark white that added to the painting's three-dimensional quality, so that the word appeared to hover in the air.

One more cohesive/noncohesive element was the signage dotted throughout the park by New York artist Stephen Powers who, interestingly, also lists a

Venice Biennale exhibition (2001) on his bio. A former graffiti artist who still uses his tag ESPO ("Exterior Surface Painting Outreach") in his artwork and signage, Powers's work doesn't have a single signature look, but explores the ways words and images can be combined, from the simplest of statements to those where a jumble of elements in every possible style are crammed into a single space. From "official" posted signs ("WINNING IS STRICTLY PRO-HIBITED" and "PLEASE NOTE, YOU HAVE NOT COME HERE TO TALK TO PEOPLE YOU ALREADY KNOW") to a multifaceted mural spanning more than one wall leading to the art gallery, Powers's imprint was everywhere but with a light touch that didn't dominate.

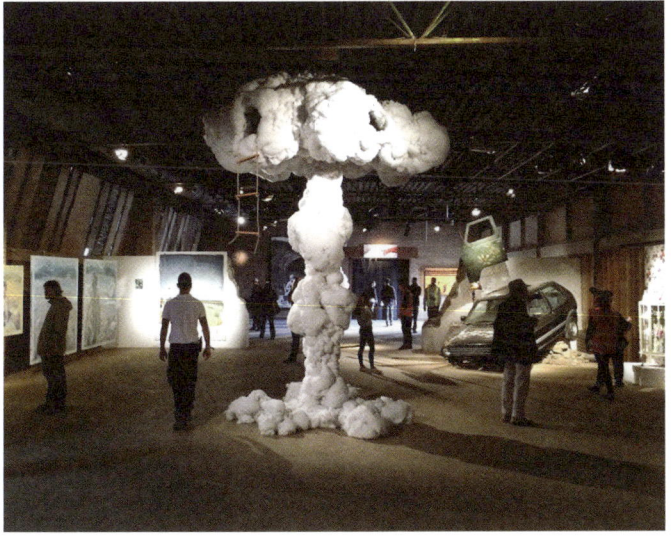

7.11
Art gallery view, *Dismaland*, 2015.
Photo: Christopher Jobson.

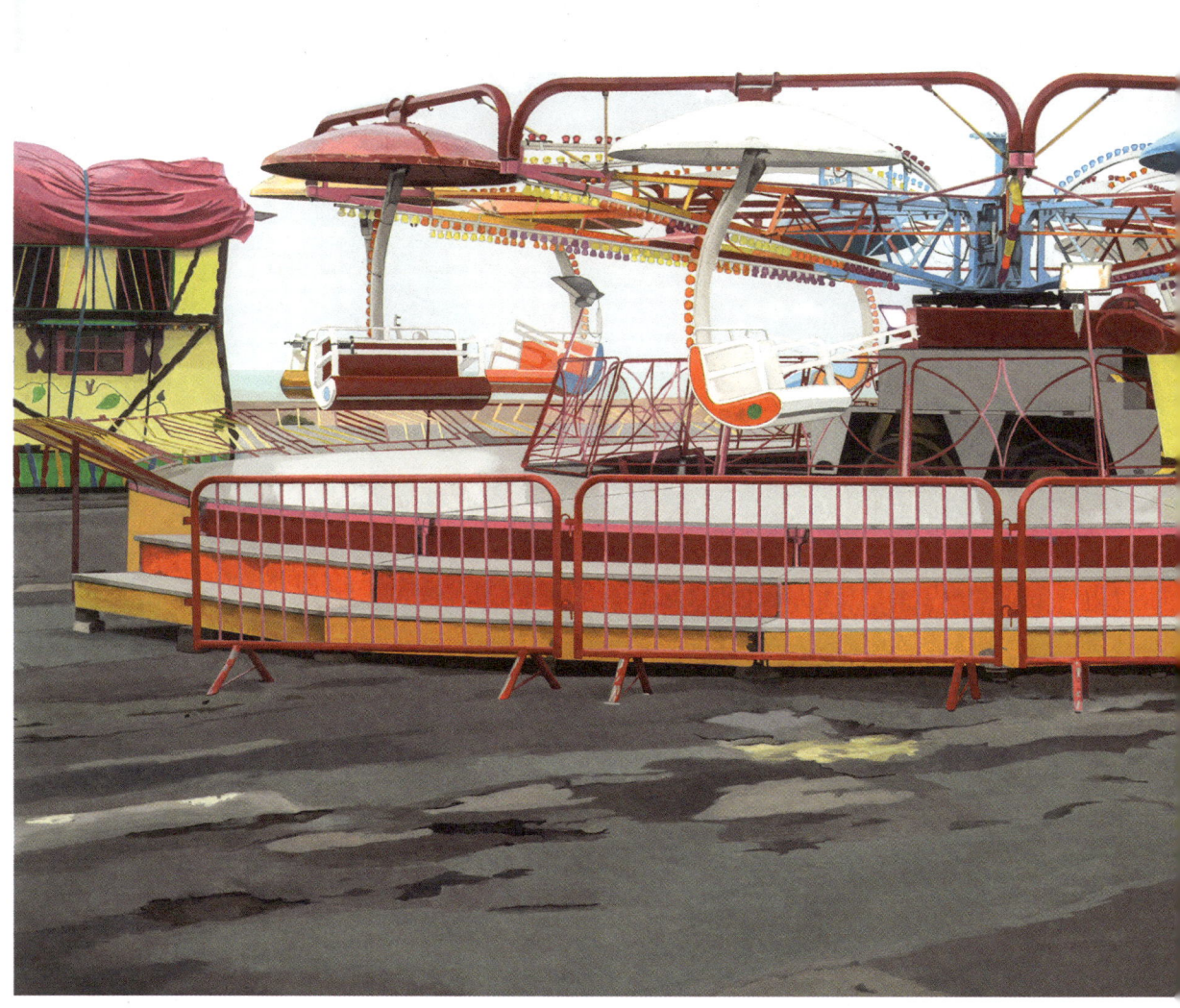

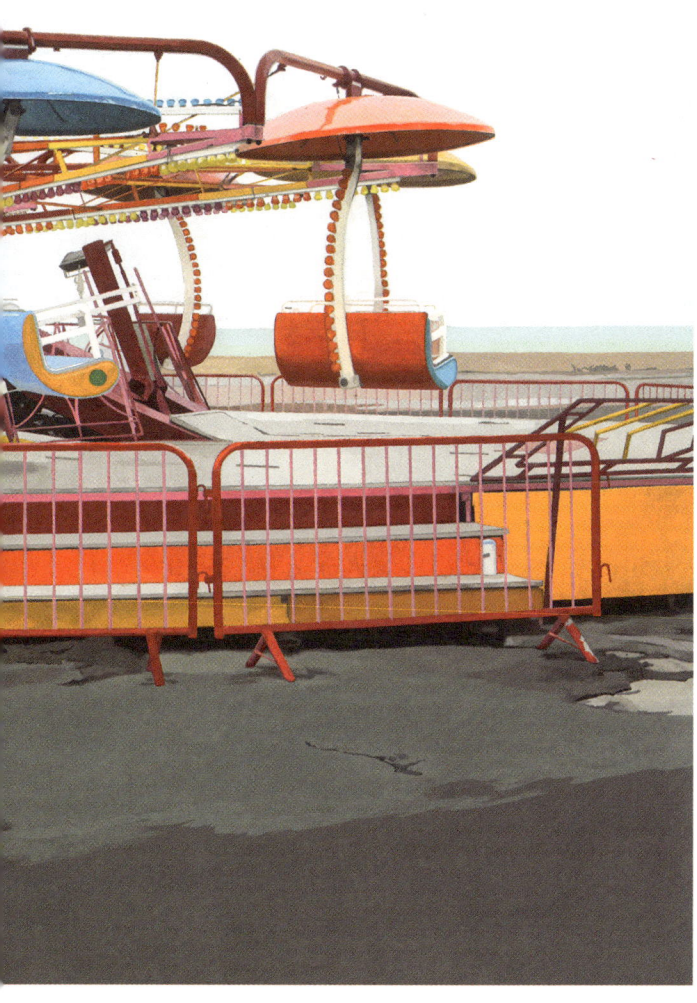

7.12

Leigh Mulley, *Paratrooper*, 2015, acrylic on canvas, courtesy of the artist.

Banksy's exercise in extreme curation was conducted entirely by email, as he kept himself secret even to the artists who participated. Chicagoan Christopher Jobson, creator of the popular *Colossal* blog, happened to be checking his spam folder while on vacation on an island in Alaska with his family when he found an email marked "private, confidential" from Banksy. "I don't know why I read it," Jobson told me, "or why I took it seriously and responded to it, but I did. He then asked if I could put together a film festival of shorts very quickly. I was freaking out, really excited, and I had about four days to do it while I was on vacation. I proposed a mix of humor, satire, animation, stop-motion, some with narrative, and some completely out in left field. They were immediately receptive of the idea, and we went from there. I sent him fifty films, and he sent me notes on all of them, putting careful thought into everything about what was going to work and why, more like this and not like this, until we came up with twenty-four, almost half of which had already been featured on *Colossal*. It was tricky, though, because I had to ask permission from all these filmmakers and animators but couldn't reveal the details. Finally we agreed that I could explain that it was going to be an outdoor theater, a lot of people would be coming, it would be an open screening in a loop, and they'd be credited, etc. It helped that I knew or had some familiarity with over half of the contributors, so they trusted me. Some we had to pay, others we had to license. One I had to keep pushing—I was a real asshole about it, but it was the one we wanted most—kept going back and forth until finally he sent me a download link to the film." The result was a whirlwind hour-long anthology of surreal interventions into real life ranging from hopeful to grim (with an emphasis on the grim), which could be encountered at any point in its continuous cycle on the outdoor screen without losing flavor or momentum.

When Folkestone painter Leigh Mulley got her email from Banksy, she told me, "It was like the opening scene in *Four Weddings and a Funeral*, where they yell, 'Fuck! Fuck!'" And then, she said, "It was 'Fuck! Fuck!' again when I realized, in a panic, that I'd committed to making four paintings in five months, all much bigger than those I usually do when, because of the detail, it takes me more than a month to complete just one small one."

The first piece I ever saw of Mulley's was the one Banksy told her he'd seen—a massive realistic painting of the head of a seagull that took up the entire side of a windowless one-story Folkestone building. Mulley figures Banksy must have then researched her work to discover that it often reflects a nostalgia, which no doubt matches his, for the seaside amusement parks of her childhood. "He said I was the first artist he contacted," Mulley told me, "which is pretty special considering the rest of the roster, but I guess my work was the right flavor. He was super casual, saying that the exhibition would be in a disused theme park, and there would be lots of beer. I never had any idea who the other artists were, and I was never given a brief, or anything like it—he told me to 'just do what you like' and that I could 'go big' because the space was large, and to get back to him when I had a plan. I could've done a huge mural—anything—it was completely up to me and that's a glorious thing for artists, the freedom to do what we want. I think his understanding of the creative process is astounding; he knew just the right things to say and do, made just the right nudges, and then would leave you to it."

The next five months, Mulley told me, were the hardest she'd worked in her art career, complicated by the fact that she couldn't tell anyone what she was doing. "I can hands-on-heart say I painted between fourteen to sixteen hours a day," she said, and then after she reported to Banksy that she'd completed the first two paintings, he sent his art handlers on the five-hour drive to Folkestone to pick them up, planning to get the others later. This may not sound like much to non-artists, but to artists, the idea of a gallery wanting to pay for more than one trip for a group show boggles the imagination.

The invitation to participate in this as-yet-undescribed exhibition also included transportation and hotel accommodations for the artists and their partners. On the date of the opening, Mulley and her partner, artist and designer Sam Millen, checked into the hotel and made their way in the rain to the seaside, planning to walk around a bit to see what it looked like from the outside before getting their artist passes. "So here we are," she said, "in this really tired seafront, this really tired location in the middle of nowhere, and we walk down the hill and see . . . the *Dismaland* sign up and a row of about a dozen high-side transit vans topped with satellite dishes—BBC, ITV, all the news agencies—and it hit me like a wave, like I'm involved in this, and, holy shit, it's massive! It was exciting and frightening all at the same time. Then we went into the gallery, the first room with the Damien Hirst piece in front, and two of my pieces were within the sightline of his. . . . Well, just seeing my work in the context of the others, it was fantastic, an incredible moment."

Mulley commented on the impeccable way the art was installed in the gallery, something a casual visitor wouldn't notice—and shouldn't, because when it's done properly it's invisible—everything configured so that nothing distracts from the art. The room, she noted, was beautifully low-lit, moody but showing the art at its best. Then there was the system by which the works were placed so that their surfaces were continuous—while hung on uneven, crumbly walls where there would be a bit of concrete, then a hole, and then some brick. Mulley concluded that the brackets that the artworks hung on must have been bespoke, so perfectly made that "if you just put your head alongside the artwork, you could see that it was hanging somewhat away from the wall, almost floating, with everything in perfect alignment." There were no wall labels, no wall text, nothing to interfere with the art, something I told Mulley I particularly appreciated. Instead the artists' names were stenciled and spray-painted on the floor beneath their works.

While Mulley said that exhibiting at *Dismaland* added to her profile and increased her work's value, ultimately what most moved her was "not only that thousands and thousands of people got to see it, but the affirmation that comes with someone you admire and respect liking what you do," as well as meeting the other artists and creating associations that have continued on social media and beyond. "What else made me happy," she added, was that "*Dismaland* was a self-funded project done outside the system, without any bullshit arts council grants, truly professionally executed, with a mix of artists, some very famous and some not, and a vibe that was outsider, anti-establishment—that was truly exhilarating."

With so much vying for attention at *Dismaland*, it was nearly impossible to take everything in, and I missed a lot in my single afternoon visit. If I'd had any idea what I was getting into—and could have been sure of getting tickets—I would have planned to visit for several days. I was very sorry to miss the Jeffrey Archer Memorial Fire Pit ("Warm yourself around an authentic real open fire ceremonially lit each day by burning one of the famed local perjurer's novels"). A former member of parliament who ran for mayor of London, the Baron of Weston-super-Mare's bio also includes shoplifting, paying off a prostitute, fraudulent investment schemes, and prison time for perjury, as well as authoring books, mostly novels for adults but some also for children, that have sold 275 million copies worldwide. Archer's Wikipedia page is definitely worth a read.

I also wish I'd seen the bus-mounted Museum of Cruel Designs, curated by Dr. Gavin Grindon, senior lecturer at the University of Essex, who later was instrumental in creating the Museum of the Wall in Banksy's West Bank hotel. "Cruel Designs" are those made for social control, items intended to manage or inhibit the activities of people who are not breaking the law but simply inconveniencing the status quo by being homeless, activist, or just unruly, as in the case of teenagers repelled by machines emitting sounds only they can hear. According to Grindon's catalog, "These objects compose and embody state and capitalist order, accompanying the formation of repressive laws and unjust social relations. . . . While they most dramatically impact the public, designs such as high-tech fences and CCTV also affect managers and police, automating their roles at the expense of their jobs as accountable figures. They outsource violence to objects, and the responsibility for them to the networks of people commissioning, designing or buying them who are all 'just doing their job.' . . . These are all bad designs. They fail to address the root causes of social problems, redefining them as 'security' problems which can be 'designed out.'" Grindon was co-curator of the Victoria and Albert Museum's 2014 exhibition entitled "Disobedient Objects" about the art and design produced by grassroots social movements; by the time it closed, it was the most visited exhibition at the museum since 1946.

Chris Jobson said he walked through *Dismaland* three times, but then hanging out at the bar in his hotel, was seeing things in the photos of others that he'd missed. That wasn't a problem for many reviewers, however, who took the easy way out by not going at all. Like turning over a rock, Banksy's *Dismaland* brought to light a gaggle of journalists (and editors, presumably) willing to put their scruples aside to gain exposure by taking advantage of Banksy's notoriety in a way that has become predictable. You'd think that the first requirement of having an opinion about any experience would be to actually have the experience. Originally tipping me off to this phenomenon in the case of *Dismaland* was a commenter in the *Los Angeles Times* who asked whether the author of the negative *Dismaland* critique, Carolina A. Miranda, who wrote, "Bansky's [sic] installations look like they were specifically crafted for Instagram" and "feel as industrially contrived as the spectacles they purportedly critique," had actually been there. Miranda later told me in a Facebook message that she hadn't, but was pressured by her editor to write about it anyway.

Then, in the *New York Times Magazine*—which, like the *Los Angeles Times*, you'd hope would know better—one Dan Brooks waxed at length on "Banksy and the Problem with Sarcastic Art," citing negative pieces by Mike Nudelman in *Business Insider* ("Banksy's 'Dismaland' Is Art about Nothing—and We're Over It"), John Trowbridge in *HuffPost* ("35 HELPFUL Things Banksy Could Have Done Instead of Dismaland"), and *HuffPost*/Canada writer Shailee Koranne ("Dismaland Is Not Interesting and Neither Is Banksy") to bolster his point—while it's obvious that neither he nor any of the other writers found occasion to visit the event (a fact pointed out by several commenters). This is especially ironic when one considers that Brooks, who fancies himself a specialist in "Ethical Dilemmas," a category on his blog, once wrote a post taking issue with people who had expressed opinions about a book they hadn't read. And the funny/not funny thing about Nudelman's piece in *Business Insider* is that he compares Banksy unfavorably to Jenny Holzer ("If it's the quips and public monumentality that draw you to Banksy, consider instead Jenny Holzer's 'Truisms'") without realizing that Holzer's *Truisms* were a prominent and well-publicized part of *Dismaland*. As R. J. Rushmore, who actually did go to *Dismaland*, observed in his *Hyperallergic* review, "The only thing hipper right now than liking Banksy is hating him."

Recalling the effect the Johnny Thunders concert had on my son Matt, I'm beginning to think that appreciating Banksy has everything to do with the relative health of your inner teenager. Rushmore concluded, "*Dismaland* did something for me that art should do but museum exhibitions almost never do: transported me back to an unburdened teenage state of mind. Now, back home in Philadelphia, it's like I'm still in a state of euphoria, reinvigorated with the kind of energy usually only provided by cheap thrills, stupidity, and drugs. I suspect it did something similar for some actual teenagers too. . . . For every random tourist who snaps 10,000 unthinking photos at *Dismaland* and leaves with nothing but the satisfaction of saying they've been there, some kid is going to be inspired to use art to take on social issues, to go down a path that felt previously unavailable to them. . . . Fuck art school. Go to *Dismaland*."

Unlike the end of his New York residency, this time Banksy didn't live up to his advice to "just walk away quietly and don't make any fuss," but topped *Dismaland*'s weekly evening entertainment series with a masked ball—masked so the host could attend incognito—a truly *grand finale* complete with fireworks and headlined by the Russian activist punk group Pussy Riot, spoken word performer Kate Tempest, and the venerable De La Soul, with a surprise cameo appearance by Damon Albarn, of Gorillaz and Blur.

A Pussy Riot fan named Emily described the group's *Dismaland* performance on her blog *Bell Jar*:

> moody, bass-heavy music dropped and shouting was coming from in front of the castle, we made our way round to see three balaclava-clad members of Pussy Riot performing from a cage to one side of the castle. Meanwhile, in the center, there were actor protestors trying to fight their way through a barrier of riot police armed with shields and truncheons. Four never-before-heard songs were performed covering political topics of migration and police/government corruption. The majority of the performance was in Russian with English subtitles projected onto the side of the castle. . . . Over the duration of Pussy Riot's set, the violence between police and activists heightened and eventually the entire group of protestors break through, get hold of the truncheons and chase the police officers into the castle. It was entertaining, hard-hitting.

Time described Pussy Riot's song, dedicated to the 750,000 refugees who had thus far arrived in Europe in 2015, and written for the occasion with footage from the performance later made into a music video, as a "bleak yet fanciful takedown of European governments."

Pussy Riot, "Refugees In"

Met in Europe by razor wires
Governments here fucking liars
Desperate people who need to flee
Seeking refuge by land and sea
Push for borders, get no peace
Fuck the police like we're in Greece

Cage me in cage me out
Refugees in, Nazis out
Governments here should feel the shame
Fucking liars, you're to blame

Fuck the police
Like we are in Greece
Destroy piece by piece
This conservative disease

Huff and puff and smash it up
Burst, blast, blow it up
Cage me in cage me out

Refugees in, Nazis out
Governments here should feel the shame
Fucking liars, you're to blame

Cage me in cage me out
Refugees in, Nazis out
Governments here, should feel the shame
Fucking liars, you are to blame

Bombing people out of homes
We want peace, not fucking drones
Push, push borders away!
Push borders, do it today!
Human beings, not a swarm
Injustice—government norm

Cage me in and cage me out
Refugees in, Nazis out
Governments here, should feel the shame
Fucking liars, you're to blame

Pussy Riot's performance could not have been more apropos. Just a few weeks before, the humanitarian crisis had captured worldwide attention with the release of the horrifying photo of the body of Syrian toddler Alan Kurdi washed up on a Turkish beach, while droves of migrants based in a rapidly growing encampment called the Calais Jungle in France were attempting to enter England via the Channel Tunnel by stowing away on trucks, cars, or trains.

Meanwhile at *Dismaland*, as one of the "bemusements" offered, Banksy had constructed a pool that replicated the Channel near the white Dover cliffs, the first sight of England for those crossing the Channel from France. There for £1, visitors could control toy boats crammed with migrants, while the lifeless face-down bodies of those who didn't make it floated by and a toy yacht looked on. As Banksy described it, "In the remote-control boat pond at Dismaland it randomly switches the boat you operate—so you have no control over whether your destiny is to be an asylum seeker or a western super-power." The *Independent*'s Chris Green, who was there on the first day, found the work "deeply unsettling, yet bizarrely entertaining," summing up, for him, the experience of *Dismaland* as a whole.

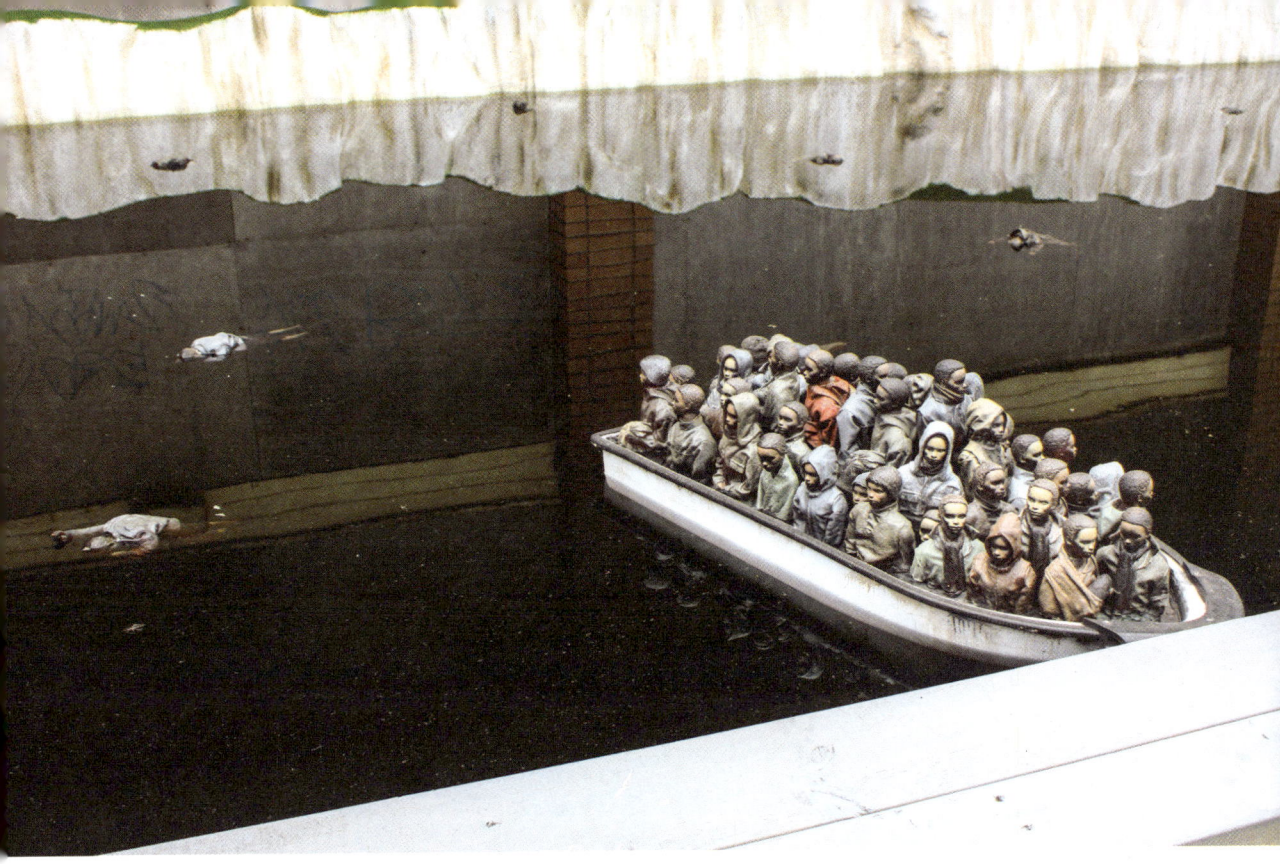

7.13
Banksy, installation, *Dismaland*, 2015.
Photo: Sam Millen.

7.14   *following pages*
Banksy, spray painting (Steve Jobs),
Calais, 2015, courtesy of Pest Control
Office.

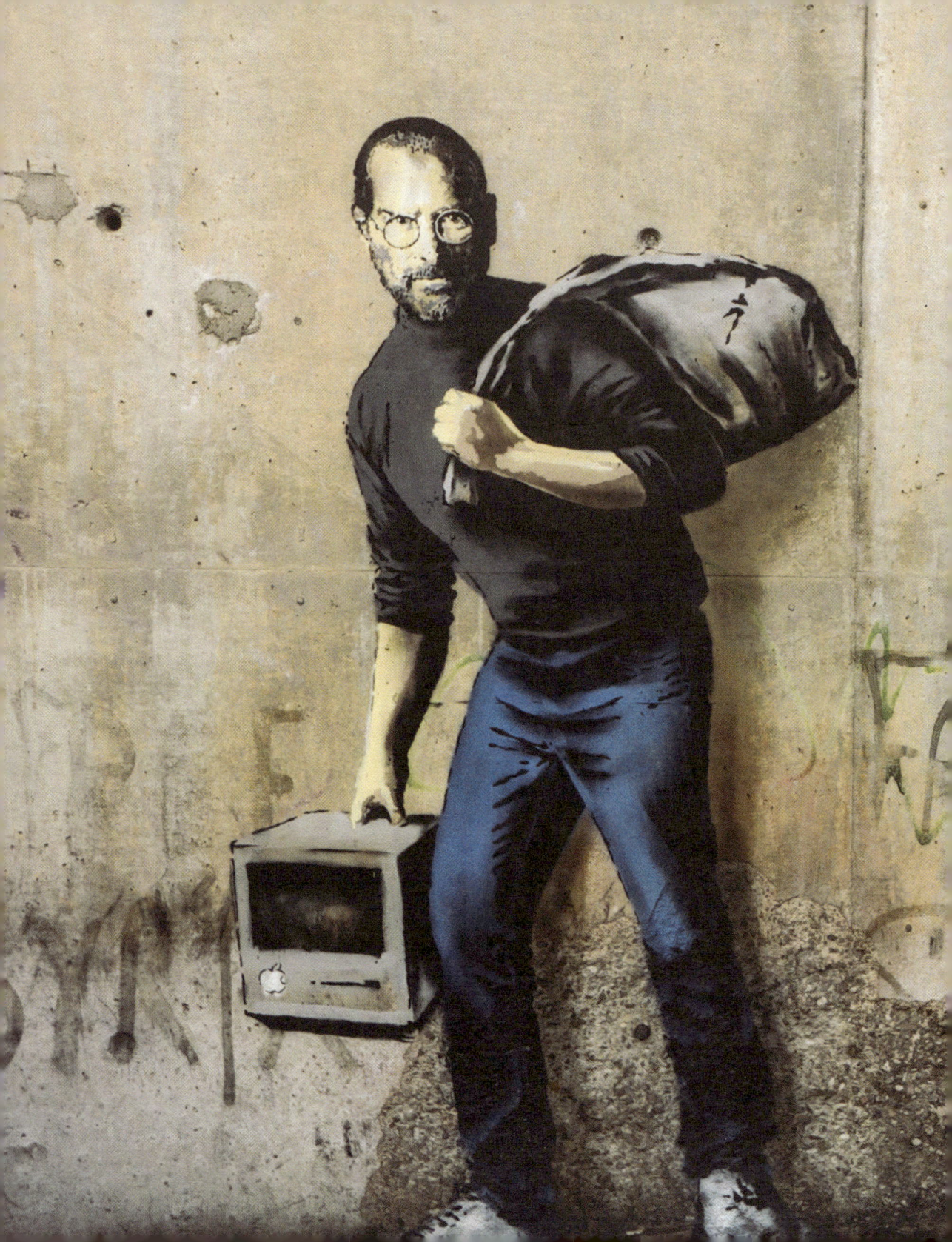

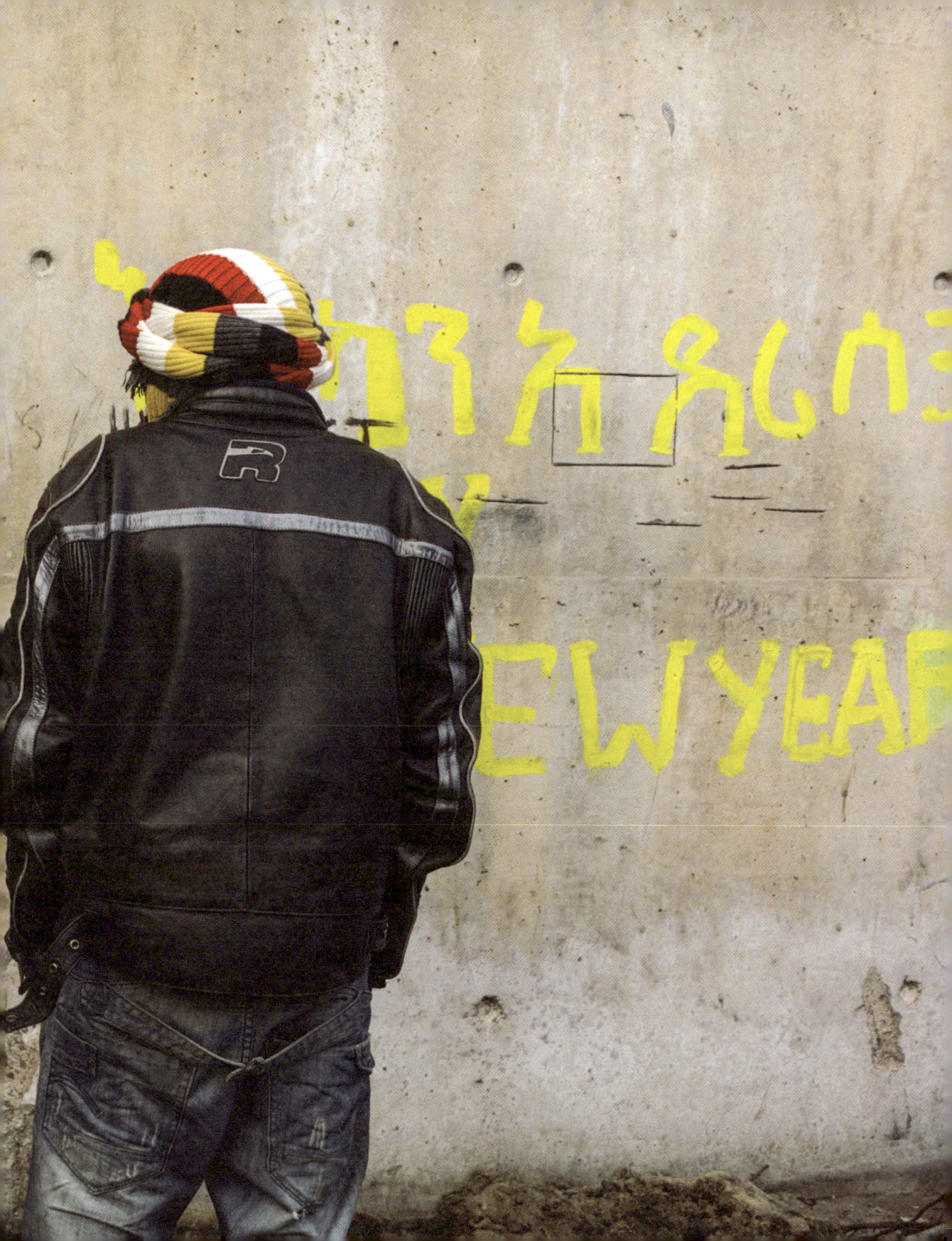

When *Dismaland* closed on schedule, after earning an estimated £20 million for the businesses of Weston-super-Mare, Banksy announced that once it was broken down, the materials would go with a team to build shelters at the "Jungle" refugee camp near the French port of Calais, now home to around five thousand migrants from countries including Syria, Libya, and Eritrea. The *Dismaland* sign, which was altered to say "Dismal aid," was sent as well, staying up until it was stolen. The group built twelve permanent structures and a makeshift playground, while Banksy left four new artworks, most notably one featuring Steve Jobs in his trademark black turtleneck carrying the original Macintosh computer and a refugee's sack over his shoulder (Jobs was adopted, and his biological father was from Syria). In an accompanying online statement, Banksy wrote, "We're often led to believe migration is a drain on the country's resources but Steve Jobs was the son of a Syrian migrant. Apple is the world's most profitable company, it pays over $7 billion a year in taxes—and it only exists because they allowed in a young man from Homs." In another piece, Banksy took off on French painter Théodore Géricault's famous 1819 *Raft of the Medusa*, depicting a group of refugees on a sinking raft as they try to hail a modern cruise ship on the horizon.

On the *Dismaland* website, Banksy posted an image of his burned-out Cinderella's castle superimposed on a photo of the migrant camp, with the announcement: "Coming soon . . . Dismaland Calais. All the timber and fixtures from Dismaland are being sent to the Jungle refugee camp near Calais to build shelters. No online tickets will be available."

Claire Breukel, a curator, must have taken Banksy seriously, thinking he was actually transplanting the park complete to Calais, when, as one of seventeen "art world luminaries" asked to comment on *Hyperallergic*'s "Best and Worst of 2015," she chose *Dismaland* for "worst": "Banksys's [sic] *Dismaland* raked in more than 20 million pounds for the town of Weston-super-Mare, yet Syrian refugees are gifted the leftovers of this gloom and doom fairground by the mega-star artist . . . presumably to lift their spirits!? Not only is the fairground a flatulent attempt at addressing social wrongs, making 'Jungle' camp refugees players on an art projects [sic] publicity campaign is just tacky. Being anonymous still makes you accountable." (When I emailed asking to interview her about her experience at *Dismaland*, Breukel wrote back, "My sentiments about Dismaland are not positive so I would prefer not to spend time and energy talking about the project," yet her Facebook page shows her jaunting from El Salvador to Miami to Bern, Switzerland, during the time *Dismaland* was up.) Did Breukel really believe a malfunctioning Ferris wheel was part of the lot sent to Calais? One also wonders how she thinks Banksy might have made more money for the refugees—or if she knows any other artists who have made £20 million for anyone, or were more actively bringing global attention to the refugees' plight. Regardless, it's unlikely Banksy is wasting any time worrying about this club that won't have him as a member—especially when he can make his own club.

With the materials shipped off, the Tropicana boarded up again, and personal thank you notes written to the participants, Banksy took down the *Dismaland* website and was on to his next chapter.

From the *Dismaland* catalog: *If you do just one thing today, that might not be enough.*

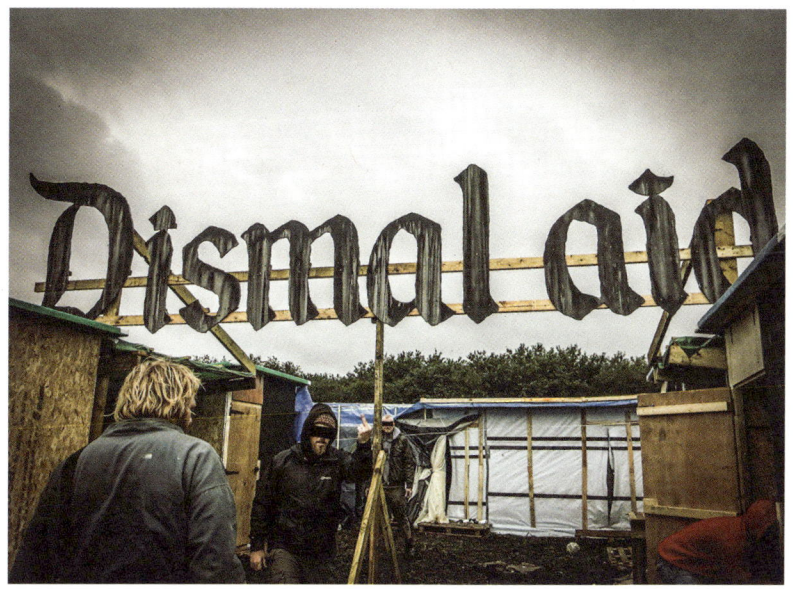

7.15
Banksy, *Dismal aid* at the Calais refugee camp, 2015, courtesy of Pest Control Office.

Banksy in Bethlehem

Palestine has been occupied by the Israeli army since 1967. In 2002 the Israeli government began building a wall separating the occupied territories from Israel, much of it illegal under international law. It is controlled by a series of checkpoints and observation towers, stands three times the height of the Berlin wall and will eventually run for over 700km—the distance from London to Zurich. Palestine is now the world's largest open-air prison and ultimate activity holiday destination for graffiti artists.

Banksy, *Wall and Piece*

In March 2017, Banksy announced his biggest project since *Dismaland* and one even more ambitious: *The Walled Off Hotel*, a fully functioning hotel with eight guest rooms in one of the most conflicted areas in the world. Named for its location in the West Bank city of Bethlehem and only twelve feet from the wall separating Israel and Palestine, *The Walled Off Hotel* offers ultimate physical comfort matched by a décor which, only somewhat mitigated by Banksy's skewed humor, serves as a perpetual reminder that others are not so blessed. Sited under one of the many Israeli military watchtowers atop the twenty-eight-foot-high wall with the windows of its "scenic" guest rooms opening onto the barrier's expanse of gray concrete, Banksy's twisted version of the Waldorf lives up to its promise of offering "the worst view in the world." A protest in the form of an artwork you can stay in, *The Walled Off Hotel* includes a bookshop and museum, both focusing on the history of the wall, and a gallery of contemporary Palestinian art overseen by a Palestinian curator and art historian—as well as a shop next door, the Wall*Mart, which sells paint, stencils, and other supplies so visitors can add their own statements to the much-graffitied barricade. In addition, the hotel arranges twice-daily walking tours to the nearby Aida refugee camp.

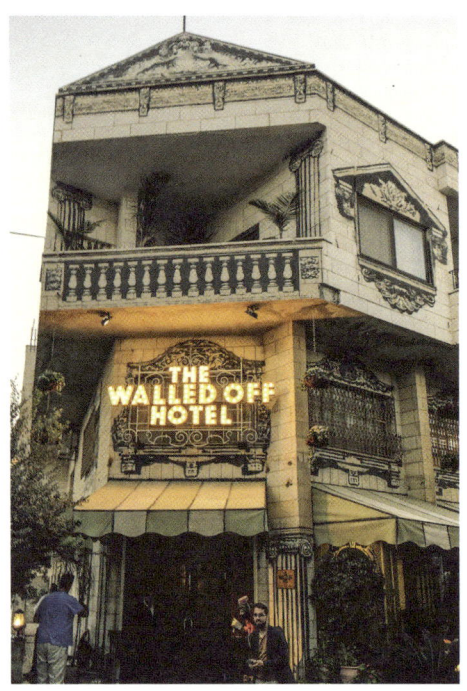

8.1

Banksy, exterior stenciling, *The Walled Off Hotel*, Bethlehem, Palestinian West Bank, 2018. Photo: author.

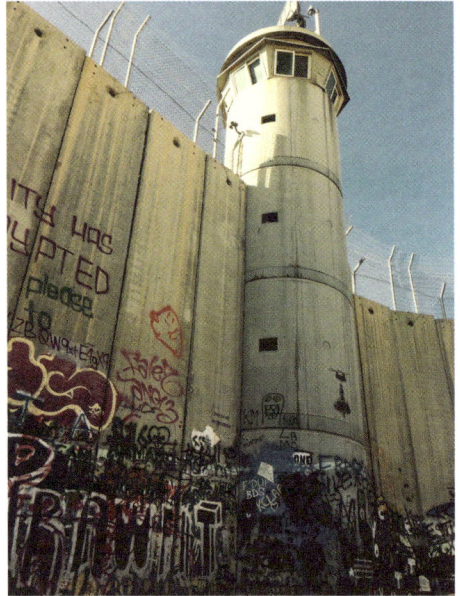

8.2

Guard tower, Bethlehem, Palestinian West Bank. Photo: author.

8.3

"The worst view in the world": view from a guest room, *The Walled Off Hotel*. Photo: author.

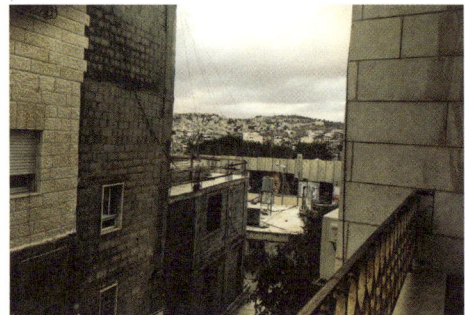

Developed over fourteen months and, like *Dismaland*, in complete secrecy, Banksy timed the opening of the hotel to coincide with the centenary of the Balfour Declaration of 1917 that supported the establishment in Palestine of a national home for the Jewish people. The declaration served as the basis for the British Mandate of Palestine, which was approved in 1920 by the League of Nations, a precursor to the UN. Referring to the fact that at the time of the mandate, Palestine was already home to a population who had been there for hundreds of years and faced displacement, Banksy said in a statement announcing the opening of the hotel, "The British didn't handle things so well here. When you organise a wedding, it's best to make sure the bride isn't already married." He added, "I don't know why, but it felt like a good time to reflect on what happens when the United Kingdom makes a huge political decision without fully comprehending the consequences"—no doubt also referring to the United Kingdom's vote on Brexit.

Politically, the West Bank belonged to Jordan before Israel took control in the war of 1967. It is inhabited by over two million Palestinians, many of whom have been uprooted from their homes by the several hundred thousand Jews who have built settlements on their land—hence, the refugee camps, nineteen in all. The vast separation wall was begun in 2000 and its total length upon completion will be approximately 708 kilometers or 440 miles—or, as Banksy has pointed out, the distance from London to Zurich. Conceived by the Israelis as security against Palestinian terrorism, the wall is viewed by Palestinians as an apartheid wall and a land grab that has turned the West Bank into what they describe as an open-air prison. Indeed, in materials and construction, the wall's appearance matches that surrounding a penitentiary which can be spotted on the road from Tel Aviv to Bethlehem. Both the wall and the over two hundred Jewish settlements dotting the West Bank are considered illegal by international law and are sources of seemingly unresolvable contention. And while the term "settlement" sounds quaint, these are really cement urban enclaves with substantial infrastructures and their own walls, sited on what was previously arable Arab land with olive groves hundreds of years old. "I was once the Berlin wall," reads a placard in the hotel's museum dedicated to the history of wall. "But the beer was better there." Written in the hand we've come to associate with Banksy, this reminder of a similar wall that was ultimately destroyed offers a rare flicker of optimism.

When I first visited Bethlehem in 1983, before the first major Palestinian uprising against Israeli occupation of the West Bank and Gaza, the little city was thriving. Easily accessed from Jerusalem only six miles away, the storied birthplace of Jesus and home to many Muslims as well as a large Arab Christian community (random fact: the mayor is required by law to be Christian), was a bustling destination for pilgrims and tourists. Since Bethlehem has been isolated from Jerusalem and the rest of Israel by the wall, bypass roads, and an Israeli military checkpoint—as well as laws forbidding Palestinians to enter Israel and Israeli citizens to enter areas under Palestinian control without prior approval—the town has deteriorated to the point that chef and writer John Gregory Smith, in an account of his visit to the hotel, described it as "a dwindling beauty within a concrete beast."

The press release announcing the opening of *The Walled Off Hotel* outlined Banksy's vision for "a three-storey cure for fanaticism, with limited car parking." Because tourism, Bethlehem's main industry, has diminished since the wall was constructed, its holy sites now visited by day trippers from Jerusalem, the hotel was intended to encourage foreign visitors to stay overnight and become acquainted with life surrounded by the wall, as well as give a much-needed boost to the local economy. -

My first direct experience with the hotel was with its extraordinary customer service while making my arrangements, as my emails inquiring about accommodations, airport car service, and tours were answered instantly, as if by text message. After making elaborate plans and flying halfway across the world, my immediate worry upon landing was, would our pickup actually be there? Which of course he was, ready to whisk my friend and me the thirty-five miles from Tel Aviv through the armed checkpoint to the hotel where its cartoon-like entrance— polka-dotted lighted sign, a stuffed chimpanzee posing as a bellboy—contrasted dramatically with the authoritarian concrete monster of a wall looming next to it. At reception (or rather "Rejection," as was engraved on the brass plate—it *is* a Banksy hotel, after all) we were immediately brought complimentary lemony drinks along with a printed greeting from Banksy that began, "You made it!" which made me feel that whoever he was, wherever he was, he knew the relief and excitement I was feeling. "We hope your stay is an enjoyable and enriching one," the note concluded, "but you should be mindful that the hotel's corporate mission statement is taken from the words of Eleanor Roosevelt: 'The role of art is to comfort the disturbed and disturb the comfortable.' So please don't bother complaining about the pillows."

There would be nothing to complain about. The hotel, while not luxurious, was supremely comfortable—if measured by the best beds, the best linens, the best towels, and hands-down the best breakfast ever to be included with the price of a room. Choosing as much as I wanted from the extensive menu, every morning I had a freshly made three-egg omelet, falafel, hummus, mint tea, coffee, and a fresh fruit plate that included sliced persimmons and kiwis, while my companion opted for the pastry selection. Ask for milk with your coffee and you get hot milk. Banksy designed the hotel to be like a British colonial gentlemen's club with wood paneling, flocked wallpaper (Banksy loves flocked wallpaper to the point that I think it may be his premier symbol of decadent capitalism), velvet drapes, sparkling crystal decanters on the bar, intimate round tables, potted palms, and tufted couches—all contributing to what the website calls "an air of undeserved authority." By enjoying such comfort in the midst of others whose lives have been tragically disrupted, you just might see yourself in the role of colonist. The clublike atmosphere extends to more than the furnishings; even without conversation, there's a certain sense of compatibility with the other guests who, no matter where they're from, may be assumed to share similar outlooks and values. Add to that a Palestinian staff who treat you like family and clearly see themselves as part of a shared larger mission, and you just might want to stay forever.

Really, the only physical discomfort during our four-day stay was beyond the hotel's control—the smell of sewage that would occasionally waft from our bathroom, a reminder that we were in an area where access to water, among other essentials, is severely restricted.

But just as Banksy clearly put considerable effort into ensuring his guests' physical comfort, he exerted even more into making sure they don't become complacent. His artworks, which dominate every surface, are visual manifestations of the occupation and its burdens; you cannot forget it. The fire in the hearth of the main room that also serves as lobby, reception, lounge, and café, contains a hazard sign and flickers from concrete rubble that spills out onto the floor.

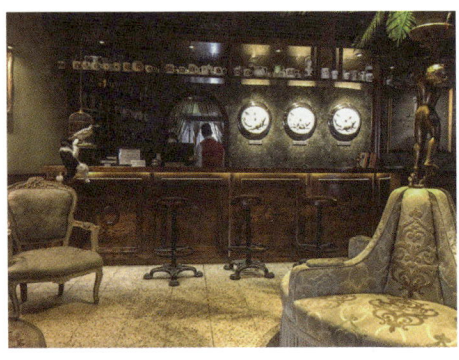

8.4

Reception, *The Walled Off Hotel*.
Photo: author.

8.5

Breakfast at *The Walled Off Hotel*.
Photo: author.

8.6

Reception, *The Walled Off Hotel*.
Photo: author.

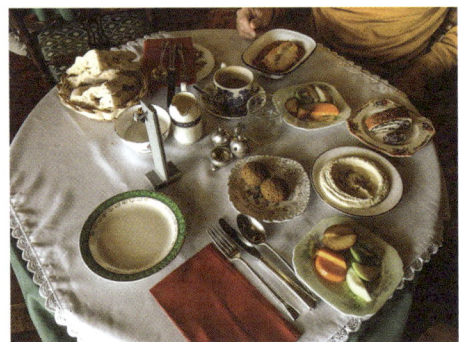

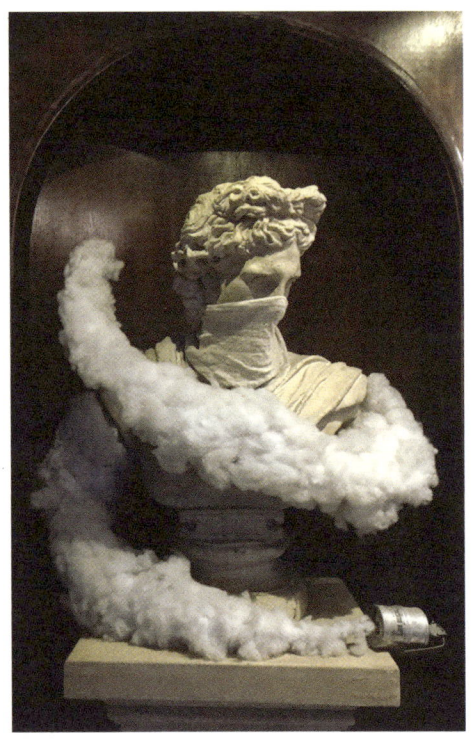

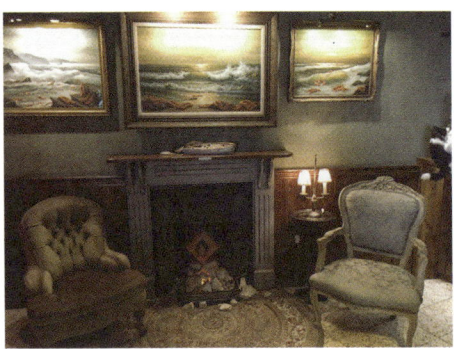

8.7

Banksy, Apollo sculpture, *The Walled Off
Hotel*. Photo: author.

Above the mantel is a series of traditional seascapes that would be tranquil to contemplate but for the abandoned life jackets of refugees that have washed up on the shore. Next to the reception desk a stuffed cat is trying to get at a stuffed dove inside a cage, while on the wall behind it, painted rats race around clocks showing the time in New York, London, and Jerusalem. On the far side of the desk, a painting of children swinging from one of the ubiquitous guard towers hangs near a recreation of Banksy's famous graffiti of a protester hurling a bouquet, which in this case consists of fresh-cut flowers, replaced daily.

The corner archway contains a pedestal holding a classical bust of Apollo wearing a protective cloth over his nose and mouth while wreathed in a swirl of tear gas from a metal canister like those that can sometimes be found, along with spent rubber bullets, in piles of debris on the street outside. Consistent with Banksy's recurring portrayal of children as the innocent victims of adult conflict, Apollo is known, among other things, as the protector of the young.

Then there's the trophy wall where, instead of the taxidermy that inevitably adorns men's clubs, we find wooden plaques mounted with the heads of surveillance cameras, now looking strangely anthropomorphic. This technological sophistication contrasts with the row of slingshots beneath it, the primitive weaponry of the Palestinian resistance, interrupted by a pair of crisscrossed sledgehammers. Below all of this high- and low-tech defense (or aggression, depending on how you look at it) is a row of British commemorative royalty plates placed on edge on a shelf and resting precariously against the wall, causing these royal portraits rendered in porcelain to appear particularly fragile.

The ghost of Banksy hovers throughout; he is everywhere and nowhere. Not only does the mystery of his anonymity add to the eerie atmosphere, the décor cultivates this suggestion of an unseen presence. Under dangling cutouts of cherubs wearing gas masks, a black baby grand piano plays itself—automated compositions created especially for the hotel by such music stalwarts as Elton John, Brian Eno, Trent Reznor of Nine Inch Nails, and Massive Attack. The high-resolution performances were so realistic I never got used to them; every time I turned around, I expected to see someone at the piano bench. Unlike the hotel's other furnishings, no doubt collected from British flea markets and car boot sales and therefore slightly worn as if they'd been there for decades, the elegant piano is shiny and new. Yamaha? Steinway? We will never know, as the label has been obliterated with a swipe of white enamel paint, complete with drip.

Clearly an expression of Banksy's contempt for corporate logos (as in *Dismaland*, you will not find any brand identification in the hotel), on such a pristine and costly instrument this spontaneous gesture feels almost violent—and spooky; the brushstroke's glossy finish looks as if it could still be wet, just painted, and you missed it when you weren't looking.

The slightly haunted atmosphere continues on the way to the guest suites, to which there is no visible entrance from the main room. We are given our key, attached to an oversize fob designed to look like a slice of the barrier wall, and shown to a bookshelf holding a small replica of the Venus de Milo. Point the end of the fob to her breasts and—voilà!—they light up with two red dots while the fake bookcase to our left slowly and silently swings open to reveal the stairway. Our room was on the second floor, off a lounge with chairs and small tables stacked with trays set with porcelain tea services and bowls of fresh apples, as if someone is about to come along and deliver them to the rooms—an arrested

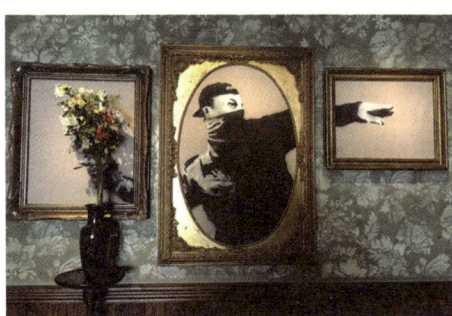

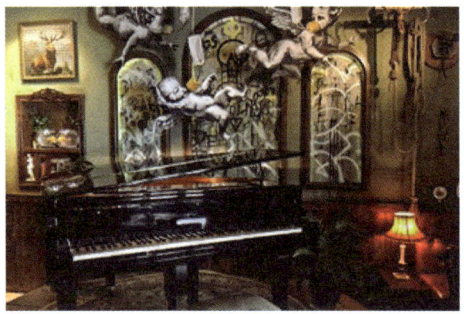

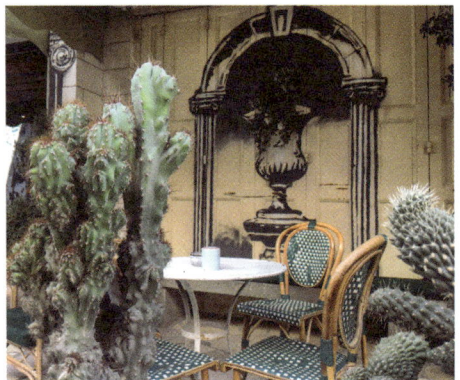

8.8

Banksy, *Love Is in the Air (Flower Thrower)*, screen print triptych, *The Walled Off Hotel*. Photo: author.

8.9

Lobby piano, *The Walled Off Hotel*. Photo: author.

8.10

Café, *The Walled Off Hotel*. Photo: author.

expectation, as there is no such room service. Across from this display is an elevator . . . well no, actually not, but stainless-steel elevator doors partly open to reveal a cement block wall, with a dangling hand-lettered cardboard sign that reads "Out of service" next to push button lights that flash excitedly from 1 to 3 and back. Gilt-framed pictures decorate the walls: bucolic landscapes covered with metal grates signifying no access, and some with no image at all, just stenciled words indicating what might be pictured there—"DOG," "TWO DOGS," "FRUIT," "NAVAL BATTLE," or "AMATEUR WATERCOLOR BY A FRIEND OF THE OWNER"—as well as, more ominously, canvases that have been burned out to reveal the words "RURAL LANDSCAPE."

It was only after a couple of treks up the stairs that I noticed the small, plain, dark wood frame hung at eye level directly across from the hidden door in the otherwise empty stairwell. It contained a quote, printed on paper with carefully hand-torn edges: "We artists are indestructible; even in a prison, or in a concentration camp, I would be almighty in my own world of art, even if I had to paint my pictures with my wet tongue on the dusty floor of my cell. Picasso, *Der Monat*, 1949."

I'd had a mad scramble to secure a reservation only a month before our trip—the rooms kept disappearing under my fingertips as I tried to get the website to take my credit card (not the hotel's fault)—so I missed getting even one night in the top-floor palatial Presidential Suite ($482.50 to $965, depending on whether it's a weekend), which sleeps up to four adults and is "equipped with everything a corrupt head of state would need—a plunge bath able to accommodate up to four revelers, original artwork, library, home cinema, roof garden, tiki bar, and a water feature made from a bullet-riddled water tank. Comes with a complete set of Dead Sea bath minerals and an in-room dining service available upon request." At the other end of the spectrum, and still available, were cots in the hostel-style Budget Barracks (sixty dollars per person), "outfitted with surplus items from Israeli military barracks. . . . No frills, includes locker, personal safe, shared bathroom" as well as complimentary earplugs, to protect guests from the snores of five or so others.

We scored one of the three "Scenic Suites" ($225), the only one left, and could not have been happier. The hotel website quotes American photographer Diane Arbus, who once said, "to live with an artwork is something different, to glimpse it from the corner of your eye." While our room was without site-specific works by Banksy (or the other two artists he commissioned to create rooms, Sami Musa from Palestine, who also participated in *Dismaland*, and Dominique Pétrin from Montreal), everything it contained was so idiosyncratic and carefully chosen that it was like living in a Banksy installation. The spacious room's most definitive characteristic, and its most sharply modern, was the color of the walls and ceiling: a vibrant true green, which could be seen as a leaf green (to make up for the lack of leaves in the view off the balcony, perhaps) or what a painter would describe as cadmium green—intense and invigorating, but also soothing, in a woodland sort of way. Rugs, lampshades, and accessories in various shades of dark pink and red lent a festive air as well as, given the flea market aesthetic, a rather faded elegance. Collections of old books, chosen for their vintage covers rather than their contents, were everywhere, with stacks of books supporting the lamps on either side of the king-size bed and an antique camel sculpture on the coffee table in front of the couch. Complete with a red feather in the inkwell, old-fashioned writing accessories graced the desk, while the water glasses and decanter were crystal (no plastic for Banksy!); opening the desk drawers revealed not a bible, but collections of old German postcards.

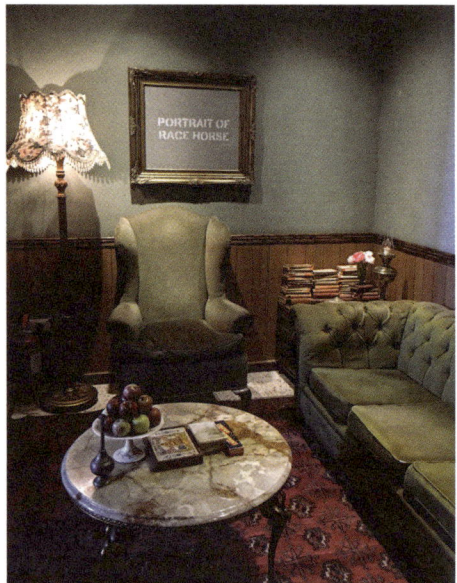

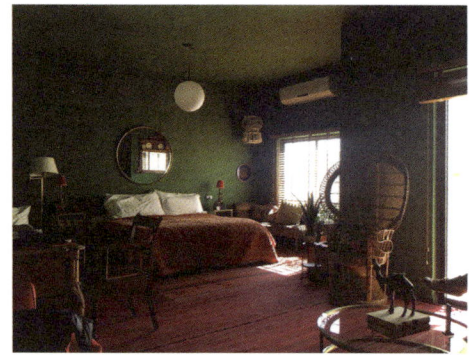

8.11
Second-floor lounge, *The Walled Off Hotel*. Photo: author.

8.12
Scenic Suite, *The Walled Off Hotel*. Photo: author.

The sparkling white-tile bathroom, with a panoply of variously shaped frameless antique mirrors arranged on the walls, was similarly ornately appointed, with extra rolls of toilet tissue heaped in a baroque chamber pot under the sink (clearly a mini Banksy joke). I had the feeling that anyone who cleaned the room was given photographs or diagrams detailing to the millimeter exactly where everything was to be placed, down to the angle of the pillow on the seat of that ultimate emblem of British colonialism, the thronelike rattan fan chair. The hotel was taking no chances with theft; every item was detailed in an extensive inventory that we were required to sign and turn in at the beginning of our stay, along with a $1,000 credit card deposit to be refunded after a fifteen-minute room check before we checked out.

However, one artwork that cannot be purloined is the exterior of the hotel, which has to be Banksy's largest stenciled work. With the exception of the ancient stone buildings in and around the holy sites, architecture in the area is drab, utilitarian, and constructed of concrete blocks—with the only variations being the size of the blocks and, if you're lucky, some decorative iron work. The three-story hotel is no different, but at least is somewhat asymmetrical, with the entrance at the corner. Fortunately, there's nothing like a concrete wall to inspire a street artist, and Banksy has taken full advantage, using stencils and spray paint to transform the building into a Roman villa, complete with ornate *trompe-l'oeil* balustrades, pediments over the windows, columns next to the front door, and carved arches surrounding unused doors on the ground floor.

Missing no opportunity for architectural ornament, a structural pediment has been added to the roof from which flies what appears to be a shredded black flag. Potted palms and other plants on every balcony add a striking lushness, as do the gaily striped awnings that hang over the entrance and outdoor seating on the narrow veranda—a touch both decorative and ironic, as if the sunlight wasn't already blocked by the immense wall, reaching the hotel only twenty-five minutes a day.

It's likely that Banksy's interest in art hotels began when he was invited to paint a room in one of the first such ventures, the Carlton Arms Hotel just north of New York's East Village, where he stayed on and off for a couple of years in the 1990s. Facilitating its transformation from flophouse to guest house, artists were invited to decorate the Carlton's fifty-four rooms, staying at the hotel for free as they worked. Several of my friends at the time also created rooms for the hotel, which since its opening has hosted over two hundred artists. While Banksy's room has long been painted over, one of his works still exists in a corridor. And, of course, his invitations to the two other artists, Sami Musa and Dominique Pétrin, to create guest rooms for *The Walled Off Hotel* follows in this tradition.

Banksy:

My guide: You could paint here—there are no guards in the watchtowers, they do not come until the winter.

Me: (returning to the car after painting for twenty-five minutes) What's so funny?

Guide: (laughing hysterically) Of course the guards are in the watchtowers, they have snipers with the walkie-talkies.

Banksy was active in Palestine long before the *The Walled Off Hotel*, spurring an industry in the marketing of unofficial guided tours to view his works, as well as unauthorized souvenir items featuring his most well-known images, found at nearly every stand that sells tourist trinkets—to the point that the Palestinian Minister of Tourism has called him "half-Palestinian." His first foray into the Palestinian territories was in 2005 when he created nine paintings on the wall, including one of his most famous, the silhouetted little girl in a dress being lifted over the barrier by a cluster of balloons. In a video from an unknown source, Banksy can be seen on a long ladder painting the girl in broad daylight, helped by a couple of assistants and a man with a rifle standing by. Banksy's early efforts inspired both local and international street artists to leave their own marks, with the result that today the length of the wall as it cuts from Bethlehem to Jerusalem is almost completely covered with graffiti and murals. At the time he told the *Independent*: "If you like dancing you go on holiday to Ibiza, if you like walls you go to Palestine. The segregation wall is a disgrace. On the Israeli side it's all manicured lawns and SUVs, on the other side it's just dust and men looking for work. The possibility I find exciting is you could turn the world's most invasive and degrading structure into the world's longest gallery of free speech and bad art. And I like to think I can help with that bit."

In 2007 Banksy organized a project in Bethlehem called Santa's Ghetto. It was based on a series of pop-up or "squat art concept stores" of the same name featuring work by Banksy and his POW Gallery friends, which had opened in

London in 2002 and had run for several years in different venues at Christmas time. "I felt the spirit of Christmas was being lost," Banksy said of the London project. "It was becoming increasingly uncommercialised and more and more to do with religion, so we decided to open our own shop and sell pointless stuff you didn't need." Described as a "festive extravaganza of cheap art and related novelty goods from lowbrow artists and trained vandals," the stores' object was to make art available at reasonable prices for those who couldn't otherwise afford it.

For the Bethlehem iteration of Santa's Ghetto, local supporters worked into the night to transform a dilapidated former chicken restaurant in Manger Square, the town's central plaza, into a rustic three-story gallery. There, for one month during Bethlehem's bustling Christmas season, more than twenty-five artists from Palestine, England, Spain, Italy, and the United States offered paintings and sculptures for sale and created images on the barrier wall, with the intention of helping revitalize tourism in the area. Of the eight works Banksy painted for the event, his most well-known are *Stop and Frisk*, a little girl patting down a soldier for weapons and, on a wall outside the Palestinian Heritage Center, what has become a symbol of the desire for peace in the area, a spread-winged dove with an olive branch in its beak wearing a bulletproof jacket and a target over its heart.

A statement on the now-disappeared Santa's Ghetto website said, "We would like to make it very clear Santa's Ghetto is not allied to ANY race, creed, religion, political organization or lobby group. As an organisation the only thing we'll say on behalf of our artists is that we don't speak on behalf of our artists. This show simply offers the ink-stained hand of friendship to ordinary people in an extraordinary situation. Every shekel made in the store will be used on local projects for children and young people. Not one cent will go to any political groups, governmental institutions or, in fact, any grown-ups at all." Emphasizing that tourists need not fear visiting the West Bank, Banksy wrote: "It would do good if more people came to see the situation here for themselves. . . . If it is safe enough for a bunch of sissy artists then it's safe enough for anyone." Within a few short weeks, the project claimed to have raised $1 million from art sales, which was donated to charities benefiting Palestinian children including, as one source reported, putting "40 kids from the area through university."

In February 2015, Banksy sneaked, allegedly through a smuggling tunnel, into an area that's decidedly not safe and where tourism is definitely not encouraged—the Gaza Strip, where 1.8 million people are hemmed into an area twenty-five miles long and five miles wide along the Mediterranean Sea, seventy-one miles across Israel from the West Bank. There, Banksy painted works on four slabs of rubble left standing after homes had been destroyed six months before by Israeli air strikes in a war between the Gaza's Islamist Hamas rulers and Israel. Israel was criticized for the large number of Palestinian civilian deaths during the conflict. Critics included its main ally, the United States, when over 2,100 Palestinians were killed during the fighting, most of them civilians and many of them children—compared to the deaths of 67 soldiers and 6 civilians on the Israeli side.

The Banksy image in Gaza most circulated by the news services depicted, in the middle of the destruction, a ten-foot-high painting of a fluffy white cat with a pink bow and sad eyes with, as its plaything, a ball of actual tangled rusted wire. Another features a theme Banksy has echoed many times since—children swinging from a guard tower as if it were an amusement park ride (similar to Ben Shahn's work *Liberation* from the end of World War II, where children are swinging from rope ladders around a pole in the midst of a bombed-out city). Accompanying the image on his website, Banksy wrote, "Gaza is often described as 'the world's largest open-air prison' because no one is allowed to enter or leave. But that seems a bit unfair to prisons—they don't have their electricity and drinking water cut off randomly almost every day." The third work, entitled *Bomb Damage*, painted on the padlocked door of a building, the rest of which was destroyed, depicted a crouching woman with her head in her hands, which a tweeter noted was clearly inspired by a sculpture of Niobe, a symbol of mourning in Greek mythology, whose children were killed out of spite; in her grief, she was turned into a rock that was constantly weeping.

Banksy documented his effort in Gaza with a 1:55 minute video on his website (since removed but posted by fans on YouTube), in which images of the devastation were paired with titles as if from a travel advertisement: "Make this the year YOU discover a new destination. . . . Welcome to Gaza. . . . Well away from the tourist track (access is via a network of illegal tunnels). . . . The locals like it so much they never leave (Because they're not allowed to). . . . Nestled in an exclusive setting (surrounded by a wall on three sides and a line of gun boats on

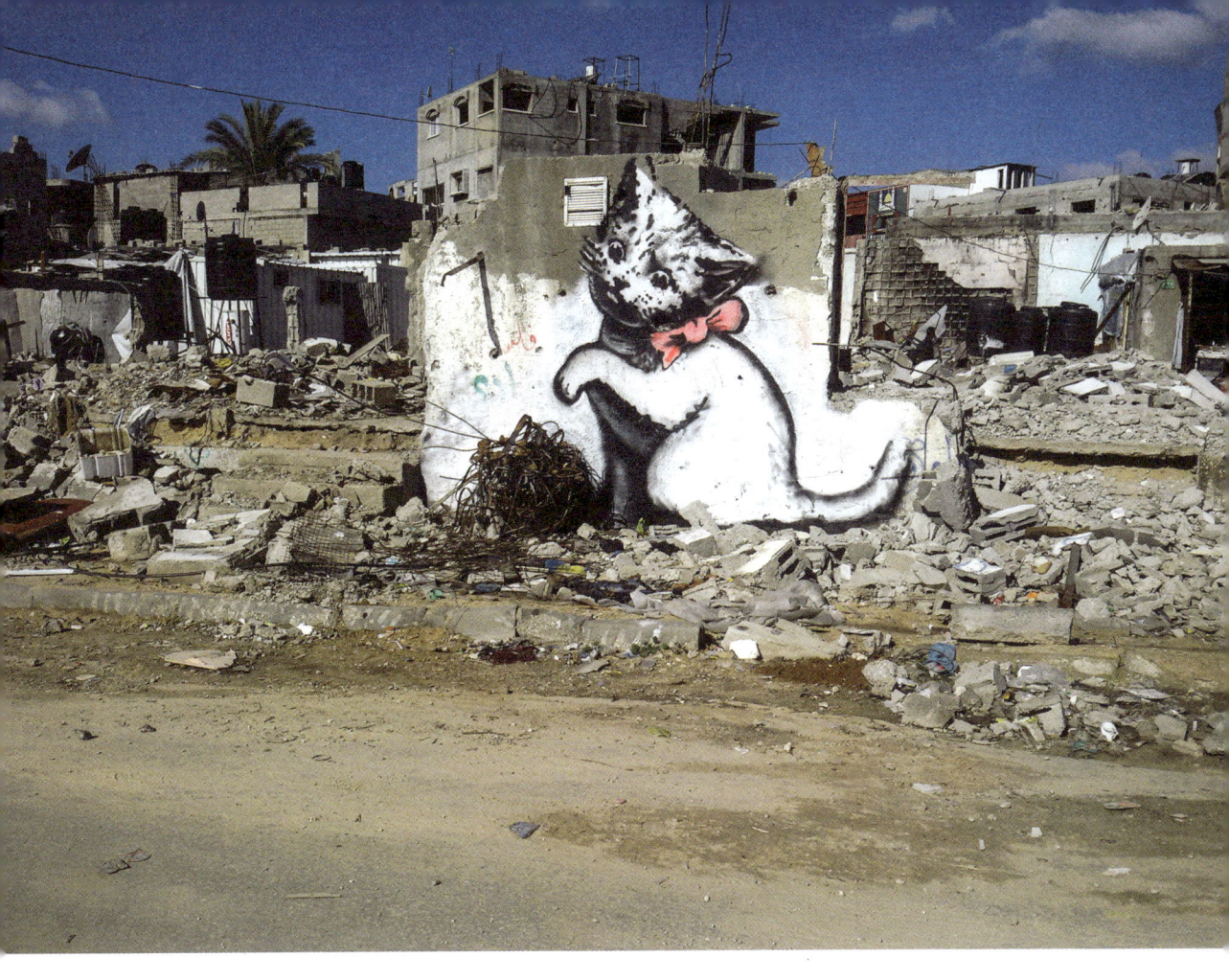

8.13
Banksy, (Gaza Kitty), Gaza, 2015, spray painting,
courtesy of Pest Control Office.

the other). . . . Watched over by friendly neighbors (in 2014 Operation Protective Edge destroyed 18,000 homes). . . . Development opportunities are everywhere (No cement has been allowed into Gaza since the bombing). . . . Plenty of scope for refurbishment." We hear a man say in Arabic, "This cat tells the whole world that she is missing joy in her life. What about our children?" The video ends with a shot of a wall with these words from social-justice educator Paulo Freire painted in red: "If we wash our hands of the conflict between the powerful and the powerless we side with the powerful—we don't remain neutral."

Only a concrete bathroom wall of the four-room house where Abu Shadi Shenbari had lived with sixteen other family members remained after Israeli forces flattened the neighborhood. In the *New York Times*, Shenbari said he watched Banksy create the image of the kitten in about forty minutes, along with a coil of metal the artist collected from the rubble. "Banksy asked us to protect his privacy, and we promised our loyalty," Shenbari said, adding that his children brought the artist tea and water while he worked. "He told us to let the people of Palestine know that his art is dedicated to them."

Referring to the painting of the cat, Banksy wrote on his website, "A local man came up and said 'Please—what does this mean?' I explained I wanted to highlight the destruction in Gaza by posting photos on my website—but on the internet people only look at pictures of kittens."

The image, in its innocence and simplicity, is confusing at first. Was Banksy shaming our internet habits? Or was it intended as a gift to the children of Gaza whose toys had been destroyed? Then, too, feral colonies of dispossessed cats are ubiquitous signs of life in devastated areas as they scavenge for food. Or it could refer to all of the above, as well as being an ingenious PR move—using a thoroughly incongruous and unthreatening image to get the conservative media to pay attention to a subject so controversial they'd do almost anything to avoid it.

As painter Wesley Kimler posted on Facebook:

This is the piece that changed my mind and made me take the artist known as Banksy seriously. Forget all the well-coiffed university-driven social practice virtue-signaling do-gooders showing in high-end galleries, hanging out with the billionaires. If you want political art, here's the man. The Gaza kitty works on so many levels simultaneously: it's cloying, insipid and ingratiating, out of place, and then bitter, laughing in anger at the increasingly stupid art world, while raging against tyranny and ultimately, because of the blown-up land it resides in, the ghosts of so many lost lives. Banksy transforms this Koonsian image into something Jeff Koons could never achieve—a generic figure that embodies great anguish and sorrow. It's everything a good painting should be, done just well enough to pull it off."

In 2005, Wisam Salsaa, eventual co-founder and manager of *The Walled Off Hotel*, was recommended by friends to be Banksy's guide. Salsaa was unemployed at the time due to the economic decline that had accompanied the completion of the wall, which had caused armed uprisings to rage across the occupied territories and made tourists too fearful to visit Bethlehem's holy sites. The two stayed in touch and developed a friendship, working together on the Santa's Ghetto venture. Salsaa became especially impressed with Banksy's commitment to the Palestinian people when the artist went to Gaza to paint in the war zone. "It's that act," Salsaa said in an interview with the Middle Eastern online magazine *The National*, "which proves that Banksy is not simply looking for kudos, or is even worried about alienating his fan base. When Banksy comes to Palestine he puts himself in danger, but what showed he's passionate and cares about it was when he went to Gaza." Salsaa added: "He went through tunnels, he went through Egypt—that was crazy. No artist—or anyone else—would put themselves in [that kind of] danger. Banksy is not a normal human being. He does not need more fans. He's making some people angry, but he doesn't care about that."

Salsaa had always dreamed of an enterprise that would bring attention to the Palestinians for something other than being terrorists or victims, and then in 2014, Banksy came up with the idea of the hotel. Salsaa found the location—a large building that had formerly housed a pottery workshop but was abandoned for fourteen years as the once-bustling street became more rundown, potholed, and a regular patrol site for Israeli soldiers. "The families had all left, because of the soldiers and the tear gas and bullets," Salsaa told *The National*. "It took me a long time to convince the owners to lease it to me." The location was ideal in that it was not only walking distance from the checkpoint, but easily spotted off the main road from Jerusalem. Also, it was classified as being in "Area C," one of the few parts of the West Bank under Israeli control where, at least theoretically, Israelis are allowed to visit. I say "theoretically" because while it's okay for Israelis to stay once they're there, getting there—to be authorized to enter the Palestinian territories at all—presents its own administrative and bureaucratic challenges.

While both he and his wife worked ten hours a day, Salsaa kept Banksy's involvement a secret throughout the gut renovation, positioning it as an ordinary guesthouse with a cheap-looking sign over the entrance that read: "Opening soon . . . Bethlehem Flowers Guest House." "We looked so stupid in front of everyone," Salsaa told *The National*. "No one expected me to do such a stupid guesthouse in such a stupid location." Salsaa said Banksy "thought of everything" related to the design. "I don't know how his mind works—he's a freak . . . he even told us how to put out the salt and pepper."

Toward the end of the renovation, after having selected the furnishings and sent them along with his artwork from the United Kingdom, Banksy stole into the hotel and continued to work there for several weeks, to the point that Salsaa said, "I called this hotel the Banksy prison. I used to sneak food in and trash out."

Dominique Pétrin, the Montreal-based artist who was invited to create one of the rooms, echoed Salsaa's characterization of the experience. After spending a month confined to her room, not allowed to see the rest of the hotel, she told CNN, laughing: "It's been pretty mental to be honest . . . a crazy journey just [being] locked in here." Like the *Dismaland* artists, Pétrin was skeptical of the invitation, admitting, "For a long time I thought it was a scam—until I got some money in my bank account." Knowing only that it was to be a hotel, but not the location or political context, Pétrin prepared as much as she could based on dimensions and pictures of the room and the one-line statement: "British colony on the verge of collapsing." After researching different elements of ornamental history, wallpaper, and architecture, which would be typical colonial decor elements, she said, "I made this room like a nice, lushy, colonial room but when you look at some details, you see something is really going wrong." When Pétrin was flown back to Bethlehem to see the completed hotel, she told Montreal's *Cult*, "it was mind-blowing to see that my work fit in the context. It was an amazing project, and it's giving me so much attention . . . a great reward after working so hard for so many years."

With his work complete, Banksy exited surreptitiously, leaving a team to finish in a marathon twenty-four hours before the opening and trusting Salsaa to be the spokesperson as the international press descended. In his statement to *The National*, Salsaa made it clear that he and his business partner are not anti-Israel but anti-occupation, saying, "When things get better here, when the occupation is over, Banksy will be the first one to do activities in Israel."

Speaking for himself, Salsaa explained, "Everything that I do here is something that I believe in. We are here to make our people stronger, to bring life to a dead area, to employ forty-five people, and to support forty-five families. We're educating tens of thousands of people around the world about Palestine, we're making the Palestinian voice heard, with no casualties. So many of our friends and kids have been killed to make people hear us. We're encouraging the creative resistance, the nonviolent resistance. We are making [things] much better for everyone, for the region and for Israel too. What matters is that Palestinians and Israelis learn how to respect each other."

Almost a year later, in an emailed interview, Banksy told the *Financial Times* that he undertook the hotel project for Salsaa, whom he characterized as his "fixer," saying, "The occupation was making him so fed up he was on the verge of leaving Palestine for a job washing dishes in Rotterdam. This is a man who has run several businesses, speaks five languages, employed half a dozen people, who is intelligent, brave and funny. I thought, it's vital people like him don't leave. . . . Plus I didn't want him coming to sleep on my couch."

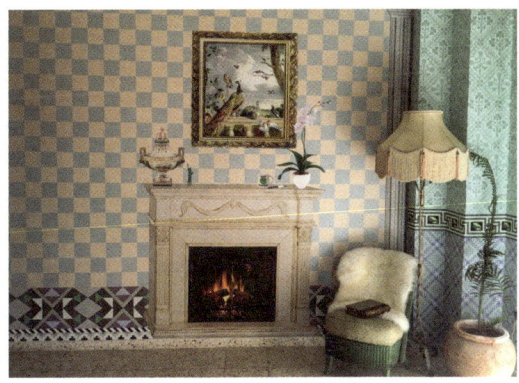

8.14
Guest room designed by Dominique Pétrin,
The Walled Off Hotel. Photo: author.

The Walled Off Hotel was originally billed as a "pop-up" with a commitment to run through the end of 2017, but now, a few years in, its success has turned it into Banksy's first long-term project. A magnet for tourists and a regular stop on many of the tours to Bethlehem's holy sites, the hotel brings work to tour guides, taxi drivers, shops, gas stations, restaurants, and—given that it has only eight guest rooms—other local hotels. Even more importantly, it has engendered new awareness of the political situation to those who formerly would have zipped in and out of Bethlehem on tour buses, which are rarely stopped at the border checkpoint. Along with seeing Banksy's work in the lobby/café, visitors are encouraged to view the Palestinian art gallery and, for a minimal fee (free to hotel guests), tour the three-room museum that tells the story of the wall.

The entrance to the museum is watched over by a Tussaud-like figure of British Foreign Secretary Arthur James Balfour, seated at a desk with his mechanical hand continuously signing the fateful 1917 letter expressing the British government's support for a Jewish homeland in Palestine. Sent to Britain's most illustrious Jewish citizen, Baron Lionel Walter Rothschild, the document, which became known as the Balfour Declaration, resulted in Britain's administration of Palestine—and the tension between the Israelis and Palestinians that continues to this day. The museum was curated in collaboration with Dr. Gavin Grindon from the University of Essex, who had created the Museum of Cruel Designs at *Dismaland*, and in true Banksy style, is hardly didactic. Instead, through local

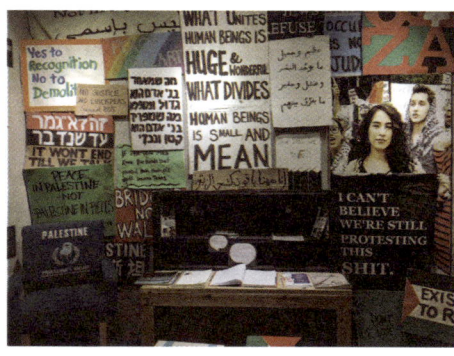

8.15
Museum wall, *The Walled Off Hotel*.
Photo: author.

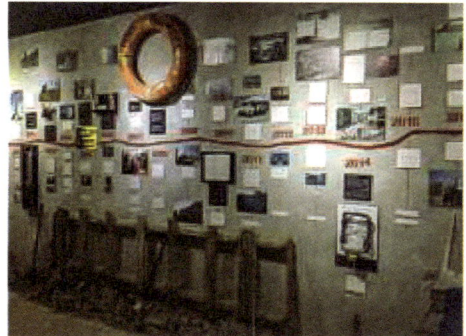

8.16
Museum wall, time line, *The Walled Off Hotel*. Photo: author.

stories, artifacts, and testimonies, including retired security cameras, remnants of bombed facilities, protest signs, and more, the museum provides a glimpse into the conflict from the emergence of nineteenth-century Zionism and the stirrings of Arab-Palestinian nationalism up to the modern-day threat that expanding Jewish West Bank settlements pose for a solution. Within the museum, a little cinema plays excerpts from the Oscar-nominated documentary *Five Broken Cameras* (2011; directed by Emad Burnat and Guy Davidi), with one of the actual bullet-damaged cameras on display. One alarming interactive feature is a constantly ringing telephone; when you pick up the receiver, a recorded male voice tells you that your house is about to be bombed and you have five minutes to get out. Masterful timing and Banksy's skewed humor sustain what would otherwise be an intolerable barrage of grim material, ending with a placard that reads, "Museums usually show things lost or far away, not things outside the window. But this museum remembers the wall for the day when it is no longer there."

Naturally, the museum's exit is through the gift shop, which is actually a closet-size bookstore claiming to contain every book written about the wall, including those by Angela Davis and Noam Chomsky. As guests, we were encouraged to borrow books overnight by the women who tended the shop, who told me they had read almost all of them.

Like dutiful tourists, we visited Bethlehem's holy sites and went with a friend on Sunday to mass, conducted in French and Arabic and attended by local families, at the Church of the Nativity. I'm not Catholic—far from it, a Quaker—but moved by the music and the hope such rituals convey, my inchoate emotions finally came to the surface and I was grateful to have that ceremonial space in which to process all I was seeing—and feeling—as in only a few short days, I had developed an affection for the people I'd met. It may sound corny, but I have never known people so full of heart. The Palestinians' warmth and generosity, especially under such straitened circumstances, was profound, as was their appreciation of our interest in coming to see how they were living.

The previous day had taken us to the Aida refugee camp on one of the twice-daily walking tours offered by the hotel. Our guide led us on the road along the graffitied wall, stepping over rubble from the crumbling sidewalks, occasionally mixed with spent rubber bullets and tear gas canisters, through a desolate cemetery to the camp's entrance. When I thought of a refugee camp, I had pictured a temporary site, perhaps filled with tents, but this was decidedly urban,

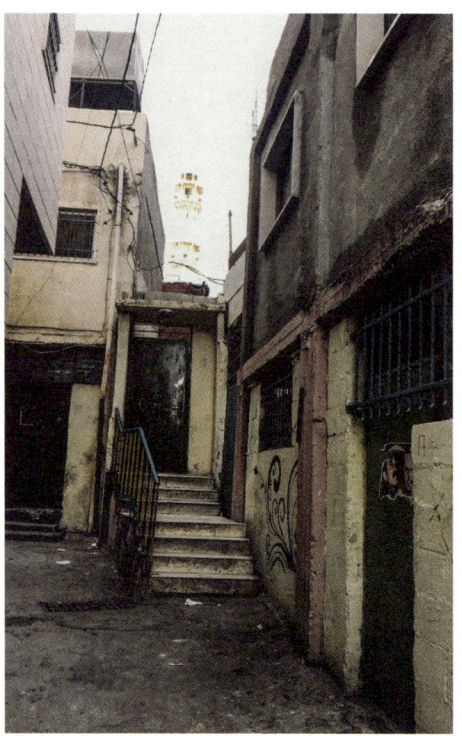

8.17

Entrance to Aida refugee camp, West Bank.
Photo: author.

8.18

A street in the Aida Refugee Camp.
Photo: author.

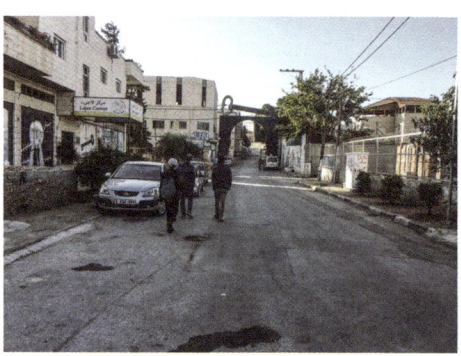

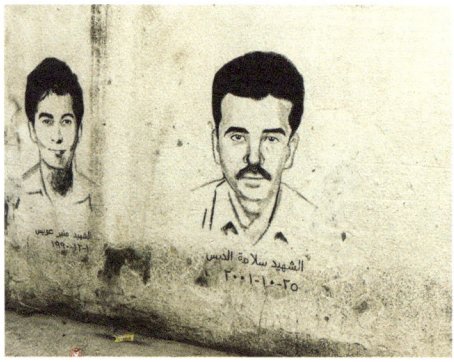

8.19

Memorial portraits on a wall in the Aida
refugee camp, West Bank. Photo: author.

8.20

Memorial to children killed by Israeli
attack in 2014, Aida refugee camp,
West Bank. Photo: author.

crowded with buildings multiple stories high, where some families have lived since the camp was established in 1950. I'd also assumed refugees were those uprooted from other countries, whereas here most have come from villages around Jerusalem and Hebron, just a few miles away. The massive iron key atop the keyhole-shaped arch at the camp's entrance, said to be "the largest key in the world" and certainly the heaviest, at two tons, symbolizes the camp residents' "right to return," as supported by international law, to the homes from which they were driven after the establishment of Israel as the sovereign homeland of the Jewish people—homes, no doubt long bulldozed, but to which they still hold keys. I'd been concerned that I would feel uncomfortable on the three-hour tour, perhaps seen as an "occupation tourist," a privileged person viewing the tragedy of others as some kind of spectacle. As it turned out, however, it was just the two of us, along with a young Japanese woman who spoke little English. Led by Anas Abu Srour, the director of the camp's youth center who took over as our guide, our visit felt surprisingly personal and our interest warmly received.

Beyond the gate were cinderblock buildings housing over six thousand people, half of them children, densely packed along narrow streets and alleyways into just 0.71 square kilometers (175 acres). With so many people cut off by the wall from the Israeli job market, unemployment is at 43 percent and the poverty level is high. Services such as water and electricity are erratic, medical facilities scarce, and inhabitants are subject to regular Israeli military raids to the point that constant tear gas exposure constitutes a major long-term health hazard.

One of the first things we saw upon entering the camp was a poster of a thirteen-year-old boy who had been shot and killed on his way home from school, and Srour recalled how as a child, before starting to play, he and his friends would figure out a place to hide in case they were subjected to a tear gas attack. Here in the Aida camp, "street art" consists of numerous painted portrait memorials to those lost—one was of Srour's neighbor, a father of eight, who was shot while standing at his window having his morning coffee. Another wall is dedicated to the names of hundreds of children killed in Gaza during the Israeli bombardment of 2014. The school has windows blocked out with concrete, its walls are marked with bullet holes, and the entire area is surveilled by the six military watchtowers that overlook the camp. Yet, despite all this, life goes on in that weird persistent way life does, with neighbors yelling greetings, parents pushing infants in strollers, children playing, and commerce taking place in the meager shops.

We ended up where we began, at the youth center near the key-arched entrance. Srour showed us around the center and described its programs, always circumscribed by a lack of funds. One program is a ten-day summer camp, supported by *The Walled Off Hotel* in recent years, which provides activities for 120 children aged six to fifteen, including field trips to nearby Hebron and Ramallah—the first time outside the area for many of the children, and even for some of the volunteer instructors. Srour explained that the camp doesn't have the kinds of problems usually associated with teenagers in poverty-stricken areas, such as gangs, drugs, and delinquency—also true of Bethlehem as a whole, which has a very low crime rate and minimal Palestinian police presence. As Srour was speaking, I realized that, except for the ominous atmosphere created by the military towers with their blacked-out windows, I have never felt as comfortable and safe traveling anywhere as I did in Bethlehem, and would not hesitate to visit there alone, the only danger on the streets being the insanely speedy motorists and lack of crosswalks—at least those acknowledged by drivers—along with sidewalks that have deteriorated to almost nothing. You see neither beggars nor homelessness; it seems everyone is taking care of everyone else.

Srour took us up treacherous uneven steps, slippery with rubble, to the open flat roof of the youth center. From there he pointed out a factory that had to be abandoned because it couldn't ship products out. We looked down on a jumble of gray buildings topped with water tanks, wires, tangles of metal, satellite dishes, hanging laundry, greenhouses, raised rooftop beds, and the thin white minaret of the mosque, all crowded up against the winding thirty-foot-high concrete wall that edges the camp, making for a sudden, shocking contrast with the open space and neat rows of symmetrical red roofs of the Jewish settlement on the other side.

In the youth center's gift shop, which sells local crafts as well as unauthorized Banksy souvenirs, there was a display of antique garments decorated with distinctive Palestinian embroidery, and I realized that I owned such a silk robe. It was handed down from my great-aunt Elma, whose Quaker father took her on a Grand Tour to Egypt and the Holy Land following her graduation from Swarthmore College in 1906. I knew about their trip from family photos, but didn't realize until now how extraordinary that was, first for a female to be given such a trip—then a tradition for college-educated males—and second, to a destination outside the usual comfortable European circuit. The random connection, the knowledge that I owned a piece of Palestinian history and that Aunt Elma had been in this very spot, reinforced my attachment to the place.

That night after dinner, we returned to *The Walled Off Hotel* and a surprising sight—a football match being projected on two panels of the wall that are apparently kept clear of graffiti especially for that purpose, with hotel guests and neighbors gathered on the veranda cheering the Spanish teams. The incongruity of this tool of oppression being repurposed for entertainment boggled my mind. It felt symbolic; the projection made the wall appear transparent, filling it with light, movement, and life, as if it had disappeared.

Banksy:

Old Man: You paint the wall, you make it beautiful.

Me: Thanks.

Old Man: We don't want it beautiful. We hate the wall. Go home.

Local opinions about the wall and Banksy's contributions are varied—is he profiting from the occupation or offering a form of resistance that contributes positively to the lives of Palestinians? For some, the hotel and the paintings on the wall are constant reminders that there's an international community standing with them. M., a trauma therapist, and her daughter, an art school graduate who teaches art to young children, friends of a Facebook friend, whom we visited in their comfortable Bethlehem home, see the hotel as a valuable artistic contribution and are glad for the economic boost Banksy brings to the area. However, B., a local internationally exhibited artist with whom we also spent time, is skeptical, to put it mildly, annoyed at having to walk past the cartoon-like facade of *The Walled Off Hotel* every day. He sees the hotel, along with the paintings on the barrier wall, as aestheticizing and simplifying the conflict—as well as framing it through European eyes. Originally he made paintings on the wall, but destroyed the last one the day the hotel opened. "The more we work on the wall," B. said, "the more it becomes the image of the place." I was interested to note that he didn't object to the wall being used to watch football because, as he said, "It doesn't simplify the message. Also, any pleasure you can get here, you should take." And while B. didn't mention it, I can imagine it might be irritating to have this drastic situation so strongly associated with a foreigner who, no matter how well-intentioned, isn't enduring what he is, and can freely come and go.

Local perception is also influenced by misunderstandings about Banksy. For instance, because not everyone knows that the hotel is Palestinian-owned and run, people assume Banksy is benefiting from their misfortune. Meanwhile, I'm thinking of how Damien Hirst recently decorated a Las Vegas hotel suite that rents for $200,000 a night, and that if Banksy really wanted to make money, the disadvantaged West Bank might not be the place to choose. Then there was the confusion created by Banksy's former dealer, Steve Lazarides, when he coordinated his unauthorized Banksy exhibition in Tel Aviv to coincide with the opening of *The Walled Off Hotel*, which made it look as if Banksy was playing both sides.

Wisam Salsaa sees the hotel as generally well-received, and believes that it's the best way to garner international attention. "It's about highlighting the wall and keeping it noticeable," Salsaa told the *Palestinian Monitor*. "[Before,] no one even mentioned the wall." Salsaa made a point of saying that the majority of people who come to the hotel are not politically motivated as much as they are art lovers and Banksy fans, which gives the hotel an opportunity to educate them about life under the occupation. "From here," he said, "they discover Palestine."

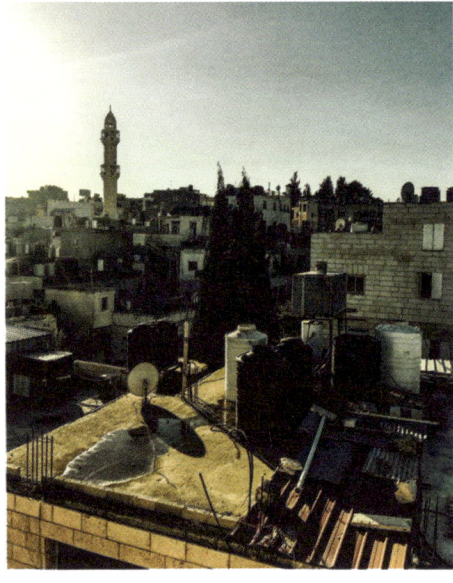

8.21
Rooftop view of the Aida refugee camp, West Bank. Photo: author.

Chapter 8

There's no way I can assess what the hotel means to the Palestinians—there are plenty, I'm sure, to whom it means nothing. I can speak only of what my stay there meant to me, which was a lot. I can't imagine what else could have motivated me to visit a region so conflicted and portrayed so negatively in the press. And even if I had been impelled to go there, I wouldn't have had the personal and informative encounter the hotel provides—nor would I now have this opportunity to share my experience here with so many others who, like me previously, may not be so aware of the situation. I can't say that my visit gave me hope for humanity—it didn't. Perhaps it gave me less hope. But it put me in touch with extraordinary people and provided insight into the ways art can be used toward greater understanding. It's here that Banksy's anonymity is especially powerful because the art is just the art, and doesn't get mixed up with gossip about his personal life or his politics. The artwork itself is similarly objective. If Banksy is despairing and angry at a particular person or group, he doesn't reveal it, but keeps his focus on a single inanimate object: the wall. His art doesn't show us conflict, but the detritus of conflict—life jackets, surveillance cameras, gas masks—that make a potent statement when placed in the context of privilege: the porcelain tea cups, crystal decanters, flocked wallpaper, and velvet drapes that indicate status and superiority. Banksy's message continues to be aspirational, holding out the possibility of a world not tainted by the insanity of adults and where, as symbolized by his painting of cherubs prying the wall apart, there are no separations.

Larry, an Australian executive leadership coach in his fifties, had come over from doing business in Tel Aviv just to spend a night at the hotel. Later, he wrote to me, "Beyond the comfort and security of the hotel, I was struck by the misery and ugliness of separation, the brutality of strength versus the weakness of oppression, the story that seemingly has no end, the short-sightedness, stupidity and perfidy of the British (again), and the young Israeli conscripts' apparent lack of both awareness of what they're doing and empathy for their fellow men and women. I'm telling friends that *The Walled Off Hotel* is surely the most important hotel in the world today."

Entering Israel at the Tel Aviv airport had been a breeze, aided by instructions from a friend not to mention Banksy. However, passing through the checkpoint leaving the Palestinian territories to return to Israel was dicier. We had purchased unlimited edition Banksy prints at the hotel (the only authorized Banksy

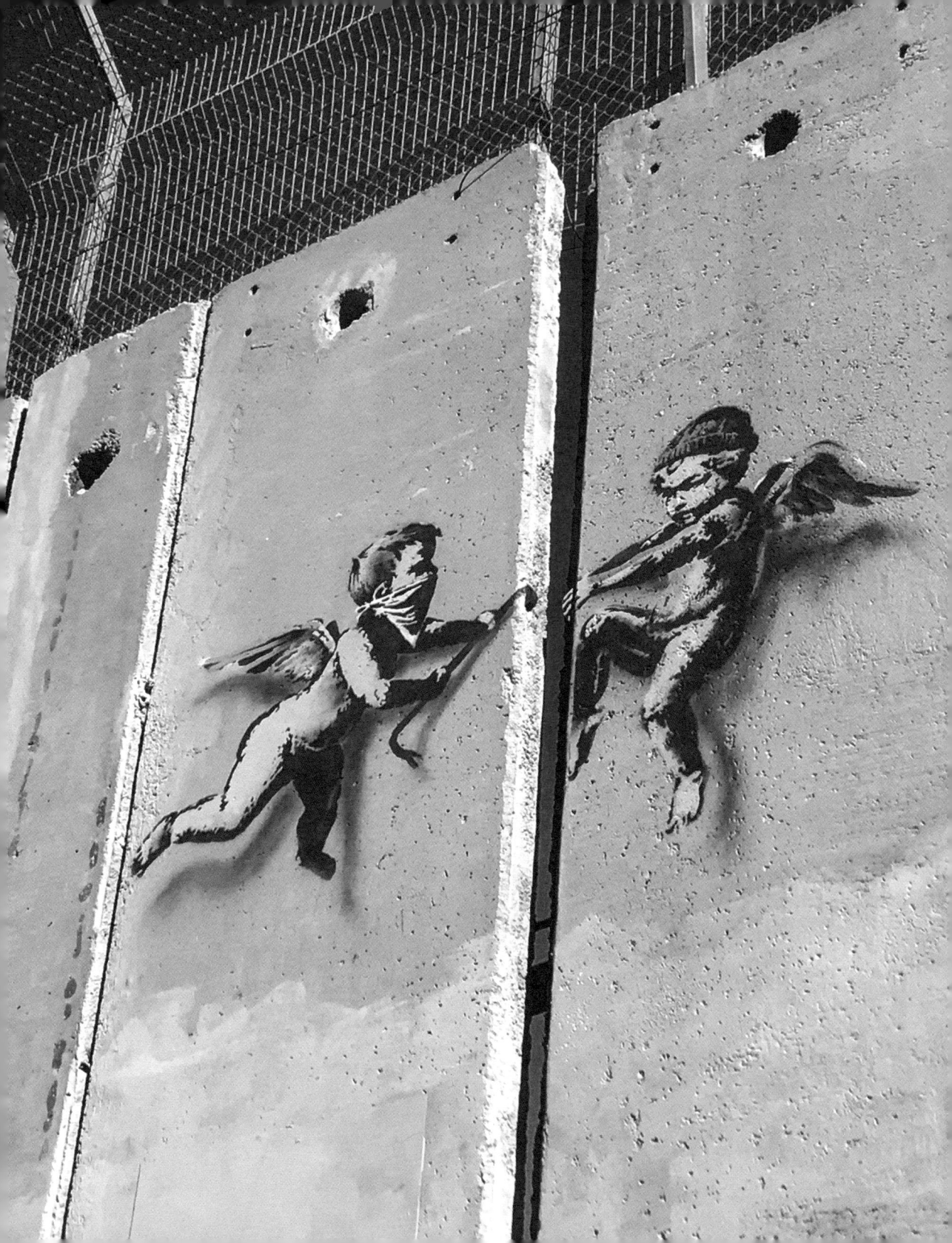

art available for sale anywhere in the world), and did not want our luggage searched, especially as the friend who advised us once nearly had his Banksys confiscated. I was also aware that they look carefully at anything unusual, and that our unconventional pairing could arouse suspicion—an older American woman traveling with a much younger British man all the way to the Middle East for just four days. So I dressed strategically. Wearing all black, a cross on a chain around my neck, I explained to the young woman at the checkpoint—who couldn't have been more than eighteen, spoke little English, and was surrounded by equally young men with giant guns slung over their backs—that I'd always wanted to visit the holy sites and, since his mother was my good friend, her son had agreed to accompany me. It worked. She nodded when I said "friend of his mother" and we sped through. Whew! What a relief. Finding the whole experience overwhelming and claustrophobic, I couldn't wait to get out.

But once I was out, I couldn't wait to go back.

8.22
Banksy, (Cherub Wall), 2017, spray painting, Bethlehem, courtesy of Pest Control Office.

Conclusion

It wasn't my plan to write a book about Banksy. What got me going was sheer annoyance with my art critic colleagues' lack of professionalism, publishing articles critiquing Banksy without doing their homework. They complain about the hegemony of the mega-galleries (like Gagosian, with, prepandemic, seventeen outlets in New York, London, Paris, Basel, Beverly Hills, San Francisco, Rome, Athens, Geneva, and Hong Kong), yet when an artist comes along who isn't part of that system, they neglect to do what they would otherwise consider basic research. Surely if they were writing about a Gagosian artist who, like Banksy, had made an Academy Award-nominated film, they would have taken the time to watch it (especially since it can be viewed for free on YouTube). They would also have considered it part of their job to check the posts on the artist's website, which in the case of Banksy's New York "residency" were an intrinsic part of the art, as well as become familiar with his book *Wall and Piece*. I was baffled by their failure to do so. Was it because it was street art? Or simply too popular with the public to be taken seriously? But then if Banksy is so inconsequential, why cover him at all? I never found an answer, while seeing the phenomenon repeated again and again, like the plethora of writers who panned *Dismaland* without having been there. (Perhaps for the next Whitney Biennial, I should propose to *Art in America* that I review it, and ask if it would be okay if I didn't go.) However, these critics' loss was my gain, as they say, because it prompted me to delve into the breadth of Banksy's output, and what started out as a diversion became an essay, then a lecture, and then . . . I couldn't stop.

9.1 *following pages*
Banksy, *Devolved Parliament*, oil on canvas, 2009,
courtesy of Pest Control Office.

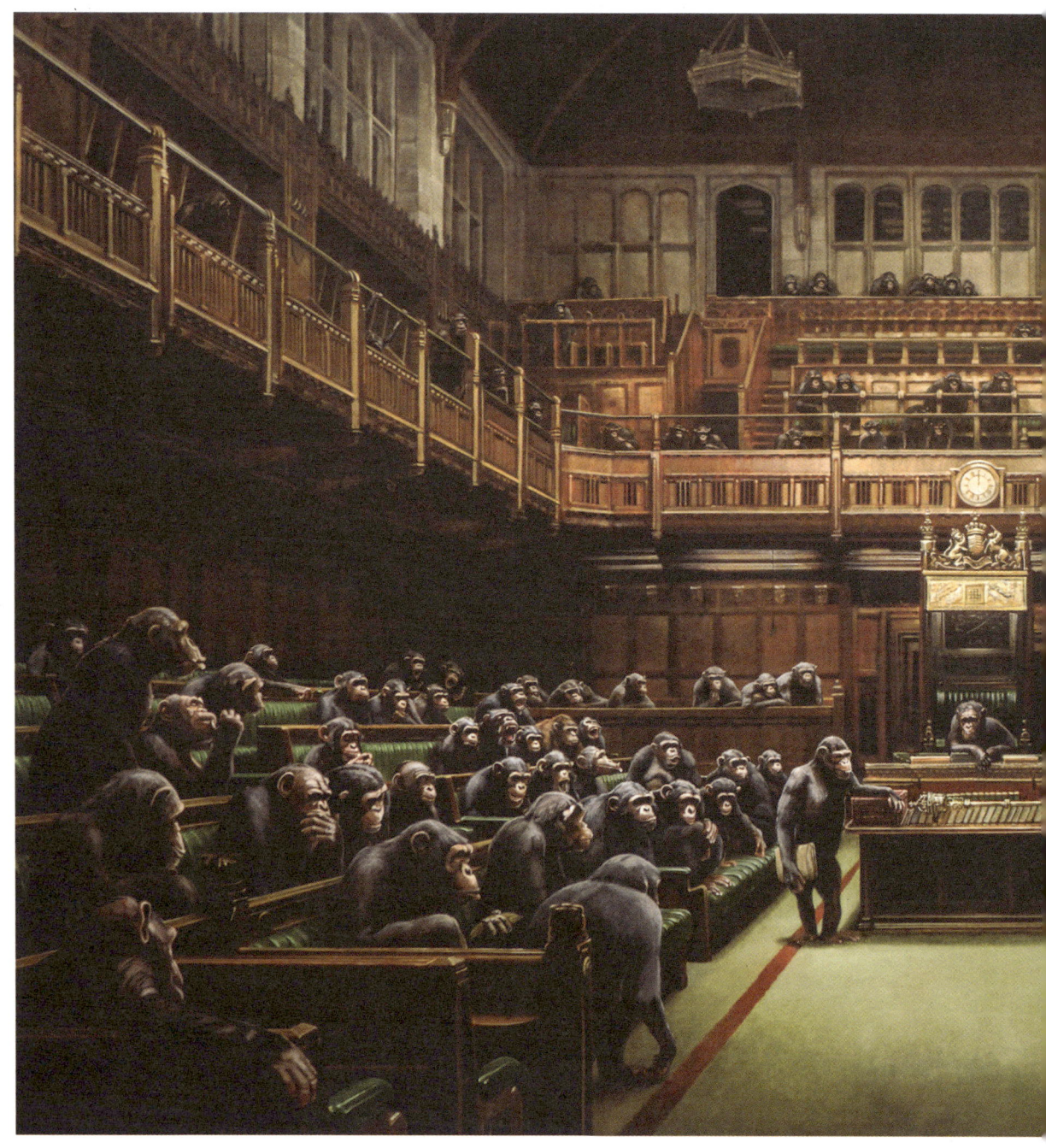

Conclusion

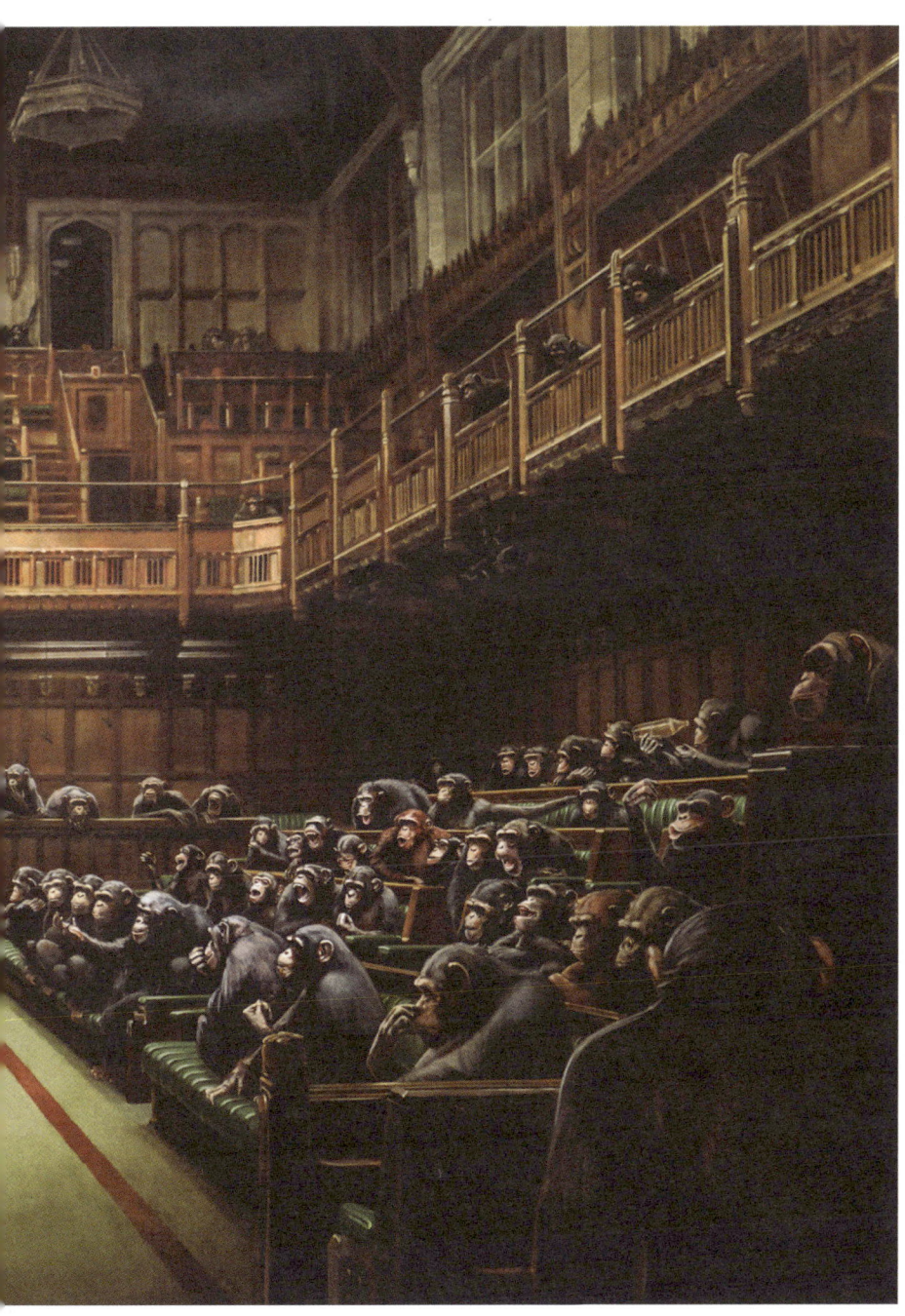

Conclusion

The clincher for me, the indication that there was more depth to his work than anyone had guessed, was Banksy's painting at Housing Works during his New York sojourn, the found landscape by an obscure artist onto which he'd inserted a Nazi officer seated on a bench. As discussed in chapter 1, Banksy's title, *The Banality of the Banality of Evil*, referenced the work of Holocaust escapee Hannah Arendt, whose theories about human nature had haunted me for years. In her book about the 1961 trial of Holocaust facilitator Adolf Eichmann, subtitled *A Report on the Banality of Evil*, Arendt posited that evil cannot just be blamed on monsters such as Hitler; the ordinary people who carry out their atrocities share the blame—like Eichmann, who insisted he never killed anyone but was simply in charge of efficiently running the trains that took the Jews to the death camps. Arendt's thesis is that such evil is not necessarily the result of belief or ideology, as we tend to assume. Instead, she portrayed it as a not abnormal human tendency that can be more circumstantial than intentional. Unconscionable deeds can be facilitated by the actions of otherwise ordinary people who are just following along and doing their jobs, while somehow justifying or otherwise disassociating themselves from the consequences: i.e., "Evil comes from a failure to think."

Today I'm reading about the New York City police who aggressively arrest people for minor crimes in the subway, such as a man they wrestled to the ground for peddling candy. To the cops who put an Ecuadoran mother of five in handcuffs for selling homemade pastries without a permit, Sarah Lustbader, writing for a criminal justice website, hypothetically asks, "Is this what you grew up dreaming you'd do someday? What is the point of your presence here? And who would be harmed if you simply walked away?"

I once had a conversation with a friend's daughter, a recent college graduate who had also read Hannah Arendt. She had just taken a job with a major mortgage company which, she discovered after she got there, was involved in nasty home foreclosures on poor people. She told me, to illustrate Arendt, "You wouldn't believe how nice the people are who work there and what terrible things they're doing." The reason this story has stayed with me is because, even though she made the connection, my lovely young friend continued to work for the mortgage company for another couple of years before going to law school—to specialize in public interest law. It's complicated.

Of course there are truly malevolent, demented people out there, no question. However, the possibility that much of the harm we see might not be deliberate but might instead be perpetrated by people who are acting due to unexamined self-interest, convenience, or perhaps simply the need to survive suggests to me—optimist that I am—that if they can be made aware of a better way, they just might take it. Banksy exposes our common, and often unintentional, complicity with the systems that reinforce society's inequities (like the art critics unconsciously supporting the status quo they probably really do resent), but avoids conflating them with personalities or political groups—no caricatures of Trump or Netanyahu here—which would encourage the taking of sides. Placing a kitten or Dumbo into a violent situation doesn't intensify the violence, but uses extreme contrast to dramatize its pointlessness and futility. In Israel and Palestine, Banksy focuses on an inanimate object—the barrier wall—because although the players who maintain it may come and go, as long as it exists, the wall continues to separate and oppress. Rather than get into a dispute that justifies or demonizes those who built it, it is the immorality of the wall's existence that impels Banksy's cherubs with crowbars to try to pry apart its panels.

Once I was hooked, Banksy kept my interest going. I became intrigued with how he has found notoriety through a practice of marketing where the first premise is not marketing—starting with his insistence on anonymity in an age of celebrity that pounces on the most minute details of a public person's life. Instead of endless press releases, advance promotion, and advertisements, we get surprise announcements and cryptic messages on Instagram, to the point it appears that the less Banksy communicates with the public, the more attention he receives. Indeed, Banksy is maintaining the ethos of street art while applying it to such ambitious endeavors as a five-week theme park or a hotel. Like graffiti, which appears on a wall without fanfare, his events pop up, and when their time is past, they pop down. And, as with street art, Banksy doesn't attempt to direct the outcome but leaves its reception to chance—or, as in the case of the hotel, to be managed by people other than himself. I marvel at how someone can be such a micromanager that they specify exactly how the salt and pepper shakers should be placed on the tables in *The Walled Off Hotel* café, yet leave town before the opening, trusting a partner with no previous experience to negotiate the onslaught of international press attention—as Wisam Salsaa did so successfully.

Which brings into the mix another aspect of graffiti: teamwork. Given that the work is illegal and often dangerous, graffitists have traditionally formed crews based on deep trust to look out for one another. I imagine the Banksy phenomenon to be one giant international crew with teams that come together to produce whatever project is at hand. More than any other well-known contemporary artist I can think of, Banksy continually arranges to bring attention to other artists, as with his Santa's Ghetto projects in London and Bethlehem, or his 2008 Cans Festival (featuring aerosol cans instead of Cannes) where he invited artists from all over the world to transform an abandoned Eurostar taxi tunnel, which turned into a huge media event. And then, of course, *Dismaland*, which was truly a collaborative effort involving fifty-eight other artists, where Banksy chose to feature artwork other than his own, down to putting artist James Joyce's unhinged smiley face on the cover of the program.

In fall 2019, Banksy made headlines with a painting sold at auction for a record £9.9 million ($12.1 million), almost five times the estimate. This is a canvas too big to shred: a thirteen-foot-long, classically rendered oil painting depicting a wood-paneled chamber in the House of Commons filled with debating MPs portrayed as chimpanzees. Although Banksy had nothing to do with the sale and certainly didn't profit from it, the timing of its exposure couldn't have been more apropos, at a moment when, more than ever, those in the governments of both the United States and United Kingdom appeared increasingly out of touch and distressingly comical. I'm guessing many would say that chimps would do a better job.

The painting is an update of Banksy's 2002 spray painting entitled *Laugh Now*, his first to feature chimpanzees. A nineteen-foot-long backdrop for a Brighton bar, it depicted a row of ten chimps wearing "see no evil" blindfolds and sporting sandwich boards with stenciled letters spelling out, "Laugh now, but one day we'll be in charge."

The newer painting of chimpanzees in Parliament, originally entitled *Question Time*, has an odd history. Made for Banksy's official exhibition at the Bristol Museum in 2009, it was sold in 2011, and then lent back by its anonymous owner for display in 2019 to mark the exhibition's ten-year anniversary—which happened to coincide with "Brexit Day," March 29, 2019, the date Britain was originally scheduled to leave the European Union. However, when the painting went back on exhibition, certain elements had been changed and it even had a new name: *Devolved Parliament*. With the permission of the owner (according to Sotheby's), Banksy had painted out the bright chandeliers, which caused the painting's mood to "devolve" into one even darker and gloomier; in a further indication of uncharacteristic pessimism, a banana held by one of the chimps, which once turned up, was now pointing down. On Instagram, Banksy announced its reexhibition with the statement, "Laugh now, but one day no-one will be in charge."

Since the rise of Boris Johnson and Donald Trump, many of us have felt that time has already come—that the structures we've relied on have fallen away (or were never really there in the first place) and the adults have left the room. But perhaps that's a good thing, an opportunity for the old hierarchical models to be replaced with those more democratic, humanitarian, and not identified with particular individuals, as they were in the past. We've seen the rumblings, from the loosely networked, decentralized, grassroots movements of Occupy Wall Street and Extinction Rebellion, as well as those behind Bernie Sanders' presidential campaign ("Not me. Us.") in the United States and the massive, worldwide "Black Lives Matter" outpouring, at once focused and decentralized. In this atmosphere, it's no wonder that the most significant artist of our time is amorphous, nameless, and not aligned with a specific ideology but exhibits a strong sense of inclusivity and humanism that crosses political and cultural boundaries—one whose work urges us not to be facilitators of the status quo, but rather to become agents of change.

The conclusion is that there is no conclusion. The questions Banksy has raised over the last twenty or so years about the uses of public and private property, the role of the global "corporatocracy," governmental incursions into privacy, the never-ending wars, and the gap between artworks as luxury goods and as vehicles of social expression will continue to gain currency. Banksy has found his way to address these issues and now we must find ours.

What happens next is up to us.

Banksy: It takes a lot of guts to stand up anonymously in a western democracy for things no one else believes in—like peace, justice, and freedom.

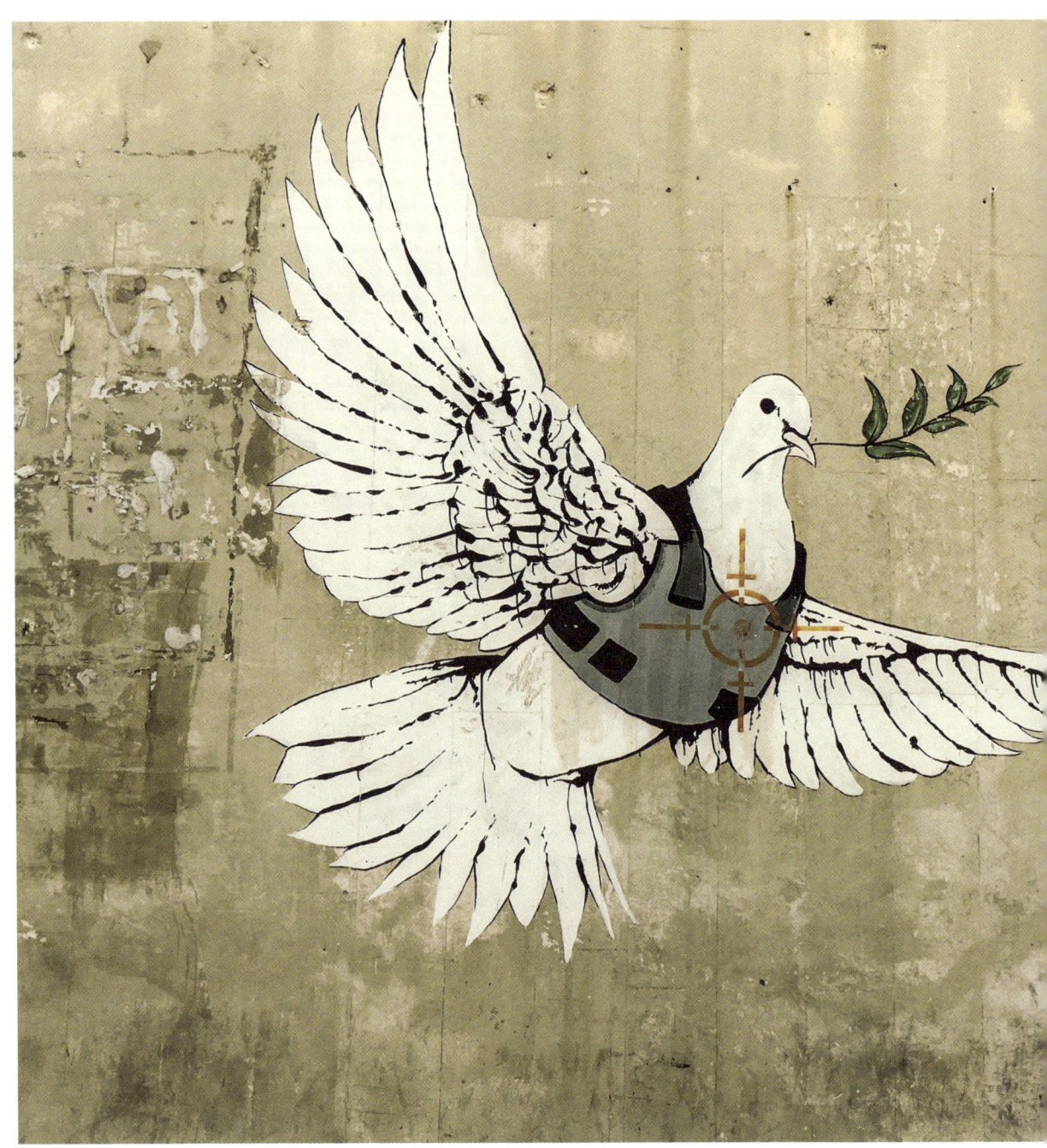

Conclusion

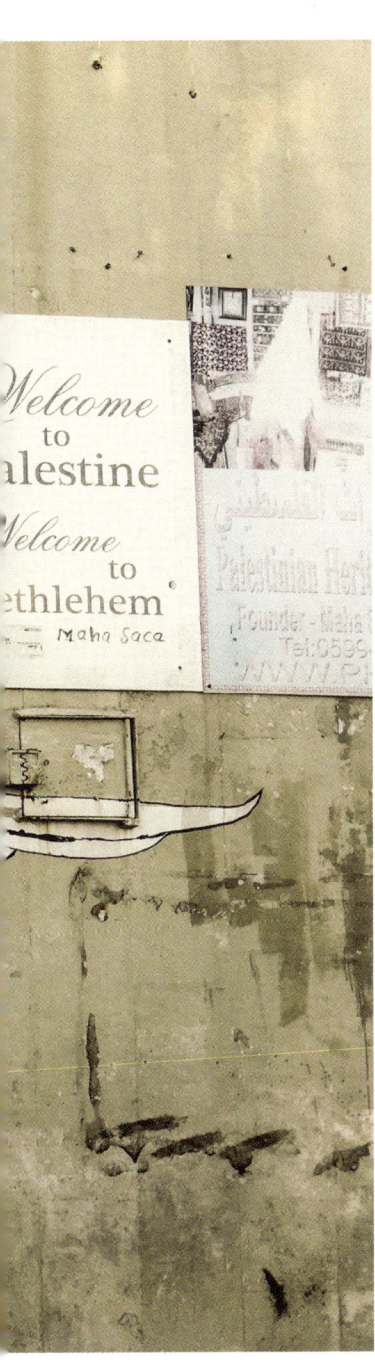

9.2
Banksy, *Armored Dove of Peace*, 2007,
Bethlehem. Photo: author.

Acknowledgments

I am grateful to those who have contributed their talents and funding beyond anything I could have imagined to bring this book to life—starting with Christopher Sweet, who connected the book with the perfect publisher and whose steadfast belief in the project has kept me energetically afloat; Alex Ross, an artist with an inspired literary eye who helped me shape it; Terry Perk, sounding board and frequent collaborator, whose conversations over the years led to the perceptions about art that propelled me to write about Banksy; Lucy Holland, all-around ally and chief cheerleader; John Spiak at the Grand Central Art Center in Santa Ana, California, who gave me a place to work before I knew what the project was and arranged for the first lecture at CSU/Fullerton; the remarkable individuals who spontaneously offered to fund my trip to the Middle East as well as others who have supported the work in so many ways: Caren Bayer, Eric Brenner, Lucie Castaldo, Jack Curletti, Deedee Diehl, Carrie Grossman, Margaret Heilbrun, Linda Hirshman, Arthur Hochstein, Carroll Janis, Susan Jennings, Tej Kaur Khalsa, Christine LaPorte, Barry Mayo, Eileen Mooney, Christopher Natrop, Paul Rapp, Susan Sultan, Jim Torok, and Chris Watford. And love to my sons, Matt and Adam Diehl, their wonderful spouses, Michelle Nishikawa and Molly Maiers Diehl, and my grandsons Aki and Alex.

Special gratitude to Mike Berthet, Lacy Davisson, Nancy K. Kalodner, Ericka Elaine Schiche, Charles Schulze, and the rest of the 185 backers of my Kickstarter fundraiser. The campaign succeeded because Seth Jordan and Wesley Kimler each took on the Kickstarter project as his own, along with Erica Spizz's videography and Jackson Whalen's music in the video.

And, of course, my biggest thanks to Banksy, whose depth of substance sustained my curiosity and made writing about him/her/them fun to the very end.

References

Where not otherwise cited, quotations from Banksy have come from his website (banksy.co.uk), his Instagram postings (@Banksy), and material from Pest Control Office from its website (pestcontroloffice.com).

Introduction

"The poet produces poems . . .": quoted in Dave Simpson, "Crowds, Vandals, Chaos: What Happens When Banksy Sprays Your Wall?," *Guardian*, January 18, 2019.

"vandalized warehouse extravaganza": Peter Bowes, "'Guerrilla Artist' Banksy Hits LA," *BBC News*, September 14, 2006.

"world's first street art disaster movie": Kenneth Turan, "Movie Review: 'Exit Through the Gift Shop,'" *Los Angeles Times*, April 16, 2010.

"Britain's newest national treasure": Peter Bradshaw, "Exit Through the Gift Shop," *Guardian*, March 4, 2010.

"family theme park unsuitable for children": Alice Canter, "Banksy's Dismaland: 'A Theme Park Unsuitable for Children'—in Pictures," *Guardian*, August 20, 2015.

"There are people out there pushing these artists like IPOs . . .": quoted in Katya Kazakina, "Art Flippers Chase Fresh Stars as Murillo's Doodles Soar," *Bloomberg*, February 6, 2014.

"national treasure": Mark Hudson, "Banksy, Dismaland, Weston-super-Mare, Review: 'Gleeful, Adolescent, Despair,'" *Telegraph*, August 21, 2015.

"He uses art as a weapon . . .": Rachel Campbell Johnston, quoted in Lizzie Crocker, "Why Banksy's Art Is Such a Deadly Political Weapon," *Daily Beast*, April 13, 2017.

"Banksy should have been put down at birth": quoted in Tom Brookes-Pollock, "Brian Sewell's 9 Most Withering Put-Downs," *Independent*, September 19, 2015.

"puerile and idiotic": Matthew Collings, "Banksy's Ideas Have the Value of a Joke," London *Times*, January 28, 2008.

"he appeals to people who hate the Turner Prize": Jonathan Jones, "Best of British?," *Guardian*, July 5, 2007.

"ostentatious": Roberta Smith, "Cascades, Sing the City Euphoric," *New York Times*, June 27, 2008.

"We can't do anything to change the world . . .": Banksy, *Wall and Piece* (London: Century/Random House, 2006), 204.

"are scarcely recognizable as the products of creative activity": Harriet and Sidney Janis, "Marcel Duchamp: Anti-Artist," *View*, 1945.

"Mr. Duchamp said it was okay": Carroll Janis, interview with the author, ca. 1984.

"create their own expression, which comes from the inside, not the outside . . .": quoted in Carol Diehl, "Sidney Janis Goes Graffiti," *Art & Antiques*, September 1984.

"GET BANKSY!": *New York Post*, October 17, 2013.

compared Banksy to eighteenth-century political satirist William Hogarth: Deborah Solomon, "Art Talk: Graffiti—Virtuosity or Vandalism," *New York Times*, October 25, 2013.

1 Banksy: Completed

"People like Banksy because other people have liked Banksy . . .": Jerry Saltz, "Jerry Saltz on Graffiti Artists, Banksy, and Al Jazeera Fear," *Vulture*, October 24, 2013.

"But what of these works as art?": Roberta Smith, "Mystery Man, Painting the Town," *New York Times*, October 30, 2013.

"the subject of a big-time documentary film": Jerry Saltz, "Banksy Is in Town, and He Could Make You Rich, Rich, Rich," *New York*, October 16, 2013.

"a complete clown": Cited in Ciar Byrne, "The Big Question: Just Who Is Banksy and What Is All the Fuss about His Work?," *Independent*, November 2007.

"should be like a net to catch a fish . . .": John Cage, quoted in Richard Kostelanetz, *Conversing with Cage* (New York: Routledge, 1966), 119.

"Another day, another Banksy . . .": Saltz, "Jerry Saltz on Graffiti Artists."

"You are in Midtown Manhattan . . .": YouTube audio, "Banksy 'You Complete Me,' New York City Audio Guide," *StreetArtNews*, October 3, 2013.

"Graffiti is a sign of decay . . .": Mara Gay, "The Daily Politics," *New York Daily News*, October 16, 2013.

"GET BANKSY!": *New York Post*, October 17, 2013.

"dirty and disheveled stranger . . .": Banksy, *Wall and Piece* (London: Century/Random House, 2006), 54.

"If one wishes to deceive the man . . .": Jacques Lacan, *The Four Fundamental Concepts of Psychoanalysis*, trans. Alan Sheridan (New York: Norton, 1978), 112.

"Adept at creating and unmasking deceit . . .": Lewis Hyde, *Trickster Makes This World: Mischief, Myth, and Art* (New York: Farrar, Straus & Giroux, 1998), 17, 10, 13, 265.

"What you see before you is a sculpture entitled *Shoe Shine*": YouTube audio, "Banksy, 'McDonalds' New Installation for Better Out Than In"—Audio Guide #7, *StreetArtNews*, October 16, 2013.

"theoretical reckoning . . .": Raillan Brooks, "Banksy Taking in the View in Gramercy," *Village Voice* (blog), October 31, 2013.

"terribly and terrifyingly normal": Hannah Arendt, *Eichmann in Jerusalem: A Report on the Banality of Evil* (New York: Viking, 1963), 276.

"The greatest crimes in the world are not committed . . .": Banksy, *Wall and Piece* (London: Century, 2005), 51.

"failure to think": Amos Elon, introduction to Hannah Arendt, *Eichmann in Jerusalem: A Report on the Banality of Evil* (New York: Viking, 1963), xiv.

"Banksy's art is conventional political realism . . .": Jerry Saltz, "Watch Jerry Saltz Hold an Impromptu Art Class at Banksy's Latest," *Vulture*, October 31, 2013.

"cash for credibility"; "It's a bit weird . . .": Patrick Potter and Gary Shove, *Banksy: You Are an Acceptable Level of Threat and If You Were Not You Would Know about It* (UK: Carpet Bombing Culture, 2012), n.p.

"anarchy-lite": Jerry Saltz, "Banksy Is in Town and He Could Make You Rich, Rich, Rich," *New York*, October 16, 2013.

"another crap advert": Banksy, *Wall and Piece* (2006), 125.

"It's unclear what this is supposed to mean": Raillan Brooks, "The Banksy Diaries: Relive All 31 Days of His New York Takeover," *Village Voice* (The Voice Archives), October 9, 2018.

"Commenters believe the clip . . .": Liam O'Brien, "Dumbo Gunned Down in Banksy's New Rebel Rocket Attack Video," *Independent*, October 8, 2013.

"There's some speculation that the video is a reference . . .": Julie Zeveloff, "Rebels Shoot a Flying Cartoon in Banksy's Latest Work," *Business Insider*, October 7, 2013.

"The clip has been criticised online . . .": Martin Zavan, "'Banksy Parodies' Syrian Rebel Videos," *9News.com.au*, October 8, 2013.

"The video has been received poorly by Syria-watchers . . .": Max Fisher, "The Awkward Politics of Banksy's Satirical Syria Video," *Washington Post*, October 7, 2013.

"Many close observers of the conflict in Syria . . .": Robert Mackey, "Banksy Parodies Syrian Rebel Videos," *New York Times* (*The Lede* blog), October 7, 2013.

"It's a view of war from the eyes of the child": https://www.reddit.com/r/videos/comments/1nui1v/banksy_made_an_interesting_clip/ccm9xme/.

"None of that is related to art . . .": quoted in Mackey, "Banksy Parodies Syrian Rebel Videos."

"When the time comes to leave . . .": Banksy, *Wall and Piece* (2006), 79.

"Well, this is the last day of the show . . .": Hrag Vartanian, "Last NYC Banksy Is Full of Hot Air, Cops Arrest Potential Thieves," *Hyperallergic.com*, October 31, 2013.

"And that's it. Thanks for your patience. It's been fun. Save 5pointz. Bye": quoted in Brooks, "The Banksy Diaries."

2 Banksy in Folkestone

"rich cultural history and built environment . . .": http://research.uca.ac.uk/1842/.

"criminal damage": Roisin O'Connor, "Banksy Art in Folkestone Vandalised by Graffiti," *Independent*, October 13, 2014.

"What are you all doing drinking in here . . .": Diane Dever, interview with the author, October 2016.

"It's being sold because the Goddens . . .": quoted in Matt Leclerc, "Folkestone Banksy, Art Buff, Removed from Payers Park and Sold amid Protests," *KentOnline*, November 1, 2014.

"People flocked to it . . .": Diane Dever, interview with the author, October 2016.

"be connected to Folkestone . . .": Martin Spring, "Folkestone, Mon Amour," *Building*, September 20, 2007.

"I've lived all over the world . . .": Andi Elliot, interview with the author, October 2016.

"living soap opera": "A Life Full of Ambition and Drama," https://www.highbeam.com/doc/1P2-31141931.html.

"the end of an era": http://www.warrenpress.net/FolkestoneThenNow/The_Demolition_of_The_Rotunda__Folkestone.html.

"Straight forward shrewd broker . . .": *KentOnline*, reprinted in *Joyland Books Forum*, March-April 2012.

"I do feel sorry for Jimmy Godden . . .": Paul Clarke, "Poor Jimmy Godden," Paul Clarke's blog, April 9, 2008.

The girl's parents' marriage broke down: David Sapsted, "Girl's Funfair Death Led to Her Father's Suicide," *Telegraph*, February 20, 2003.

"hurt him more than anyone will ever know": *KentOnline*, March 28, 2012.

"It was the opportunism that really got us . . .": Diane Dever, interview with the author, October 2016.

"keeping his name in the public eye": https://www.nationalartsprogram.org/news/big-interview-art-dealer-robin-barton-restoring-banksys-spy-booth-cheltenham-and-his-incredible.

"This show has got nothing to do with me . . .": quoted in Michael Kaplan, "Building Owners Are Making a Fortune from Banksy's Art," *New York Post*, April 15, 2018.

"a signed confession on a letterhead": Rachel Corbett, "Keszler & Banksy, Pest Control Stymies Keszler Gallery Sales," *Artnet*, October 12, 2011.

"We have warned Mr. Keszler . . .": ibid.

"We do not know why Pest Control . . .": ibid.

"I would view that as grave-robbing": "Hacked Off: The Art Show That's Driving Banksy Up the Wall," Guy Adams, *Independent*, October 25, 2011.

"I work on handshakes only . . .": "Art Dealer: 'Mistake' to Auction Banksy Folkestone Mural," *BBC News/England/Kent*, January 25, 2016.

"no reasonable prospect of establishing . . .": Eileen Kinsella, "London Judge Orders $720,000 Banksy 'Art Buff' Mural Back to UK," *Artnet News*, September 11, 2015.

one of the first cases to consider the ownership of street art: Tim Maxwell, Becky Shaw, and Andrew Bruce, "Who Owns Street Art?," *Law Society Gazette*, September 21, 2015.

"People should fight to keep these works . . .": Hannah Ellis Peterson, "Banksy Artwork Set to Return to Folkestone after Lengthy Legal Battle," *Guardian*, September 11, 2015.

"massive high five": Kate Boyden, "The Rise and Fall of Folkestone's Banksy and Whether It Will Ever See the Light of Day Again," *Kent Live*, March 22, 2018.

"regeneration tiptoes into gentrification . . .": Matt Rowe, interview with the author, October 2016.

"a documentary of despair"; "in questionable taste at the very least . . .": Stephen Armstrong and Maruxa Ruiz del Árbol, "Why the Digging Has Never Stopped in England's Gold-Rush Town," *Guardian*, April 16, 2015.

"But at the same time, I struggle . . .": Matt Rowe, interview with the author, October 2016.

"empty plinth": https://www.bbc.com/news/uk-england-kent-29415116.

"It was dark . . .": Terry Perk, interview with the author, October 2016.

"We shouldn't install it . . .": ibid.

"solidified France's place at the center of the European Union . . .": Dan Bilefsky, "Banksy's View of 'Brexit'? It's in the Stars," *New York Times*, March 8, 2017.

"a little bit on the grotty side . . .": Kent on Sunday (North & West), *Kent News*, May 13, 2017.

"I told the minister how much it is loved . . .": Sam Lennon, "Arts Minister John Glen Asked by Dover MP Charlie Elphicke to Save Banksy Brexit Mural," *KentOnline*, July 20, 2017.

"as a matter of urgency": Sam Lennon, "Call by Charlie Elphicke MP to Dover District Council to Use Planning Powers to Save Banksy Mural," *KentOnline*, August 30, 2017.

3 The Case for Graffiti

"Stop thinking about art works as objects . . .": Brian Eno, *A Year with Swollen Appendices* (London: Faber & Faber, 1996).

"radical qualities art used to have . . .": Michael Kimmelman, "Biennial 2006: Short on Pretty, Long on Collaboration," *New York Times*, March 3, 2006.

"Art is not like other culture because its success . . .": Banksy, *Wall and Piece* (London: Century/ Random House, 2006), 170.

"GET BANKSY!": *New York Post*, October 17, 2013.

"a sign of decay and loss of control . . .": Michael Bloomberg, quoted in Mara Gay, "The Daily Politics," *New York Daily News*, October 16, 2013.

"The people who truly deface our neighborhoods . . .": Banksy, *Wall and Piece* (2006), 8.

"Brandalism . . .": Banksy, *Wall and Piece* (London: Century, 2005), 160.

"When people in power believe something firmly . . .": Noam Chomsky, lecture, Massachusetts Institute of Technology, Cambridge, MA, quoted in Patrice Milillo, "Graffiti and Street Art Can Be Controversial, but Can Also Be a Medium for Voices of Social Change, Protest, or Expressions of Community Desire. What, How, and Where Are Examples of Graffiti as a Positive Force in Communities?," *TheNatureofCities.com*, March 23, 2016.

"It is . . . telling that from 1972 to 1989, New York City spent . . .": Adam Mansbach, quoted in Milillo, "Graffiti and Street Art Can Be Controversial."

"Imagine a city where graffiti wasn't illegal . . .": Banksy, *Wall and Piece* (2006), 97.

"Graffiti that is sanctioned by authority . . .": Paul Downton, quoted in Milillo, "Graffiti and Street Art Can Be Controversial."

"needs the law so that it can function outside of it . . .": Lu Olivero, "Graffiti Is a Public Good, Even When It Challenges the Law," *New York Times*, July 11, 2014.

"When graffiti isn't criminal . . .": Keegan Hamilton, "Village Voice Exclusive: An Interview with Banksy, Street Art Cult Hero, International Man of Mystery," *Village Voice*, October 9, 2013.

"The more you can muddy the waters around the meaning of a work . . .": quoted in Andy Beckett, "A User's Guide to Artspeak," *Guardian*, January 27, 2013.

"This language has enforced a hermeticism of contemporary art": ibid.

"In contemporary art magazines . . .": Sven Lütticken, "Deconstructing Liam," *Texts and Other Projects* (blog), May 2009.

"living artists who did not yet have wide public exposure or critical acceptance": *Newmuseum. org* (History).

"Writing graffiti is about the most honest way . . .": quoted in Tristan Manco, *Stencil Graffiti* (London: Thames & Hudson, 2002).

4 Banksy and "Real Art," Part I

"If you think my graffiti is overrated, you'd be right . . .": Banksy, *Graffiti Wars* (television documentary), dir. Jane Preston, Channel 4, 2011.

"Banksy is no longer hot": Jonathan Jones, "Should Banksy Be Nominated for the Turner Prize?," *Guardian*, April 15, 2009.

"People are stupid . . .": Jonathan Jones, "Britain's Best-Loved Artwork Is a Banksy. That's Proof of Our Stupidity," *Guardian*, July 26, 2016.

"The world is full of vulgar purists . . .": John Ruskin, *The Stones of Venice* (London: Smith, Elder & Co., 1851–1853).

"is depicted as a simplified black shadow on the wall": Jones, "Britain's Best-Loved Artwork Is a Banksy."

"One anecdote he does tell about his origins is . . .": Jonathan Jones, "Best of British?," *Guardian*, July 5, 2007.

"Better the rudest work that tells a story . . .": John Ruskin, *The Seven Lamps of Architecture* (London: Smith, Elder & Co., 1849).

"Art that repels is didactic": Joseph Campbell, "The Way of Art," recorded lecture, Theater of the Open Eye, New York, December 1, 1990.

"The political content of Banksy's art is generally so accepted"; "This satire is in the tradition of Aesop's fables": Jonathan Jones, "Banksy Wanted Clacton-on-Sea to Confront Racism— Instead It Confronted Him," *Guardian*, October 2, 2014.

"It's not art unless it has the potential to be a disaster": Banksy, *Dismaland* poster, 2015.

5 Banksy and "Real Art," Part II

"To be an artist is not a matter of making paintings or objects at all . . .": Robert Irwin, *Notes Toward a Conditional Art* (Los Angeles: Getty Publications, 2017).

"the object existing not in a vacuum of its own meaning": Robert Irwin, quoted in Carol Diehl, "Doors of Perception," *Art in America*, December 1999.

"the turd in the plaza": ibid.

"monumental or ephemeral, aggressive or gentle"; "if you do it right, it makes perfect sense and looks as if it's been there forever": ibid.

"So when you walked into this thing . . .": ibid.

Lawrence Weschler's book about Irwin: Lawrence Weschler, *Seeing Is Forgetting the Name of the Thing One Sees: A Life of Contemporary Artist Robert Irwin* (Berkeley: University of California Press, 1982).

"the most famous piece of immersive art in the world": Will Gompertz, "Olafur Eliasson: Will Gompertz Reviews the Danish-Icelandic Artist's Show at Tate Modern," *BBC News*, July 13, 2019.

"The time after a show is just as interesting to me": quoted in Michael Kimmelman, "Art: The Sun Sets at the Tate Modern," *New York Times*, March 21, 2004.

"fragile, sensual, and temporary character": Christo, *christojeanneclaude.net*.

"Do you know that I don't have any artworks that exist": Mark Getlein, *Gilbert's Living with Art*, 6th ed. (New York: McGraw Hill, 2002).

"Christo doesn't do commissions": Christo and Jeanne-Claude meeting with the author, ca. October 1988.

when I blogged about Black artist Kara Walker's gigantic sculpture: Carol Diehl, "Dirty Sugar: Kara Walker's Dubious Alliance with Domino," *Art Vent* (blog), June 16, 2014.

"innovative, site-specific, socially engaged artworks in the public realm": *CreativeTime.org*.

"Koch Brothers of South Florida": "The Fanjuls: The Koch Brothers of South Florida?," *Florida Independent*, January 19, 2016.

"Hello, and welcome to lower Manhattan . . .": YouTube audio, "Banksy 'You Complete Me' New York City Audio Guide," *StreetArtNews*, October 3, 2013.

"'Banksy' on Twitter: 336,000, #banksy on Instagram: 42,110": https://hyperallergic.com/92081/a-look-at-the-social-media-impact-of-banksyny-residency/.

"I think there were genuine conversations that happened . . .": Hrag Vartanian, quoted in Zachary McCune, "A Look at the Social Media Impact of #BanksyNY Residency," *Hyperallergic*, November 6, 2013.

"I've learnt from experience that a painting isn't finished . . .": quoted in Andrew Anthony, "Banksy: The Artist Who's Driving to the Wall," *Guardian*, April 20, 2014.

"Nobody ever listened to me . . .": Banksy, *Wall and Piece* (London: Century, 2005), 13.

"I don't know why people are so keen . . .": quoted in Will Ellsworth-Jones, *Banksy: The Man Behind the Wall* (New York: St. Martin's Press, 2013).

"I have no interest in ever coming out . . .": ibid.

"I don't think artists like myself . . .": quoted in Michael Kimmelman, "Roy Lichtenstein, Pop Master, Dies at 73," *New York Times*, September 30, 1997.

"You'd be surprised what comes out of your mouth . . .": quoted in Christopher Bollen, "Guerrilla Girls," *Interview*, February 15, 2012.

"I'm still very interested in testifying . . .": quoted in Sandro Ferri and Sandra Ferri, "Elena Ferrante, Art of Fiction No. 228," *Paris Review*, Spring 2015.

"Every time I think I've painted something slightly original . . . ": quoted in Matilda Battersby, "Blek le Rat: Streetwriting Man," *Independent*, April 25, 2012.

"simplicity is desirable in political tracts . . .": Cal Revely-Calder, "Banksy's Latest Reindeer Stunt Is Cute, but His Politics Still Leave Us Cold" (previously titled "Overpriced, Obvious and Ubiquitous: What Is the Point of Banksy?"), *Telegraph*, December 11, 2019.

"Brits' favourite painter of all time": Jonathan Jones, "Banksy Is the Brits' Favourite Painter of All Time—Is This Status Deserved?," *Guardian*, July 15, 2019.

6 Banksy and the Art Market

"What strip mining is to nature . . .": "What to Say About: Robert Hughes," London *Times*, August 11, 2012.

"Banksy-ed . . .": Scott Reyburn, "Banksy Painting Self-Destructs after Fetching $1.4 Million at Sotheby's," *New York Times*, October 6, 2018.

"He is arguably the greatest British street artist . . .": quoted in Anny Shaw, "Sotheby's 'Banksy-ed' as Painting 'Self-Destructs' Live at Auction," *Art Newspaper*, October 5, 2018.

"Banksy pranked the insidious auction world . . .": Jerry Saltz on Twitter, October 7, 2018.

"It isn't even noon": Comment on Saltz's Facebook post, since deleted.

"Good morning, Sotheby's . . .": Jerry Saltz on Twitter, October 9, 2018.

"categorically no collusion . . .": quoted in Matta Busby, "Shredded Banksy: Was Sotheby's In on the Act?," *Guardian*, October 13, 2018.

"no prior knowledge of this event . . .": Anny Shaw, "Banksy Seller's Stringent Instructions for Sotheby's Revealed," *Art Newspaper*, October 17, 2018.

"the first artwork in history to have been created live . . .": quoted in Alex Greenberger, "Sotheby's: Self-Destructing Banksy Piece Officially Sold, Is Now a 'Newly Completed Work,'" *ARTnews*, October 11, 2016.

"rehearsals": Alex Marshall, "Banksy's Shredding Prank Misfired, He Says: 'In Rehearsals It Worked Every Time,'" *New York Times*, October 18, 2018.

"he is a master manipulator and that his word cannot be trusted": "Art Assignment: Behind the Banksy Stunt," *PBS Digital Studios*, November 1, 2018.

"People often say . . .": quoted in Shaw, "Banksy Seller's Stringent Instructions."

"and that's part of the joke . . .": ibid.

"self-constructing and self-destroying work of art": "Jean Tinguely, Fragment from Homage to New York," Moma.org/collection/works.

"Can We Just Admit . . .": Ben Davis, "Can We Just Admit That Banksy's Art-Shredding Stunt Is Actually Really Good?," *Artnet News*, October 10, 2018.

"a tiresome bit of attention-seeking": "Banksy's Self-Shredding Stunt: Avant-Garde Prank or Cynical PR?," *Frieze*, October 8, 2018.

"an empty gesture": Andrea K. Scott, "The Empty Gesture in Banksy's Self-Destructing Art Work," *New Yorker*, October 8, 2018.

"Feels a bit like a publicity stunt by an artist . . .": Sarah Rose Sharp, "Was Banksy's Recent Stunt a Hoax?," *Hyperallergic*, October 9, 2018.

"disaster struck—and many of our artists . . .": Pictures on Walls, *picturesonwalls.com*, accessed November 17, 2020.

"absurd as the banking crisis": quoted in Marion Maneker, "Gerhard Richter v. the Art Market," *Art Market Monitor*, October 6, 2011.

"He is estimated to have a net worth upwards of $20 million . . .": Danielle Rahm, "Banksy: The $20 Million Graffiti Artist Who Doesn't Want His Art to Be Worth Anything," *Forbes*, October 22, 2013.

"Most commonly, it is suggested that he has amassed a fortune . . .": "How Does Banksy Make Money?," *Microsoft News*, September 15, 2014.

"given that his work now sells for millions of dollars . . .": "Banksy Net Worth $50 Million," *The Richest*, 2019, accessed November 17, 2020.

"publicity stunt": Sophie Robehmed, "Banksy Sells Original Works Worth a Fortune for £38 Each in New York Booth," *Guardian*, October 13, 2013.

"been at loggerheads for years": quoted in Will Sloan, "An Inside Look at the $35-Million Banksy Exhibit in a Warehouse on Sterling Road," *Toronto Life*, June 14, 2018.

"The anonymous artist includes his . . .": Louis Miner, "'Banksy: Genius or Vandal?' Exhibition in Lisbon," *Euronews.com*, June 17, 2019.

"He is a messenger . . .": quoted in ibid.

"$35 million worth of art": Sloan, "An Inside Look at the $35-Million Banksy Exhibit."

"The unwary consumer who decided to spend . . .": Kate Taylor, "Unauthorized Banksy Show Strips Street Art of Its Power While Cashing In on Its Fame," *Globe and Mail*, June 13, 2018.

"Copyright is for losers": Banksy, *Wall and Piece* (London: Century, 2005), copyright page.

"the event, however risible . . .": Lee Rosenbaum, "Banksy's Hanky-Panky at Sotheby's: Letting the Hot Air Out of Punctured Balloon—Part I," *CultureGrrl*, October 9, 2018.

"was sufficiently iconoclastic . . .": Dore Ashton, quoted in ibid.

7 Dismaland

"over 50,000 Europeans die prematurely . . .": James Elismoor, "Cruise Ship Pollution Is Causing Serious Health and Environmental Problems," *Forbes*, April 28, 2019.

"the aura, effects, affects, and spectres of capital": "56th Venice Biennale 2015, Okwui Enwezor: All the World's Futures," *Universes in Universe*, 2015.

"unsuitable for children": Alice Canter, "Banksy's Dismaland: 'A Theme Park Unsuitable for Children'—in Pictures," *Guardian*, August 20, 2015.

"festival of art, amusements and entry-level anarchism": "Banksy: I Think a Museum Is a Bad Place to Look at Art," *Guardian*, August 21, 2015.

"shadowy group of Seals, Delta troops and CIA": Chris Hughes, "Shadowy American Special Forces Unit Sent to Take Out al-Qaeda's Network," *Mirror*, May 5, 2011.

"family-friendly theme park": "Funland at the Tropicana, Weston-super-Mare," *visitbristol. co.uk*.

"I gave it a lot of deep thought . . .": quoted in Mark Brown, "Banksy's Dismaland: 'Amusements and Anarchism' in Artist's Biggest Project Yet," *Guardian*, August 20, 2015.

"meeting the comedian Jack Black . . .": Elise Bell, "Three Years On, We Look at the Strange Legacy of Banksy's Dismaland," *Dazed*, August 21, 2018.

"the UK's most disappointing new visitor attraction": Laura Wagner, "Banksy's 'Dismaland' Living Up to Its Name with Ticket Debacle," *NPR International*, August 21, 2015.

"I would like to think I had a part . . .": quoted in Kevin Holmes, "Meet the 'Slumscape' Painter Who Inspired Banksy's Dystopian Theme Park," *Vice*, June 28, 2016.

"This is not a small group show!": quoted in Becky Parker, "Meet the Dismaland Artist: Bill Barminski," Weston *Mercury*, September 14, 2015.

"It is just amazing having this much sarcasm . . .": Mark Brown, "Banksy's Dismaland: 'Amusements and Anarchism' in Artist's Biggest Project Yet," *Guardian*, August 20, 2015.

"thin, threadbare and, to be honest . . .": Jonathan Jones, "In Dismaland, Banksy Has Created Something Truly Depressing," *Guardian*, August 21, 2015.

"The rise of the far-left and hard-right parties . . .": quoted in Robert Booth, "David Cameron: I Feared 'Xenophobic' Trump Could Win after Brexit Result," *Guardian*, September 18, 2019.

"I got an email from Banksy's manager . . .": In Sasha Bogojev, "Interview: Smiley Faces and Not So Smiley Faces with James Joyce," *Juxtapoz*, December 19, 2018.

"a gut-wrenching Easter egg": Melia Robinson, "Many Are Finding This Shocking Piece Hidden inside Banksy's 'Dismaland' Installation Gut-Wrenching," *Business Insider*, August 21, 2015.

"I don't know why I read it . . .": Christopher Jobson, interview with the author, May 2016.

"It was like the opening scene . . .": Leigh Mulley, interview with the author, September 2019. (Continuing in following paragraphs.)

"These objects compose and embody state and capitalist order . . .": Gavin Grindon, *The Museum of Cruel Design at Banksy's Dismaland*, catalog, 2015.

"Bansky's [sic] installations look like they were . . .": Carolina A. Miranda, "Banksy's 'Dismaland' Theme Park Installation a Singular Blend of Dystopia and Hype," *Los Angeles Times*, August 18, 2015.

Dan Brooks waxed at length: Dan Brooks, "Banksy and the Problem with Sarcastic Art," *New York Times Magazine*, September 10, 2015.

Mark Nudelman, "Banksy's 'Dismaland' Is Art about Nothing—and We're Over It," *Business Insider*, August 24, 2015.

John Trowbridge, "35 HELPFUL Things Banksy Could Have Done Instead of Dismaland," *HuffPost*, August 21, 2015.

Shailee Koranne, "Dismaland Is Not Interesting and Neither Is Banksy," *HuffPost*, August 28, 2015.

"If it's the quips and public monumentality . . .": Nudelman, "Banksy's 'Dismaland' Is Art about Nothing."

"The only thing hipper right now . . .": R. J. Rushmore, "Slouching towards Banksy's Dismaland," *Hyperallergic*, September 25, 2015.

"*Dismaland* did something for me . . .": ibid.

"just walk away quietly and don't make any fuss": Banksy, *Wall and Piece* (London: Century/Random House, 2006), 79.

"moody, bass-heavy music . . .": Emily, *The Bell Jar* (blog), September 27, 2015.

"bleak yet fanciful takedown": Sarah Begley, "Watch Pussy Riot's New Music Video about the Refugee Crisis," *Time*, November 18, 2016.

Pussy Riot, "Refugees In": see https://www.youtube.com/watch?v=FDoVdLjCjoM.

"deeply unsettling, yet bizarrely entertaining . . .": Chris Green, "Dismaland: Banksy's 'Bemusement Park' Is Deeply Unsettling . . . but Bizarrely Entertaining," *Independent*, August 21, 2015.

"Banksys's [sic] Dismaland raked in more than 20 million pounds . . .": Claire Breukel, quoted in "We Ask Some Art World Luminaries to Pick the Best and Worst of 2015," *Hyperallergic*, December 28, 2015.

8 Banksy in Bethlehem

"Palestine has been occupied by the Israeli army . . .": Banksy, *Wall and Piece* (London: Century, 2005), 110.

"The British didn't handle things so well here . . .": quoted in Beckett Mufson, "Banksy Explains Why He Built a 'Walled Off Hotel' on the West Bank," *Vice*, March 10, 2017.

"a dwindling beauty within a concrete beast": John Gregory Smith, "My Night at Banksy's Walled-Off Hotel in Bethlehem," August 10, 2018, *johngregorysmith.com*.

"a three-storey cure for fanaticism . . .": see https://www.theguardian.com/world/2017/mar/03/banksy-opens-bethlehem-barrier-wall-hotel.

"My guide: You could paint here . . .": Banksy, *Wall and Piece* (2005), 113.

"If you like dancing you go on holiday . . .": quoted in Louise Jury, "Banksy: A Guerilla in Our Midst," *Independent*, August 6, 2005.

"I felt the spirit of Christmas was being lost . . .": quoted in Mark Brown, "Season's Greetings from Banksy and Friends," *Guardian*, November 30, 2006.

"festive extravaganza of cheap art . . .": Charlotte Crips, "Graffiti with Bells On," *Independent*, December 1, 2003.

"40 kids from the area through university": Josh Jones, "Feature: A History of Pictures on Walls, London's Legendary Street Art Print Shop," *Juxtapoz*, January 1, 2018.

"Gaza is often described as 'the world's largest . . .'": quoted in Alexander LaCasse, "What Is Banksy Doing in Gaza?," *Christian Science Monitor*, February 26, 2015.

"Make this the year YOU discover . . .": quoted in Sabrina Toppa, "Banksy Releases Video Shot in Gaza," *Time*, February 26, 2015.

"Banksy asked us to protect his privacy . . .": quoted in Majd Al Waheidi and Isabel Kershner, "Banksy Finds a Canvas and a New Fan Base in Gaza's Ruins," *New York Times*, April 30, 2015.

"It's that act which proves . . .": quoted in Ashleigh Stewart, "'I Don't Know How His Mind Works': What It's Really Like Working with the Elusive Street Artist Banksy," *National*, December 22, 2018. (Continuing in following paragraphs.)

"It's been pretty mental to be honest . . .": Dominique Pétrin, quoted in Oren Liebermann, "Banksy's Boutique Art Hotel Opens Its Doors in Bethlehem," *CNN*, March 3, 2017.

"it was mind-blowing to see that my work . . .": quoted in Lorraine Carpenter, "Dominique Pétrin, from the Zine Scene to Banksy's Hotel," *Cult*, April 9, 2017.

"When things get better here . . .": quoted in Stewart, "'I Don't Know How His Mind Works.'"

"the occupation was making him so fed up . . .": quoted in Jan Dalley, "Banksy Goes to Bethlehem," *Financial Times*, December 15, 2017.

"Old Man: You paint on the wall . . .": Banksy, *Wall and Piece* (2005), 110.

"It's about highlighting the wall . . .": quoted in Ruth Regan, "One Year since Opening, What Is the Banksy Hotel's Impact in Bethlehem?," *Palestine Monitor*, February 23, 2018.

Conclusion

"Evil comes from a failure to think": Amos Elon, introduction to Hannah Arendt, *Eichmann in Jerusalem: A Report on the Banality of Evil* (New York: Viking, 1963), xiv.

"Is this what you grew up dreaming . . .": Sarah Lustbader, "I Never Thought Selling Corn Could Lead to Being Torn from My Family," *Appeal*, November 12, 2019.

"It takes a lot of guts . . .": Banksy, *Wall and Piece* (London: Century/Random House, 2006), 29.